THE
MEANING
OF
Sport

THE
MEANING
OF
Sport

SIMON BARNES

First published in 2006 by
Short Books
3A Exmouth House
Pine Street
London EC1R OJH

10 9 8 7 6 5 4 3 2 1
Copyright ©
Simon Barnes 2006

A CIP catalogue record for this book
is available from the British Library.

ISBN 1-904977-45-6
(978-1-904977-45-2)
Printed in Great Britain by
William Clowes Ltd, Beccles, Suffolk

Jacket illustration: EF

For CLW
who does the job
that actually matters

1 To be frank, I am in a state of mild terror. I am sitting at a table in a café in Lisbon, having eaten a pleasant lunch with a couple of very pleasant crisp, cold beers. The weather is overcast, cool, easy. This evening, England play Croatia: if they (should I say we? Definitely not) draw or win, they continue to the next stage of the tournament. This is the European Football Championship of 2004. If Croatia win, they go through, England go out: disgrace, ignominy, sack the lot, where did it all go wrong? If England lose, I will have no problem in seeing the ironies, no problem in sleeping tonight, no problem, absolutely none at all, in catching an early plane home and getting back to Suffolk. So why the terror?

Lisbon is full of men with very little hair on their heads and very considerable bellies. They are all wearing England football shirts, of course. On the whole, they are men I would cross the M25 to avoid. And yet my chosen life constantly brings me up against them. They care far more than I do about the result of tonight's football match. I might despise them for this, were it not for my own state of mild terror.

So I take out my book and read, closing my mind to the man who has just ordered 'Dos beers', the man with the peroxide crewcut and his one-legged friend, a frank prosthesis thrust into a limp trainer. Also drinking dos beers. Perhaps I should play the part of the exquisite, and drink Madeira or white port, being in Portugal. Perhaps I am more like them than I wish to be. Perhaps we all are.

The book is the great Portuguese novel: Fernando Pessoa's *The Book of Disquiet*: rambling, brilliant, speculative, wise, above all, unpredictable. And a phrase grasps me: ravishes me with its perfection. The more so, since Pessoa almost certainly wrote the line sitting at a café table in Lisbon. Perhaps this very one, just down the hill from the Sé or cathedral; though the table itself, plastic and wobbling, mars the sense of continuity.

'The more a man differs from me, the more real he seems, for he depends that much less on my subjectivity.' A writer's remark if ever there was one. And I who read, who digest, who sip and savour, am in a state of mild terror not because of what I must see but what I must write. And I must write not of mild-mannered book-reading Sé-visiting café-sitters, but of Wayne Rooney and David Beckham, Michael Owen and Steven Gerrard.

They are not like me, no. I do not possess the intellectual depth of a Rooney or a Beckham. I cannot compute the dynamics of the spin and curve and dip of a well-struck football, cannot construct the equations that Beckham has learned and developed and sought to perfect; I cannot work out the probabilities concerned in the collision of human bodies at speed, Rooney's speciality.

Tonight, at the moment the final whistle is blown, I must press a series of keys on this laptop, the one on which I am writing now, and it will, please God, at once fire 700 words to London in an instant of time. These words will, I trust, land at the sports desk of *The Times*: I will then call and ask if the piece has arrived safe and sound, clean and ungarbled. They will then send it on to the Home News desk, for I am destined for the front page. The match is that important.

Well, not important compared to world peace, or a cure for cancer, or the ending of the ecological holocaust. But important because a lot of people care about the result. Perhaps sport matters because it doesn't matter: a thought I shall return to. It is this factitious importance that has got to me: reduced me this state of mild terror. I would much sooner be in Suffolk than in Lisbon. Ride my horses, play with my children, hug my wife.

I could be there. I could be doing just those things. I don't have to do this: I don't have to sit here fretting about the computer cable and the mobile phone and the efficaciousness of the landline and the overwhelming question of exactly what 700 words I shall have written by the time the whistle is blown. I could have insisted on the quiet life, a column or two a week, tablets that descend bi-weekly from my personal Olympus.

But I am a chief – note that word, chief – sportswriter. I am chief sportswriter of *The Times*, and that means that I am the one who will be telling the tale tonight. And I am intoxicated by the thought: tonight, a tale will be enacted, and I am the teller of that tale. Drunk with self-importance. There is a dominance hierarchy thing, yes, of course there is, me being the chief and all. But above all there is the tale.

I am a little like Beckham in that he, too, is a slave to the concept of the dominance hierarchy. I too am going to the Estadio da Luz tonight in order to be brilliant and wonderful and ravishing: or at least, to try to be. But I am unlike Beckham in many more ways: that is why he is so real to me, so enthrallingly un-dependent on my subjectivity. Not because I read Pessoa and he presumably does not; not because he can bend a free-kick and I can't. But because he is the creator of tales, and I am the teller of tales. There is a lifetime of difference here: and with it, enough shame and glory to last a lifetime of words.

2

But let us talk of elephants. When I was in Hwange national park in Zimbabwe, I acquired the habit of visiting a certain waterhole just before sundown: stopping there for an hour or two to see who passed by. And mainly it was elephants. Now this waterhole was man-made, or at least man-managed. Water bubbled up from a pipe into a small concrete cistern which then overflowed and made a pool about 20 yards across.

The females and the young elephants all drank from the pool. Its waters were often opaque: the teenagers would bounce and frolic in the shallows and stir up the sediment. The bull elephants would not drink there at all. They would drink only from the cistern, two or three at a time, a small concrete oblong in which a trio of trunks sucked and gurgled while the rest waited their turn. The most sought-after position was right by the pipe: the coolest, freshest water for the coolest, freshest elephant. To drink there was not only tastier: it said a great deal about what sort of elephant you were.

The drinks party of females and young was always a riot: I remember one youngster so excited by all the company that he chased a flock of guinea fowl – also eager for a drink – round and round like a tiresome little boy chasing the pigeons in St Mark's Square. But it was the bulls that fascinated, because there was a mystery about them.

What did it take to drink at the pipe? What sort of an elephant did you have to be? What were the essential requirements? Size was obviously a help, along with seniority and size of tusk. You would see one elephant drinking, and then see another swaggering out of the bush, and it was completely obvious that the pipe belonged to the new arrival whenever he wanted it. And he in his turn would be displaced by yet another, still more gaudy of tusk.

Sometimes the difference was not obvious at all. One elephant would emerge from the bush and walk up to the elephant drinking at the pipe. The two would be much of a size. You simply could not guess who would defer to whom. But it was perfectly obvious to the elephants.

Did they fight? Did they trumpet, did they tussle, did they tusk and gore? Not a bit of it. One looked at the other.

And that was it. Or perhaps for about half a second, he flicked his ears: a signal. An elephant spreads his ears in order to look more fearsome. It is a statement of aggression. But the merest hint, no more. A twitch, a flicker. No need for dramatics. No actual threat: just an indication of his seriousness of purpose. And in that instant of flickering the matter was decided; and one elephant backed down while another did not. No goring and trumpeting: just a meeting of minds.

The reason why one elephant deferred to another was, then, a mystery. And I have watched this mystery over and over again in the arenas of sport, and I have never tired of doing so. Sport is not only – perhaps not at all – an examination of how good you are at running, jumping, controlling a ball. It is also a matter of who defers to whom. Sport is the most intensely physical thing that humans do, or do in public, anyway. And yet the tales we tell are not of bodies but of hearts and minds and souls.

3 There is an ancient saying in horseracing: cheap horses know it. When you invest in an aristocratic equine lineage, you are not just buying speed. You are also buying a sense of self-worth. At the end of a hard race, some horses will defer to others; another will assert his will over them all. When you buy the best stock, you are also buying a high place in the dominance hierarchy.

So let us come to the best race I ever saw: the best race,

that is, between humans. It took place in Seoul in 1988. There were eight people in it, though I noticed only two. Carl Lewis. Ben Johnson. Carl Lewis wrote about it later on, in his autobiography *Inside Track*. 'I couldn't get away from those yellow eyes. The bastard did it again.'

Johnson ran faster, it seemed, than the human body was designed to go: so much so that I half-expected his arms and legs to come flying off under the crazy stress of it all. Or at least the body to break down and leave him writhing on the red track far below me in that steeply raked stand.

How much faster could he have gone, had he not celebrated, pierced the sky with his index finger, floated those last two strides instead of running them? No matter; it is a sporting image burned onto the retina: one man's moment of total dominance.

And the other. Lewis, tortured by the thought that Johnson had an illicit advantage, was beaten before the start. While they were running, I had eyes for no one but Johnson; but, when I watched the slo-mo afterwards, I could see that Lewis swivelled his eyes round to Johnson three times. A sprinter is not supposed to do that. Ever. Especially not a champion. It costs time: it bursts the bubble of self-regard. But Lewis couldn't help himself. He knew he was beaten before he put his feet in the blocks.

Johnson knew that he would win. I don't know to what extent the anabolic steroids and human growth hormone helped his body. But it was blindingly obvious how much the drugs helped his mind. He knew he was Superman. He knew he could run faster than a speeding bullet. He knew he had something that nobody else had. Perhaps if you had given him Smarties and told him they were go-faster pills, he would have run the same impossible 9.79 seconds.

It's not about who you are. It's about who you think you are.

4

For much of my time at *The Times*, David Miller was chief sports correspondent; I was a good deal lower in the dominance hierarchy. David is a magnificent journalist; I always thought I was rather better. Then in 1985, he covered the disaster at Heysel Stadium, the occasion on which 37 people were killed. David extemporised front and back page leads over the telephone from his seat in the stadium, for this was the pre-laptop era, and did so without a note. I read the paper the next day rather in the manner that Carl Lewis was to look at Ben Johnson three years later. The bastard did it again. I couldn't beat that.

David was and is very serious about sport, believing in the importance of sport as a social and moral force. I don't share this view. For me, sport is a monstrous triviality that produces stories that people want to hear, that I want to tell. For me, sport is not moral. Truth is in the performer, in the performance. Truth is in what sport reveals about the person who does it. Compared to that, the idea of sport as a moral force seems rather small.

I do jokes. I made my early impression at *The Times* by doing jokes. David, on the whole, does not. Not when writing about sport. And so I used to maintain that there was only one writer at *The Times* who was fully serious about sport – and it was not the one that David thought.

5

Perhaps you are wondering what I did at the England–Portugal game, the quarter-final match in the European Championship. Shall I tell you how ghastly it was? But perhaps I have already alienated my readers by bringing up the very possibility that covering a big England game for *The Times* could have the remotest trace of ghastliness about it: fancy being paid to go to a football match! An England game! Blimey, can I come and carry your bag? Well, let me tell you what actually happened that night. Being as free of self-pity as possible, of course.

I got to the stadium rather more than two hours before the game: at these major tournaments, you lose your match accreditation if you fail to collect your ticket an hour and a half before kick-off. I hung about. I made phone calls: I learned that I had to file 600 words for the front page. They wanted copy after 90 minutes, 'on the whistle'. All right then. So far so easy.

That is, so long as you are prepared to overlook the obvious insanity of asking someone to write the story of a football match while the match is still going on. It can be done, of course, but the drawback is that you can't actually watch the match. Also, you don't know how the story ends until you have actually finished writing it. This makes it technically rather tricky: the more ambitious you are in your story-telling, the trickier it gets. And no one wants to read a kick-by-kick report these days: most readers have already got that sort of information from television.

So I wrote a hymn of praise to Michael Owen, who scored an early goal for England, further praise for England's doughty defence, and then as an after-thought, the fact that the Portuguese scored a late goal and the match went into extra time. In other words, the story was based on a false premise: that the Owen goal was important. It now meant nothing, but it was far too late to re-write the story. I filed the copy – that is to say, connected the laptop to the mobile phone, pressed a few buttons and there, bang on the whistle, the copy was dropping in Wapping. It might not be a true reflection of a match that was still going on, but hell, it was on time.

My second brief – the in-the-event-of-a-draw-after-90-minutes brief – was to write an additional three or four paragraphs the instant I knew the result. That at least meant that I was able to watch quite a lot of the football. There was a goal each in extra time, the match went to a penalty shoot-out: and I wrote and filed the paragraphs on England's defeat. That went through first time as well. I was on a roll. I called the sports desk and told them I had to re-write my Michael Owen piece from top to bottom, and without Michael Owen, and therefore I couldn't write a second piece for the sports pages. OK, fine.

Which gave me half an hour for 600 words. Everybody in the profession can do that: it's no great trick. The variable in the equation is quality, that's all. I finished in 25 minutes, and pressed send. It didn't work. Half a dozen more tries: no luck. I borrowed a landline from someone, plugged it in, tried to send. It didn't go. Remembered I had to re-configure the computer. Did it. Didn't work. Realised that I had done it wrong. Not my long suit, computer technology. Did it right. Copy didn't go.

'I must have my landline back.'

'All right, all right, one second.' Tried again. Didn't work.

'I need that landline and I need it now.'

'One second.' I prayed the prayer of EM Forster, and at last the machine responded.

Joy. Or relief, anyway. Had it not worked, everyone back at Wapping would have been very sympathetic; and blamed me. I'd have had to dictate to a copy-taker, and would have missed at least one edition. Still, it went.

And how horribly unsatisfactory it was. I hadn't really watched the match, and I hadn't written a piece that was anything like pleasing. And now I had to get back to my hotel. I had a beer with a couple of colleagues: a deeply gloomy gathering, a depressing tale to tell in circumstances that made the telling of it almost ludicrously unsatisfying. I eventually found the metro, and then my hotel. I drank some whisky in an attempt to compose the mind for slumber. Rang the out-of-hours travel desk and they booked me a flight for the following day.

I slept, woke, went to a press conference, wrote two pieces, went to the airport, checked in, had a beer, went to the gate, got bumped off the flight, spent three hours organising a flight for the following day and another hour finding my bag, which they'd taken off the plane. Got back home on Saturday. Went to Wimbledon Monday morning.

It was Kitchener of Khartoum who said, 'We do not make war as we would like to; we make war as we must.'

6 Who invented sport? It would be nice to know, if only to curse him. Or her: but we'll talk about sexual dimorphism elsewhere. Where did sport start, where did it all come from, and who can I blame? All questions I was inclined to ask as I left my wife and my boys and my horses and my few Suffolk acres after a heady 24 hours of hugging – it would, of course, have been nearer 48 had I not been bumped off the flight and forced to retreat – and headed for the London postal district of SW19.

Sport started less than 200 years ago, with the Victorian codification of games and the influence of the public schools. Or if you prefer, sport started a couple of thousand and more years ago, with the ancient Greeks, with their taste for naked grappling around orange vases. We'll talk about sex and the Olympic Games elsewhere too. Or again, if you prefer, sport began with deep folkloric traditions: local games, their links with religious rituals, and the overlapping of Christianity with paganism: maybe three thousand years, maybe more.

Me, I am inclined to put the invention of sport a little earlier than any of the above. I suggest that sport is about 65 million years old. The invention of sport was the result of the collision of the earth and a meteor.

That meteor, at the end of the Cretaceous era, and before the Tertiary – right on what geologists call the KT Boundary – not only possibilised sport, it also wiped out the dinosaurs and put the earth through an extended nuclear winter. When the dust settled – no metaphor this, the literal truth – the mammals found themselves in pole position to become the dominant large animals of the planet. And the invention of sport was inevitable from that moment.

Let us zip-pan from the KT Boundary to the Luangwa Valley in Zambia. I had better tell you about the Luangwa Valley: it is likely to come up again in this book. The Luangwa is a southern extension of the Great Rift. It is also a place where a piece of my heart lies, and I try and go back there reasonably often to see if it is still there. I spent an extended sabbatical there in 1992, and I have lost count of the other visits I have made.

The Luangwa River changes its mind and its course every season. It is not a tame river. There is nothing tame about the place at all. And I was parked on an abandoned bit of riverbed, a place where the river no longer flowed: a stretch of sand and beyond the short sheer cliffs of a Luangwa riverbank. Watching sport. No humans for miles around, save the two or three in the Toyota Land Cruiser with me. I was standing behind the driver holding a powerful spotlight, and I had the sporting athletes right in the middle of the beam.

Lion. No, not hunting. Hunting is not sport for a lion: it is a job and a passion. They were playing. And what they were playing was sport. It was a group we called the Fubsy

Cubs: three cubs, generally found with two or three adult females, one their mother, the others either aunties or older sisters. A pride is a female system with an attendant obstreperous sperm bank.

And, when we were lucky, the Fubsy Cubs did sport for us. They sported themselves. They played. The games were Scrag Your Brother, Pounce on Your Sister, Stalk Your Mother's Tail, and an endless variety and fusion of these three basic themes. Fighting games, hunting games, roughing and tumbling games. And it was clearly sport, because it was a metaphorical version of the real thing. It was pretend hunting and pretend fighting, just as tennis is a pretend duel and football is a pretend battle. No one was going to get hurt, save the odd bang. That was not the idea. The idea was a deeply serious kind of fun. Sport, as I said.

On one occasion, I saw one of the adults initiate play: rolling over onto her back to grab a passing cub and toss him into the air. The cub, delighted, landed heavily on a furry chest and batted at the whiskered face before him with paws like little sledgehammers, then fell over and was pounced on by brothers. Play is for the young, but not only for the young. At times of contentment, repletion, safety, adults too can indulge in sport.

For those lions, sport was fun, and sport was frivolous. It was also deadly serious: preparation for a lion's life ahead, when stalking, pouncing and scragging would become not sport but survival skills. But during this very young, very safe time, there was a feeling in the air that sport could also be pursued for its own sake. It seemed then, to me, as it no doubt seemed to the lions, that sport was an end in itself.

Young mammals play. I have never seen shrews play – the earliest mammals were insect-chasing busy little shrews – but most young mammals will play. I have never seen reptiles or amphibians or fish play; I have never seen invertebrates at play. Birds: well, I have seen birds behave skittishly. I have seen jackdaws ride a Ferris wheel of air for no reason other than their mastery of it. Birds know something about play. But I am inclined to suggest that sport is a mammalian invention.

Sport goes pretty deep in us. Sport pre-dates humankind by maybe 60 million years. We have all seen puppies and kittens at play. I have also seen foals playing: in Newmarket studs, in my own fields, and in the Luangwa Valley, where horses tend to carry stripes. I have seen elephants at play (remember those well-chased guinea fowl) and I have seen giraffes at play. I have seen baboons at play; I have heard monkeys at play on my roof. I have seen, though alas only on film, whales and dolphins and chimpanzees and gorillas at play. At sport.

Sport goes deeper than the mere human in us. Sport goes to the heart of our mammalian selves. No wonder sport transcends all cultural boundaries; no wonder sport brings 202 nations together at the Olympic Games. We are not all in sport together because we are human – we are all in it together because we are mammals, and our fellow-mammals have been doing sport for 65 million years. Hardly surprising, then, that sport is part of us. Whether we like it or not. On, then, to SW19.

7

Southfields station, SW19. A walk to the All England Lawn Tennis Club: about a mile. Merry crowds. Merry touts. The merry queue. Unmerry me. Scowling at Panamas, scowling at shorts, scowling at cotton blouses. Scowling at those who speak to me in the tout's mutter: 'Buy or sell. Any tickets.' Past improvised stalls standing in front gardens that are demure for 50 weeks of the year, and which now sell sandwiches and burgers and giant tennis balls and souvenir tee-shirts. There is always money to be made from cheerful people. Optimism makes a person vulnerable.

I was going to watch Tim Henman. So was almost everybody else: either on Centre Court, or on the big screen on the area they now call Henman Hill. Queuing up in order to watch television.

And I was neither cheerful nor optimistic. There is no ducking it: I am no more like these tennis followers than I am like the football people I scowled at in Lisbon. I like the tennis people better: they are less liable to thump you, they send out better vibes, they don't try to kill you by song. I walked past the queue and scowled at them all.

I have been writing about Henman since 1996. That was the year he beat the number five seed, Yevgeny Kafelnikov, and reached the quarter-finals for the first time. I have chronicled all his moments of incipient greatness, and all the disappointments that followed them. I have watched Henman more often than most of the people who will be cheering themselves silly and waving flags and acting up with Last Night of the Proms patriotism. I think it probable that I would sooner die than shout 'Go on Tim!'

But I want him to go on, for all that. Probably more than the Henmaniacs. I want to see it happen for the time I have invested in watching him. I want it to happen for the – purely one-sided – affection I have for him. But, above all, I want it to happen so that I can tell the tale. Tim Henman, the eternal tease of British sport, has finally delivered. No. He waited till all faith in him was dead. No. The man who has let greatness slip from his grasp every summer for nine years yesterday claimed his own. No. It was precisely now. All those other years of nearly-but-not-quite were but preparation for this moment: and yesterday it came.

No, that's not right either. But what a story. Federer said afterwards: 'He was just too good. There was nothing I could do.' How could I not want to tell this tale? I have written so many chapters of Henman's life. He deserves – it deserves – I deserve – a big finish. Alas, life is perfectly capable of continuing without you or I getting what we think we deserve. For that reason, life, and sport, often seem rather poorly organised.

8

But there is something far more despicable than Henmania. I once read an interview with some third-rate footballer who said that he hoped for great things in his life. 'I don't intend to become a typical British loser like Tim

Henman.' So far as I know, the footballer in question has yet to be rated as the fourth finest player in the world.

It is Henman's sad fate to be regarded as a loser – as something rather pathetic and hapless and hopeless; as something rather despicable and spineless and useless. We have absurdly high expectations of Henman; and still more absurdly, feel that his failure to fulfil our expectations makes him something to be despised, reviled and spat upon. If we seek to see Henman plain, then we must look somewhere between the hope and the despair.

But we don't seek to see any of our sporting heroes plain. We prefer to oscillate between undue hope and undue despair. We relish the fizz of expectation, but we also relish the anger and the sadness. Henman's annual tilt at the dragon of SW19 was part of the rhythm of national life; and so is the dragon's ultimate inevitable victory. The hope is something that builds up slowly. Even the atheists and the agnostics find in themselves a little chink of hope. Some, almost despite themselves, catch a game, a set, a match: and are reminded with something of a shock that this tosser, this archetypal British loser is one hell of a tennis player, capable of playing with a magisterial coldness. What is more, much more, he can do that most thrilling thing that tennis players can do: he can find in moments of greatest trial the greatest of his ability.

The acquisition of hope is subtle and cumulative. It is a hope that dare not speak its name: it is a murmuring within: well, he could, you know; he might; he just bloody well might. And then once again the nation is united in a long, dark tea-time of the soul: a five-set agony of nearly-but-not-quite. It has become a defining point of the summer: the day when Henman gets knocked out, and in that moment we are forced to abandon hope; in that moment we despise ourselves for the hope that we guarded within us. But, more than that, we despise Henman for the crime of *allowing* us to hope.

Henman is a first-class player. First class of the second class: a crucial phrase, to which we shall return. John McEnroe, asked why Henman hadn't won Wimbledon, said that the problem was that he 'happened to run into a god by the name of Pete Sampras'. Sampras is gone, but Roger Federer is no less god-like. If Henman was ever to win Wimbledon, he had to strike sometime between god and god.

The time came, too. In 2001, Sampras was knocked out early, the draw opened up, and Henman was in the semi-final with only a wild-card entry between him and the final. But it was not to be. To win Wimbledon you must know how to play tennis, you must know how to play your opponents, you must know how to play the crowd, and how to play the Centre Court, which can be the most intimidating arena in sport. But you must also know how to play the rain.

And, in that year, Henman's semi-final lasted three days, like a cricket match, and it was the wild card that played the rain better. 'I don't sleep,' said Goran Ivanisevic. 'Six o'clock I don't sleep, seven o'clock I don't sleep, eight o'clock I don't sleep, nine o'clock, I still don't sleep. So it is ten o'clock and I get up. Is time for Telly-tubby.'

Henman is not a loser, not in the derogatory sense of the

term. He has won more than 11 million bucks in prize money, and he achieved that by the cunning ploy of not losing tennis matches. In every Grand Slam singles tournament there are 127 losers, and 64 of them – half of them – lose in the first round. Henman has made the last eight at Wimbledon eight times and the last four four times. That year, 2004, he had already made the last four at the French Open. This is not the record of a tosser.

The fault is not with Henman. The fault is with those who hope. Henman is but the hopee. He can't logically be blamed for the hope people place in him. But sport is not a logical process. Sport is an area of life in which most of us feel that we are let off logic, if not thought of any kind.

That explains something of Henman's bitterness in recent years. He has surfed the wave of emotion on the Centre Court too often not to be grateful for the hope he inspires: but he has also been pained too often by the fury that comes in disappointment. Henman: the best we've had for 70 years. So let's despise him for not being still better. It's a hard thing to deal with: for there is a thumping and overwhelming contradiction at the heart of the matter. A sporting star is a hero, a legend and an archetype. But he is also a man.

And so I travelled from Lisbon to Wimbledon because of the hope that is annually incarnate in Henman: and I wrote up an almost serene victory in the round of sixteen, which, alas, was followed by a quarter-final defeat in which Henman did well to keep humiliation at bay.

Henman had done it again. He had spilled his guts and been despised, as ever. Yet again, he had tried and he had failed. There is a real nobility in that: in the not giving up, in the belief that his destiny lies in his annual tryst with the dragon. And if the dragon always wins: surely that is better than the not fighting. Certainly, it is better than the sneering.

9

The first thing I did after the women's singles final was to call Simon Worrall. Worrall lived then at West Egg, or possibly East Hampton, but anyway, on Long Island. You've got to write it, I told him. Now.

Worrall and I were at university together. We used to play ferocious games of psychedelic pingpong, write poems and talk about girls. He too writes for his living, not poems, and mostly for *National Geographic*. Seven years ago, he played a set of tennis against Maria Sharapova. Now Worrall fancies himself at tennis, not that this makes tennis unique. Pulverising opponents at tennis is what Worrall does when he is not writing or chasing girls. And he did a story about the Sharapova family and got to play a set with Maria, or Masha. And he got walloped. Hammered. Trashed. Sharapova was ten. He was impressed by the weight of shot, and the depth and the accuracy and the consistency. But, above all, he was impressed by the weight of mind. He didn't win because she wouldn't let him. This was Bull Elephant Syndrome: the place at the pipe goes to the one with the stronger mind. And Worrall, fit, athletic and strong (back then), was beaten by a ten-year-old girl because her will was stronger.

Seven years on, Sharapova beat Serena Williams and won the Wimbledon singles title because her will was stronger. We had feared a mismatch, feared that it would all be one-way traffic: and so it proved. But not the way we expected.

I had been dyspeptic and grumpy and out of sorts in SW19, and this girl with waist-length blond hair, playing in a nightie with a forehand that smashes down doors had charmed me out of the grumps. It was a story that made the sporting life seem good again. After telling the tale of England's inevitable defeat in Portugal and Henman's inevitable defeat at Wimbledon, here was this absurdly young thing with a glorious athlete's body smashing the crap out of the established way of things.

They say the young have no fear. What nonsense. When I was seventeen, I was eaten up with fears of every kind. The idea of fearless youth lies somewhere between impertinence and amnesia. But Sharapova went out there and rewrote the history of her sport. Worrall wrote his piece for *The Times*, and it was a belter. And I wrote mine. Lost, for a brief moment, in hope.

10

If I were a football manager and one of my players told me, 'I see myself as an artist,' I would sack him on the spot. Look, son (like bi-coloured-python-rock-snakes, football managers always talk like that), I would say. I can see you as an artist if I want to, and that's all right. But if you see yourself as an artist, then the art in you is dead. And with it the football.

Roger Federer is an artist. Everybody says it, so it must be true. Everybody, that is, except Federer. Which makes it all right. Federer is convinced – erroneously, if you like – that he is a tennis player. That he is an athlete, a sportsman, a games player, and his job is not creating art, but winning tennis matches.

And, if I were indeed a football manager, I would insist on footballers who believe they are footballers and that their task is to win football matches. Not just because such a mercenary approach would help me to keep my job, but because, unless footballers see themselves as footballers, they have no hope of creating art. I watched Federer win the men's singles final and did so in a trance of delight. It was not because I would go home at last once the match was done, and it was not because this was an especially wonderful tale to tell. It was something else entirely.

If you watch a lot of sport, you acquire a separate set of values. You watch with two distinct systems operating at the same time: a new set, to go along with the one you started with. It is something that takes a little getting used to. The first, and for the writer, the highest of these systems, is the tale. Not the excellence but the drama, the background, the beauty, the sudden shift in momentum, the break in the pattern; and, with these things, the nature of participants, and the extent to which they have a meaning for those who will be doing the reading.

The Wimbledon men's final of 2001 had all those things: the triumph of Goran Ivanisevic, the wild wild-card entry and Tim Henman's semi-final conqueror, over five melo-dramatic sets. You may recall that he kept double-faulting on match point: an afternoon of sweet agonies and tearful joys.

It was a wonderful tale to tell, and it fulfilled every possible criterion in the first set of values. It was a wonderful match to watch, it was a wonderful match to write. It was a great tennis match, and it had everything. Except, of course, great tennis.

Joe Mercer, a former football manager of some renown, once dismissed the 1966 World Cup final as 'a good spectators' match'. So it was, and I was a good spectator myself, watching on television in black and white at the family home in Streatham. The Goran final was also a good spectators' match. It was a stirring tale and I did my best to tell it stirringly.

But in 1999, I saw a men's final that failed on most of the spectators'-game counts, and it remains in my memory as the finest tennis match I have ever watched. More: it is one of the greatest sporting occasions I have been present at. It was a straight-sets win by a player most people believed was boring.

You acquire rather rarefied tastes when you take too much sport into your life, in the same way that too much womanising is supposed to bring out rather specialised tastes in the womaniser. But there is nothing of perversity in my delight in that match. It was probably the best three sets of grass court tennis that have ever been played. But it didn't touch people, in the way that Goran final did.

In 1999, Andre Agassi had his year of years. He won two

of the four Grand Slam titles that year and also reached the final at Wimbledon. He was playing tennis of white-hot perfection, and he continued to do so in the Wimbledon final. So Sampras did the only thing possible if he was to win: he went beyond perfection. Agassi played some of the finest tennis ever played, and it just wasn't good enough. It was not a match in which advantage went first one way and then the other. It was Sampras all the way.

Perhaps only someone with my number of sporting miles on the clock would have rated this game so highly. Tennis specialists would not have appreciated it in quite the same way: they love complexity of strategy and versatility of shot-making. They love what a player can do with a ball: pure tennis, if you like.

Me, I am a specialist at observing the collision of wills: and this particular collision has become a jewel in the collection. Agassi was brilliant: and was comprehensively beaten. But Sampras did not impose his will on Agassi: that is the point. Agassi did not cease for a second to play well. Sampras imposed his will on himself. He forced himself to play better than himself. He took himself to the level that lies beyond mere perfection.

It was not the most dramatic tale I have ever told, but it was an afternoon that has informed all my writing on sport ever since. It was the clearest possible demonstration of the difference between very, very good – and great. And, as I seek constantly a good tale to tell, so I seek – almost for private reasons, for personal rather than public gratification – greatness. I seek a definition of greatness, I seek an under-standing of greatness. I seek, perhaps the highest thing of all, to write greatness: and write it true. But, above all, I seek to be where greatness is. That is the greatest thing in the life of a sportswriter.

11

But we are artists, too, of course, we sportswriters, hacks, journos, scribblers, scribes and Pharisees. And no doubt every sports editor would be right to sack us on the spot should we tell him that we were artists. Such a claim would destroy the art within us.

Still, we go in for artistic tantrums. We do it all the time. The story we have written appears in an insufficiently prominent place in the newspaper; the headline – headlines are written by the subs back at the office, not by the writers – fails to reflect the writer's sense of the story; the story has been too brutally cut to fit the demands of the space; the words have been changed.

I never read my stuff in the paper any more, say some. They do such frightful things with my copy. I mean, take this morning for example... All sports editors are aware that the prime skill of the job is handling the infinitely fragile personalities of the egomaniacs they employ.

The humming neuroses of a large gathering of leading sportswriters is a strange thing to experience. We all live in constant denial of our neuroses, of course. We like to think of ourselves as a bunch of tough, robust, effective individuals. We pretend to be relaxed and cool and cynical, especially about our own work. Oh, usual rubbish, we say, when asked what we plan to write, even while wincing inwardly at such blasphemy. It's a form of politeness among egomaniacs: not to make too loud a claim for oneself.

We all pretend that the nitty-gritty of the job doesn't really matter too much to us. If that were the case, why do we all turn up for every football match at least an hour before kick-off, even when there is no official requirement to do so? Logistically, we could all manage our pre-match preparation comfortably in fifteen minutes. But the hour or more is essential. Our fragile nerves, however well concealed they might be by our cynical facades, simply could not stand being somewhere else. I mean, what if something went terribly wrong? We would never arrive at a restaurant an hour early, no matter how beautiful the woman we were due to meet.

We do artistic tantrums and we have artistic nerves, without producing art. But we are artists in the sense that we start with nothing and end up with something. Creation *ab nihilo*: a definition of both an artist and God.

People have written about the fear of the blank page: today, we journos live in fear of the empty screen, the glowing, tastefully off-white oblong whose purity is marred only by the winking of the curser. The curser that says: write something you bastard. Write *now*. The never-spoken thought that unites us all is this: what if I can't think of something to write? What if I don't have any ideas? What if inspiration – if you care to call it that – simply fails to descend? For some reason, it is not acceptable to ring the office and say: 'I'm sorry, I'm just not in the mood.'

It was Frank McGhee, former chief sportswriter for the

Daily Mirror – his by-line called him 'The Voice of Sport' – who made the remark that defines our trade and ourselves for all time. 'If you can't write a good piece,' he said, 'write a bad one.' They are, after all, the only two choices available to us.

12

Roger Federer is not an artist. He is a businessman. He does not seek to beguile our senses or to make us sigh with pleasure. He is just a man looking for the best method to win tennis matches. Yet for some reason this method is sublimely beautiful.

Federer is no more seeking to create beauty when he plays tennis than a cheetah is trying to create beauty when he pursues a gazelle. Federer is not seeking to create anything. Like the cheetah, he is seeking to destroy. His job on Friday was not pleasing me: it was displeasing Sebastien Grosjean. Tennis is not an art form: it is a stylised or metaphorical duel. It is the opposition of one will and another. But, when Federer plays, he creates a strange illusion, that he is creating a spontaneous work of art for our particular delight.

I suspect that this is because there is an illusion within the illusion. When Federer becomes the boy with the racket of fire, creating the illusion of art, he also creates an additional illusion: that his opponent is not, in fact, opposing him. That his opponent is in fact co-operating with him: conspiring with Federer to create these patterns of angle and trajectory, of curves and straight lines, of criss-crossing white-clad bodies, of singing strings made, at one moment, from cobweb, the next, piano-wire. It becomes a *pas de deux* choreographed by Federer, dancing with a man who is partner, stooge, straight man and butt: a partner who is cherished, ravished, made much of and humiliated before our eyes.

And it looks so pretty, so devoid of anger, so devoid of malice, so devoid of intention: it looks as if Federer were trying to create something pure in a naughty world. And it lifts our spirits as we watch, even while we see through the illusion and we know that all that is really (but what is really?) happening is that two millionaires are hitting a furry ball back and forth, and that one of them has a mouth that is filled with the bile of frustration.

That was the semi-final, a rain-soiled master-class. The final was quite different. Federer did not play terribly well. He was jostled and harried out of his art by Andy Roddick. Roddick used speed in part because it is a tactic, and more because the tactic is in sympathy with his own impatient nature. It half-worked, too. It worked, certainly to the extent that Roddick did not look for a moment as if he were co-operating with anybody, least of all Federer.

People are already talking about Federer as the greatest tennis player of all time. Me, I am a bit more cautious about greatness. Or perhaps I mean about tenses: perhaps we are looking at a player who, in a few years, will have become the greatest player ever. Pete Sampras won Wimbledon seven times, fourteen Grand Slam titles in all. No doubt he had greatness in him all along. And perhaps Federer is already great. But he has yet to achieve great things. He is not yet a serial winner: and so we cannot say that he has achieved greatness. In sport, greatness surely requires a sustained oeuvre: a multiplicity of championships. To call a man great too early is wrong: and besides, it leaves a writer with nowhere else to go. Greatness itself should have about it some kind of narrative.

Federer may be moving inexorably towards the Sampras level of greatness – perhaps even beyond, who knows? If so, I found that rough and disappointing final more convincing than the artistry of the semi-final. For Federer did not beat Roddick because of his beautiful hands. He won by means of his distinctly unbeautiful mind. He won because, of the two, his mind was the bloodier.

Federer was not able to impose his will on the match, he was not able to choreograph its steps or compose its music. He had to go slumming into the sordid parts of himself and come up with a – by his standards – rather ugly victory. And he took it without apology.

Federer lost a lot of points, and he lost a lot of points that he should have won. But he lost very few of the points that he needed to win. That was the difference; and, in the long term, it is the difference between very good and great. Tennis is a game in which all points are equal, but some points are a very great deal more equal than others. Break-point down on your serve is a different point from 40-love up. Multiply that by ten for set-point, by ten again for match-point, and by at least another thousand for championship point in the men's singles finals at Wimbledon. If you play those points better than everybody else, you are a champion.

And it is what a person requires in order to play those points better that concerns me. That is where the Bull Elephant Syndrome cuts in. Concerned, then, I wrote my last piece from SW19. Sharapova and Federer had filled me with joy and wonder and tales of – incipient – greatness. But I was on the train to Suffolk.

13

Have you heard about the chief sports writer with an inferiority complex? He thought he was just the same as everybody else.

When you are travelling on assignment, you get used to a certain deference: and that can make the return to domestic life a trifle sticky. You have grown accustomed to a reasonable amount of respect from your colleagues back at the office: you grow if not fat, then at least slightly plump on a diet of praise. Some of it is no doubt sincere, quite a lot of it certainly is the calculated ego-maintenance of one of the newspaper's more expensive assets: but it all slips down pleasantly enough for the one being praised. You fly business class long-haul, so they call you Mr Barnes instead of sir and they bring you stuff all the time; and it is all the more pleasant when you think about all the lesser people at the back.

It makes life on the road more comfortable: but it is not very helpful in the maintenance of humility, not to say perspective, not to say sanity. You stay in decent hotels, where you get sirred and offered room service. You can, if you wish, eat at expensive restaurants and, if the white wine isn't chilled to your satisfaction, you can call the sommelier and tear his ears off. You are an important person, are you not? You won't find anyone to give an argument.

And then you get home, dead tired but rather pleased with yourself ('you've murdered the opposition'), and you expect the same kind of deference. Instead, you are required to look after the children, cook the supper, go to the supermarket, generally muck in and – imagine this – consider other people. Other people! The mind reels at the prospect. And you find that you are now slightly behind the pace in terms of family culture: there are running jokes you don't know; there are horror stories you were not a part of, you aren't quite sure where everything goes any more, and there is a new device and you don't know how it works and you have to ask, and someone has a new craze and you haven't a clue what it means, and you love them all very much and would someone please bring me a cold beer and a sandwich while I lie down on the sofa and watch sport on the telly, because I am tired, jet-lagged and important.

'It's that word chief,' a colleague once said to me. 'That's what does it.' It becomes an addiction. You love being the chief: and, equal and opposite, you are terrified that someone else might become the chief. Like all monarchs.

For some, chiefdom takes the form of a mania: you simply have to be present at every major sporting event that takes place anywhere in the world. Partly because you feel that it won't really have happened if you weren't there, and partly because you don't want anyone else to be there instead. You don't want someone else to write the story for you. I mean, damn it all, he might do it well. He might even – impossible thought – do it better than you. Or people, being foolish, might have the extraordinary illusion that he had done so; and could you really risk that happening?

At the World Cup in Japan, three of my fellow-chiefs flew from Japan to Memphis for the world heavyweight title fight between Lennox Lewis and Mike Tyson. And back. One went for a week, and covered the whole arc of the story. Two others flew in for the fight, watched it through mad, glazed eyes, wrote their tales and leapt straight back on the plane – or series of planes – to get back to Japan in time for the next England footy match. Me, I wouldn't have crossed the road to watch it: but I have a problem with boxing. This is a problem I was forced to confront, once again, a few weeks after Wimbledon had finished.

The thing about all this travelling, all this I-must-be-there stuff, is that it changes the way you understand life. Gavin Lyall, the excellent thriller writer, often has tough but dysfunctional pilots as his heroes. One of these muses about the way that, for a pilot, 'up there' can become 'up here'. Life on the ground becomes meaningless, transitory, unsatisfactory, altogether unconvincing. That, I suspect, is what happens to chiefs who cover their sports not wisely but too well.

Not just chiefs, of course. There is also the phenomenon

of the doyen. You find him more often as a specialist: a single-sport expert who knows everybody, has seen everything and who becomes – or at least sees himself as – a kind of moral arbiter of his sport. Such people carry themselves in a different way: they expect deference not only from stewardesses but from their colleagues and for that matter, from the players. They matter more than the players; just as much as the critic matters more than the novelist.

I remember talking to Brian Glanville, a doyen *malgré soi*: 'I am just another toiler in the vineyard.' He rejected, almost fearfully, the idea that he was a doyen, and spoke of doyens he had known, explaining why he was quite different. 'There's something we used to say about such people in the 50s,' he said. 'They think it's all real.'

I like the ambiguity there. It's not clear whether they think that the concerns of their chosen sport are real, or that the act of writing about sport for a newspaper is real. Perhaps both. But it is quite clear that, the more real you think it is, the less you qualify as a human being. And therefore as a teller of tales.

This feeling of 'up here' helps to explain why it is so easy to get the bends when you surface from assignment to domestic life. My wife has the policy of treating me like an agreeable but rather difficult lunatic: expecting little, employing a degree of detachment that seems to make things work.

But then I came to chiefdom quiet late in life, and I did my mad obsessive travelling before we had children. These two things make for comparative sanity. These days I travel because I must – but what does 'must' mean? I returned home out of love. Joy it was, too: I drank champagne. Hugged wife and boys. Got ready for the Olympic Games. Because I must.

14

But my horses treated me as usual. With the same mixture of affection and indifference that so fascinates the horseman. I schooled my young horse on the ground, goal-orientated, and I rode my old mare out, free and goalless, and it was all good.

I don't compete. I used to compete: eventing, cross-country, showjumping, even a spot of dressage. Loved it. No special urge to compete now. I always explain that this is because I have enough stress in my professional life, and perhaps that's true. But perhaps it's a bit glib.

I don't want to compete. I like to work with my horses at home, without anyone getting in the way. I am – well, I'm not bad, as a horseman. I'm pretty competent. The best thing about me is that I don't get tight and stressed at difficult moments. I am quiet. I can impart a sense of relaxation to a horse: I can be a tension-killer. If a horse spooks at a rolling paper bag, I will laugh and pat, not grip extra tight and wallop. It's OK, be cool. And mostly, the horse is cool. To my quiet satisfaction.

I am tempted to go on from here and tell you all about my horsemanly skills. Fill the whole book up with my horsey adventures. Plain brown wrapper stuff. I want to do this is because, in some ways, I am more proud of my abilities as a horseman than I am of my abilities as a writer. And yet I have no illusions about my level of skills with horses: no chiefly illusions of genius, no ego buttressed by horsemanly awards.

My out-of-proportion delight in my own skills as a horseman is, I think, something to do with fear. I have known fear with horses, many times. The stuff any horse-person does with any horse on a daily basis is potentially lethal. The difference between a horse and a dog or a cat or a goldfish is that the horse can kill you. And I have picked up my injuries. Working with a young horse is particularly dangerous, because neither you nor the young horse knows precisely what it is going to do. A young horse has no framework to his life, no set patterns, no rails to run on: that is precisely what the process of training is trying to give him. One moment all is well; the next, you have a horse performing handstands.

In other words, I have to be brave. Ever so slightly brave every day, and quite seriously brave on certain days when things with a young horse get slightly, or more than slight-ly out of control. As a result, I have to face up to moments of funk. And say: all right, if you don't want to do it, don't do it. You can always give up. And you answer: well, I do want to do it, but I am quite seriously frightened. That's quite an interesting state to be in: to be really quite fright-ened of something that you know you are actually going to go on and do. Physically frightened, I mean. It's not like being frightened of public speaking (which I am, of course). I am talking here about being afraid that you might break your collar-bone, or your back, or your skull. And then doing the thing that you feared might bring this about. Interesting, as I say.

Experiencing physical fear is a big thing for anybody. One of the reasons why I feel a need to write about it here is because I am well aware that I am regarded as the great coward of the sporting round. I have it on good authority: 'You're a nice boy, Simon, but your trouble is you're a fucking coward.' Words of Hugh McIlvanny of the *Sunday Times*, and who am I to argue with such a man?

At the heart of my reputation for cowardice is my dislike of boxing. And I was to be brought right back to boxing in a little over a week's time. At least I could do so without fearing I might break my neck.

15

At the Olympic Games, the two things that worry you most are the nature of your cell and the efficiency of the transport. When I arrived in Athens for the Olympic Games of 2004, it took three hours to get from the airport to the media village, not a good sign. Especially as my cell wasn't in the media village. It was in something called Iaso 2. I was by no means sanguine about this. In Sydney, we had stayed at a hotel that served me a fat boiled egg and Vegemite toast for breakfast, and it had had a nice little bar on the top floor where I could drink Cascade beer at the end of the day. And now here, in Athens, I had a great desire, not for luxury, but for comfort. To be comforted, in times of exhaustion and stress.

I was dropped somewhere distinctly unpromising: a maternity hospital. I asked a couple of people where to go: no one knew. It would have been a great help had I known then that Iaso was a daughter of Ascelpius, the Greek god of medicine. After half an hour – very amusing it is, walking round and round the same place with the temperature in the high 80s while carrying two bags, one full of laptop and the other full of clean shirts and modern Greek literature, all the time having no idea whatsoever where you are going, and finding no one at all with any idea about anything to do with what you are trying to do – I found out where to go. Which was, yes, the maternity hospital.

Please don't think I exaggerate for effect. It was not a former maternity hospital. It was not going to be a maternity hospital as soon as the Olympic Games had finished. It was a working maternity hospital: a lobby filled with gravid women, while outside its doors men desperately sucked life from cigarettes while the floor was crossed and recrossed by doctors strutting about like film stars. I had already been in twice and given up, as this obviously was the Wrong Place.

But it wasn't. Around a couple of turns of corridor, there was a nice Greek student dressed as a Games volunteer, and after various complications, we established that, against all logic – this in the country that invented logic, logic being of course a Greek word – I had a cell on the upper floor. I was shown around by a concierge lady in a lemon yellow nursey-uniform.

It was a cell of very decent size, with a viciously shiny floor that was to lay me out a couple of days later. There was a panic button in the shower, handles for levering myself on and off the bog, and the bed was high off the ground and on wheels. It could be raised, lowered and tilted into whatever conformation I thought necessary. The only concession they had made to its non-maternal use was to take away the stirrups.

The window was large and looked out over the Olympic complex. I could see swift: good start. There was no desk, but the phone went almost immediately and I was asked to write 1,500 words on why the Olympic Games are sexy. I moved a cushion from the sofa, and placed my laptop on the coffee table, to make myself a sort of Zen prayer-desk to work at. It would do very nicely.

I unpacked, a luxury you can afford at the Olympic Games, when you are not always off somewhere else the next day. And you know something? I had changed my method. Plenty of books, yes. I had brought a small immersion heater, a mug and a box of rooibos teabags. I was pretty self-sufficient. You will get the impression, then, that a base is important. If you can make some sort of accommodation with your accommodation, the story begins to look a great deal more writable. I could, I thought, write here.

The new bit of methodology was a Walkman with speakers. I used always to travel with a Walkman, but then I got fed up with having the sound forever and inescapably dinning into my ears. It made me feel claustrophobic. More and more things do. One of these days I will refuse to get on a flight because I don't have an aisle seat. I explained this latest neurosis to a friend, who told me to get a pair of silly little speakers. The day before I left, I bought the whole lot, Walkman and speakers and all, for seventeen quid, a fact that quite doubled my delight. I had a wallet filled with favourite music, and so I tried it out. At full volume, the Goldberg Variations whispered over the ice-rink floor. But I didn't want anyone to shout, least of all Bach.

Tentatively, I began to wonder if the bizarre nature of my cell was not in itself a pleasure. A stimulus. But it was time to parturiate: time to give birth to my first piece from Athens. Sexy indeed.

16

One thing that sex and sport have in common is that stupid people like them both. One important difference is that clever people can enjoy sex – and can say that they enjoy sex – without forfeiting their right to be considered clever. However, a clever person who claims to enjoy sport will be considered less clever as a result.

I remember reading a newspaper piece on what people watch on television. AS Byatt was invited to comment: 'I'm an intellectual and obviously – except for the odd thing on BBC4 – the BBC doesn't cater for intellectuals. The only things I really watch are sport and 24-hour digital news. Everything else is too slow: telling you things you already know.'

This was a knowingly brave and challenging thing to say. True, Byatt's reputation for cleverness meant that she could get away with this without being thought less of. I suspect she enjoyed the tease: because not liking sport is seen by many as prima facie evidence for being an intellectual.

If you claim to like sport, you are knowingly stepping away from the intellectual side of life. That is one of the reasons why politicians always claim to be football fans: it makes them seem like good ordinary people. We don't want to be governed by anybody too clever, now do we? So Tony Blair has always claimed to be a fervid fan of his beloved – crucial cliché – Newcastle. The story is that Blair talked about sitting behind the goal to watch the great Jackie Millburn; Blair is too young to have seen Milburn and, anyway, there were no seats behind the goal at that time. Blair denies this story, and claims that it is an urban myth. But the story does at least illustrate the importance of sporting credentials for anyone who doesn't wish to be seen as a stand-offish intellectual.

All people in public life who have a taste for sport know that this will affect their intellectual credibility, but that it will also make them more loveable, more like the not-particularly-clever rest. If you want to set yourself up as really clever, however, it is very important to despise sport. There are the arties and the hearties: and the twain must never meet. This is an antithesis summed up for all time in *Brideshead Revisited*, when, after a long and lovely lunch, Anthony Blanche seizes a megaphone and 'in languishing tones recited passages from *The Waste Land* to the sweatered and muffled throng on their way to the river: "I Tiresias, have foresuffered all," he sobbed to them from the Venetian arches.'

The hearties later dunk Blanche in a fountain – 'nothing could give me keener pleasure than to be manhandled by you meaty boys' – to demonstrate the mutual loathing that exists between those who like sport and those who like art.

It does not take any great intellectual acuity to see that this position is absurd. It is as idiotic to dismiss sport as a concern solely of the stupid as it would be to do the same thing with sex. But then sex has always been an intellectual concern. In the early decades of the 20th century, to write about sex with shattering frankness was essential to one's intellectual credibility. When a true modernist wrote, nothing was comprehensible except the four-letter words. Bloom tossed off on the beach, Molly gloated that she had been fucked yes and damn well fucked too, while Mellors told his employer's wife that she was the best bit o' cunt left on earth and showed her some very inventive ideas about flower arrangement.

Sex is intellectually respectable, sport is not. We lack the scene in which Mellors tells Lady Chatterley about the 4-4-2 system. This is, of course, a very British thing; perhaps I mean a very English thing. In places other than England, an intellectual can like football without forfeiting claims to be an intellectual. Thrill, then, to this collection of renaissance goalkeepers: Albert Camus, Vladimir Nabokov, Yevgeny Yevtushenko, Julio Iglesias, Che Guevara and Pope John Paul II. Note that none of them is English.

It was, of course, Camus who said, 'For, after many years in which the world has afforded me many experiences, what I most surely know in the long run about morality and the obligations of men, I owe to sport.' (It was, inevitably, Brian Glanville who brought the essay that contains this line to our attention.) No English philosopher would say such a thing without a layers-deep coating of protective irony. But Camus said it, and said it plain. Note that 'most surely'. Sport, it seems, does not deal in subtleties and ambiguities when it comes to morality and obligation. Perhaps sport can only bring us subtlety when it comes to execution. But subtle or not, Camus thought sport was a big thing, a thing that somehow mattered. And he was of course, clever. But not English.

I am English, and I like sport. I write about sport for my living. Therefore, I am stupid; or at best not terribly clever, and will only look silly if I pretend to be clever. Unfortunately, I don't accept that. I don't accept the limitations that a liking for sport condemns me to. I do things like reading books. Obviously, I can't do this because I understand them, still less because I enjoy them. I can only be doing it for the sake of showing off.

Like most people, I have a wide range of cultural references. When I write about sport, I sweep them up without apology: references to the Modesty Blaise books, references to 'Allo 'Allo (of which more later), references to, perhaps, The Waste Land.

As a writer about sport I am not entitled to read The Waste Land, still less to refer to it. The idea of referring to Eliot and football in the same piece is, to some, by definition hilarious. Am I beginning to sound bitter here? Worse, a little shrill?

You're right: I am not entirely balanced about my regular appearances in Private Eye's Pseud's Corner. My feeling is that this magazine consistently confuses pseudo-intellectual with intellectual. But I will not have my agenda set by the mockers. No. I write about what I see and what I understand, the way I see it, the way I understand it. I shall continue to write as if sport, like sex, were worth the time of an intelligent person. I would see any other option as a failing of courage.

17

It wasn't Joyce or Eliot or even Waugh that got me into trouble in Germany. It was a thoughtful and deeply intellectual (pseudo-intellectual, if you prefer) reference to *'Allo 'Allo*. Being an intellectual like AS Byatt, I only watch television for sport and *'Allo 'Allo*. And a few years ago, I had to write a piece about Michael Schumacher, and why the English hate him.

I wrote with a light touch, keeping the ironies decently organised. I said that Schumacher represented for the English a traditional comic bogeyman, national archetype and pantomime villain. He was, I said, like Herr Flick, the Gestapo officer in, yes, *'Allo 'Allo*. But perhaps you are less of an intellectual than me, and you don't watch *'Allo 'Allo*; in which case I must tell you that Herr Flick is the one who always wears a leather coat, never takes his gloves off even when smoking a cigarette, and says things like: 'You may kiss me if you vish, Helga.' ('I vood razzer not.')

Next thing I knew, I had a telephone call from a German lady. Apparently it was all over the papers in Germany: *The Times* says that Michael Schumacher is like a Gestapo officer. I found myself in the ludicrous position of trying to explain English seaside-postcard humour to a German. 'Well, it's a comedy about the French resistance.' Explaining 'comedy' was hard enough. It got harder when I mentioned the war.

Actually, the German lady was delightful and clever and almost, I think, understood. I tried to explain that Hitler was a stock comic character for Englishmen and tried to explain about *Fawlty Towers*. The idea of Hitler and the funny walk was, of course, completely baffling. I tried to explain that there was a jocular element to the English dislike of Schumacher, and that the English see a huge comic element in Hitler and the Nazis. A couple of years later, Prince Harry was in trouble for dressing up in Nazi uniform for a party. Harry was at a loss as to how anybody could be under the impression that the Nazis weren't a joke.

And I wondered then if this wasn't something to do with the reason why extreme political movements have never really gone down big with the British. We too easily see the funny side of it. God defend us all, then, from the conspiracy of the humourless. PG Wodehouse himself was a victim of this conspiracy: disgraced and vilified for an error of judgment; that is to say, he spoke of trivialities on German radio in wartime. People said that made him a traitor: a fascist sympathiser. But Bertie Wooster said it all when he addressed Sir Roderick Spode, a character in *The Code of the Woosters*, based unapologetically on Sir Oswald Moseley, founder of the British Fascist Union.

Spode is the leader of k Shorts. But Bertie tells him: 'It's about time that some public-spirited person came along and told you where you got off. The trouble with you, Spode, is that just because you have succeeded in inducing a handful of halfwits to disfigure the London scene by going about in black shorts, you think you're someone. You hear them shouting "Heil Spode" and you imagine it is the Voice of the People. That is where you make your bloomer. What the Voice of the People is saying is: "Look at that frightful ass Spode swanking about in footer bags! Did you ever in your puff see such a perfect perisher?"'

God, as I believe I said before, defend us from the humourless.

18

If you write on more than one sport for your living, you need to find a formula for answering the question everyone asks: which sport do you like best? This never seems to be a question with a simple answer. For a start, there are at least three ways in which you can enjoy a sport: by doing it, by watching it, by writing about it. And within these categories, there are complex sub-categories: you can watch out of loyalty; you can watch for the pure love of seeing one will against another; you can watch in search of narrative; you can watch in search of mythic resonance; you can watch in search of beauty. My grandmother, an amateur silversmith, used to sit at the window to watch the football being played in King's Heath Park in Birmingham: 'Because it's so pretty.'

My stock answer to this overwhelming question is based

on the attorney in *Fear and Loathing in Las Vegas*, who, stoned on – so far as I remember – acid, mescaline, ether and booze, claimed mendaciously to be a professional motorcycle racer. He is asked which team he rides for. After a moment's pause, he answers: 'The really big fuckers.' He then produces a knife and asks – did I say he was in a lift or elevator? – 'Anyone want to get cut?'

Well, when it comes to watching sport, and when it comes to writing about sport, I like the really big fuckers. These come in two categories, but with a huge overlap, like a Venn diagram in which the area in common is at least as big as the area unshared. One category comprises events that are big because they matter hugely to the people who are playing, and the other comprises events that are big because they matter hugely to the people who are watching. Or more importantly, to the people who are reading.

The Olympic Games is big: a feast of really big fuckers. Back in Barcelona, in 1992, I had a revelation. A lot of the venues were grouped around Montjuic, and there was a media bus service that made a perpetual Dante-esque circle around this mountain-top, stopping at each sporting destination as it went. I was on this bus, commuting, perhaps, from the judo to the pingpong via the Greco-Roman wrestling, when I realised that I could get off the bus at any point, walk into any hall or onto any sports field, and witness the most important day in somebody's life: the few minutes for which all his previous life had been a preparation. These events matter hugely to the participants, and also to a huge number of spectators and/or readers, but they don't necessarily matter to the people I was writing for.

I find that aspect of the Olympic Games enthralling. That and the size of it. I remember when David Chappell, then *The Times* sports editor, made his landfall at the main press centre in Sydney: roughly speaking, an aircraft hangar full of thousands – no exaggeration – of desks, phone, televisions, and endless yards of pigeon-holes awaiting the arrival of endless pieces of paper. And on the next floor all the offices of all the agencies and large news organisations; and then the offices of the media people from most of the national Olympic Committees; also mysterious places that were the domain of the photographers. There were something like 10,000 officially accredited journalists in Sydney: 'I knew the Olympics was big,' Chappell muttered, a man not easily awed. 'I didn't realise it was this big.'

Of course he didn't. Nobody does. Most of us see the Olympic Games through the keyhole of television. We see the events in which there are local heroes, local medal hopes. In Britain, we never see the handball, the pingpong, the taekwando, the football, the rhythmic gymnastics, the synchronised swimming; yet all those events are contested and followed and written about and read about with as much commitment and passion as the British had for Steve Redgrave's finest hour.

There are so many things that matter in the Olympic Games: so much so that the form in which the mattering takes place becomes irrelevant. We are drawn to the mattering itself by an irresistible force. An audience of 5.9 million stayed up to watch Rhona Martin lead a British team to an Olympic medal... in curling. It wasn't the curling we stayed up to watch, it was the Olympic Games. It was not the action that made us watch, it was the mattering. In backgammon, the money you bet is adjusted by the turning of the doubling cube. At the Olympic Games, the cube turns again and again: two, four, eight, sixteen. Every final takes us to 64 and then beyond, as if the stakes were determined by a phantasmagorical cube with an endless number of faces, which turns at the very essence of it all to show the face that reads infinity. You ask Redgrave, you ask Ben Johnson. It is the mattering itself that matters.

All sports represent the collision of wills: people or teams who want the same thing and have to cause somebody pain in order to get it. The more it matters to the athletes, the more vivid the experience is for the spectator, and for the writer. And, if the writer gets it right, for the reader. That's the idea, anyway. The essence of the Olympic Games is that it demands that the writer should also be in Olympic form: the form of his life, writing things that matter more than anything else he has ever written in his life.

There has already been plenty of natural history in these notes so far, and there will be more to come. And here is what the Olympic Games is all about: biodiversity. At the World Cup, the event to which the Games is often compared, you have 32 nations, one sport and one sex: it is a monoculture, a horizon-to-horizon prairie that provides us with a single crop. At the Games there are 202 nations, 29 sports and, best of all, two sexes. There are more ways of mattering here than you find anywhere else in the world outside the rainforest. Naturally, I wanted to capture the individual species and name them. But more than that: I wanted to capture the immensity.

19

And still the Games hadn't started. It was a nice evening, and there was no sport, not yet. We could have a mild treat, could we not? So four of us travelled into town from the Olympic complex to eat. We had just arrived in Monastiraki when David Chappell's phone went. He had to leave us: a big story had broken: two Greek athletes had dodged a drugs test and gone missing. I arrived at the restaurant with Jenny MacArthur, equestrian correspondent, and Jeremy Whittle, cycling correspondent. They were to monopolise the conversation throughout the meal.

That's because my phone went, and I was asked to supply 800 words of comment on the scandal of the Greek athletes. How amusing: to produce 800 words in 45 minutes about two people, only one of whom you have heard of, neither of whose names you can spell, and about whom you know almost nothing. I borrowed a pen from Jenny and some paper from Andrew Longmore of the *Sunday Times*, now of the *Independent on Sunday*, who happened to be in the same restaurant. I then did a bit of frenzied scribbling, taking occasional distracted slurps of wine and forkfuls of what might have been nice food.

I then went into the street to dictate these words to a copy-taker, and discovered that I could actually see what I had written if I stood in the light of a shop doorway opposite the restaurant. So I read the stuff, complete with punctuation, spelling out the Greek names letter by letter, wondering why whatever you have written sounds so horribly lame when read out in this painstaking manner. The piece was a comment on what such a scandal means to a host country and it was – well, it was on time. And I was, naturally, briefly shattered by the sudden outpouring of energy. It's not a hard thing to do – though doing it well is hard, as I have said – but it's always a bit on the briefly shattering side.

I got back to the table, offered apologies and received wine and stared out in a glazed sort of a way. The headwaitress walked between me and the lit shop window. She was a little under six feet, gracile, graceful, beautiful and wearing an asymmetric skirt that was at once rendered transparent by the light behind her. It was a vision of pure and blinding beauty.

She was James Joyce's bird girl, the long-legged wading beauty that Stephen Dedalus saw as he walked along the beach, seeing his own future as an artist: 'When she felt his presence and the worship of his eyes her eyes turned to him in quiet sufferance of his gaze, without shame or wantonness… – Heavenly God, cried Stephen's soul, in an outburst of profane joy.' And like Stephen, I was touched to my soul by this piercing vision of perfect loveliness.

There was no need, and for that matter, no inclination to do anything about this: to try a chat-up, make a pass, all the routine of seduction. It was nothing to do with her: it was all to do with me. It was a revelation of beauty: and I, to whom it had been revealed, found in it great joy and wondered very deeply what it meant.

I am still wondering. But I think it meant that sport and sporting journalism do not truly matter. They only seem to do so when you are tightrope-writing your way to a humorously close deadline. Neither sport nor newspapers matter much compared to beauty. A man looks on a beautiful woman. That matters. Sport is only about life. Beauty is life.

20

Beauty, immensity. There were 10,000 journalists in Athens, as I have said. If you like, 10,000 artists, all trying to grapple with beauty and immensity. Certainly, people whose daily task was to start with nothing and, by means of some kind of relationship with beauty and immensity, to end with something. But, like footballers and Roger Federer, all journos know that as soon as we claim to be artists we fail. We have to understand that the things we create are doomed. What we write has a brief moment of life between its preliminary nothing and its ultimate destiny at the bottom of the cat-tray. A piece of journalism is a bubble, floating in the air, perhaps to blow away unseen, perhaps to provoke a crow of delight: before it pops.

Ezra Pound had it right. Literature, he said, is news that stays news. Bloom's defecation in the crazy jakes is still news 100 years (to the year) after Bloomsday: my few hundred words about the perfect beauty of Svetlana Khorkina, the Olympic gymnast have long since gone – shredded, I always hope, to create bedding for racehorses: a marvellous and fitting end. What we write in a hurry is read in a hurry and forgotten in a hurry. Our work, like certain adult, sexual forms of insect, has a life of a few hours. Our only aim – our only possible aim – is to make them good and fertile hours. The only way to make them good is by sowing a seed in the reader's mind. Like the athletes we write about, we must labour as if the work we did were the most important thing in the history of the world; and do so in the sure and certain knowledge that it is nothing of the kind. Our lives depend on that contradiction. If we cannot master both halves of it, then we are worth even less.

21

The first time I rode a competitive round of showjumping, I entered the ring, saluted the judges, cantered a wary circle and then leapt the first jump. Rather impressively, to my mind. Bong! The bell sounded at once for my elimination. I had neglected to ride through the start. I was very miffed about this at the time. I had made a three-hour journey to get there – I was living in Hong Kong at the time, and had travelled from my home on Lamma Island to the furthest reaches of the New Territories – suffered the most desperate agonies of nerves, and all for this. I thought it unfair. I thought I should have been allowed to compete. I thought someone really should have explained the protocol to me.

I now see that I was wrong on both counts. It was my own responsibility to learn the rules, and the judges were right to stick by them. This is not from rule-worship – a sad affliction, most frequently found among golfers – but because sport is by definition an artificial situation. The freedoms of real life are inappropriate here. Football is impossible if the ball and the players do not stay on the pitch. You can express yourself freely only within the confines of the rules and the white lines. The rules need to be applied in order to stress the seriousness of the whole thing. If we did not do so, we might come to the conclusion that sport wasn't serious at all, and that would never do. Sport must pretend to a seriousness that it doesn't actually possess, if it is to exist at all.

Which brings me to the Olympic three-day event. (I must say that for someone with occasional pretensions to being an intellectual, I have picked the worst possible pursuits in my life. Birdwatching, horses, sport – not entirely convincing, I think.) It was, alas, a deeply flawed competition. A three-day event takes in three phases of action: dressage first, showjumping last and, in the middle, the hardest of the three: the cross-country, the gallop over a series of fiendishly difficult obstacles. The trouble was that in Athens the fearsome obstacles weren't fearsome at all. They did not separate the good from the less good. They lumped the whole field together as average. It was too easy. The Olympics is supposed to be the best against the best: the ultimate thing. And this wasn't. The three-day event became, in effect, a showjumping competition.

Which meant that Bettina Hoy of Germany won it. It was then noted that she had done the exact opposite of what I did all those years ago. She had gone through the start twice. Her round should have been timed from when she first started: instead, the clock was stopped and re-started. This was incorrect procedure. After protests, Hoy was stripped of her gold, Leslie Law won the individual gold medal and Great Britain took the team silver behind France. Heartbreak, anger, bitterness, embarrassment: not the way we would wish to win a gold medal, the Brits all said. Humph, I said. You win things by being better than your opponents. That includes making fewer mistakes. Hoy made an error; Law didn't. That's sport. Sport is cruel. Many children learn that in the Pony Club; I learned it in the showjumping ring of the Royal Hong Kong Jockey Club; Hoy learned it at the Olympic Games. Of course sport's cruel. What on earth would be the point if it wasn't?

22

The kovacs is the most beautiful single thing in sport, and – perhaps not entirely by coincidence – it requires the most courage. It is a move in men's high bar gymnastics. You let go of the bar, somersault and then – this, of course, is plan A – catch it again. The snag is that you have to take your eye off the bar for most of the manoeu-vre, and the basic principle of catching anything is to keep your eye on the ball.

The Athens maternity hospital was reasonably close to the gymnastics hall, so I was able to get there several times. In fact, I only wrote one piece about gymnastics for the entire Games, but I went there four or five times for the simple and the complex love of it. Of course it's a flawed sport. All sports are flawed. It's subjectively judged, which opens the way for corruption and favouritism and misjudgments, though all sports are, to a greater or lesser extent, subjectively judged. Even boxing – you ask Lennox Lewis, who was denied the world heavyweight title by a bemusing split decision.

But gymnastics is beautiful and immense. Especially beautiful is the competitors' striving for impossible perfection, though even that is less beautiful than the occasional illusion that perfection has been attained.

They used to perform the kovacs only in the tuck position: I was there for the first Olympic piked kovacs, and also for the first one performed fully laid out. Each one harder, more spectacular, more dangerous.

This is a mad sport, and being mad, its mandarins recently changed the marking system weighting it in favour of the cautious as opposed to the bold. (After the Olympic Games, they changed it yet again, to an open-ended system that does away with the perfect ten. Perfection is no longer attainable or indeed, desirable: the sport now requires only an endless succession of improvement. That is perhaps more in tune with the human condition.)

I went to the men's high bar final, and it seemed very much as if this was a drab competition, to be won by the safest performer. Then Alexei Nemov came in with a glorious high-risk routine, joyful and triumphant. He got low marks for it. The crowd, incensed, booed for fifteen minutes without ceasing, until Nemov himself asked for quiet. Paul Hamm of the United States then performed a kovacs-free routine of solid safety, and was put into first position, which created even more unhappiness. And then came Igor Cassina of Italy, who threw three kovacs in his routine, including one laid out with a full twist: a move called the Cassina Straight. It was so perfectly performed that it didn't even look risky.

But then the best of the kovacs is to be found when it doesn't look daring at all: when the gymnast creates the illusion of perfect control. He takes a huge risk – people break their necks doing this sport – but makes it look like part of the pattern, following with simple inevitability from the move before, leading with simple inevitability to the move that follows. The risk itself is there, but that is not the point. The most important thing is the flight. The meaning of the kovacs is in the context – as part of a perfectly fluent routine – and it is as if the movement that takes place between handgrip and hand grip is neither fearful not ostentatiously brave. It just is. It is inevitable: beautiful, perfect, and its meaning is a form of flight. Good writing should be like that, or try to be, whether it is destined for the great libraries of the world, or the cat-tray. And, for every writer, the ground is very hard.

23 If David Beckham had been an Olympian he would be seen as a waster. Or at least, as a man who missed his destiny. A man who failed to seize his time. And that is the art of being an Olympian: the seizing of the time. The great beauty, the great perfection of an Olympian is that he or she must perform in the knowledge that there is no second chance.

The Olympic Games is, as I have said, often compared with the World Cup. This is not a sensible comparison. Beckham failed at the World Cup in 1998. He kicked an Argentinian, got sent off, England lost, and were out of the competition. Beckham became a national hate-object as a result. And there was not another World Cup for four years, so redemption would have been a very long way away if the World Cup was the only prize in football worth playing for.

But that is the way it always is for an Olympian – someone who takes part in one of the heartland Olympic sports, like athletics, swimming, rowing, gymnastics, sports for which nothing matters – nothing matters at all – except the Olympic Games. If you fail at the Olympic Games you have nothing. Nothing for four years. And that is what gives the Games that extraordinary intensity. Winning is not just about being perfect. It is about being perfect now. The unforgiving present tense of the Olympic Games dominates the hearts and minds of the competitors. If not now, when?

For Beckham, there was redemption to be found as soon as the following year. Consequently, he was able to perform one of the great self-rescuing acts in the history of sport. He refused to leave the country, as many recommended. Instead, he stayed with Manchester United and inspired them to their immortal treble of the 1998–99 season: the Premiership, FA Cup and European Cup.

But for an Olympian, there are no consolation prizes,

and, if you seek a second chance, you must wait nearly half a sporting lifetime for it. And very few athletes in any discipline have eight years at the top. If you mess up the Olympic Games, you have four years for the suffering. In Atlanta 1996, Paula Radcliffe finished fifth in the 5,000 metres. In Sydney at the 2000 Olympic Games, Radcliffe led most of the way in the 10,000 metres and finished fourth. She then reinvented herself as a marathon runner, and set some astonishing world records. But this is athletics, a heartland Olympic sport, and so naturally Radcliffe still hungered for the sport's ultimate reward. She wanted an Olympic gold medal. And this was her time. It was hers for the seizing.

The greatest seizer of them all was Steve Redgrave. I saw him win his fifth gold medal at his fifth Olympic Games in Sydney; and it will go down as the greatest piece of sport I have ever seen. I am not challenging for originality here: it was the greatest piece of sport anybody has ever seen. Longevity, it seems to me, is an ineluctable aspect of sporting greatness.

I was also at the waterside in 2004 to see Matthew Pinsent claim his fourth gold medal. And it was as fine an example of time-seizing as you could ever wish to see. There was something gloriously mythical about it: an echo of the *Odyssey*, the story of a ship cursed by the gods. The hero prevails in the end, after many tribulations and, at last, he can pause and weep an ocean of tears: just as Pinsent did.

Pinsent's boat had originally been a pair, which won everything and then inexplicably failed. They finished fourth at the World Championships of 2003. The pair was sacked, and remade as a four. It didn't work. A man was dropped. Another was injured. And then eight weeks before the Games, another member, Alex Partridge, suffered a collapsed lung and dropped out. Ed Coode came back into the four: seven weeks. An Olympic crew normally takes four years to create.

It was terrifyingly close. The British crew went side-by-side with Canada from start to finish and throughout, Canada held the slightest advantage. It was perfectly clear that this was a heroic British effort doomed to end in failure. There was a feeling of glum inevitability about the process: a feeling that your best is never, ever quite good enough, not for the things you really want. But, impossibly, the British four won in the last ten strokes, and they did so because of Pinsent. He recalls thinking: 'We're doing our best and we're still not making any inroads at all.' Desperate times require desperate measures. Great times require great people to seize them. Pinsent took the crew over the line by means of a massive outpouring of the self. He refused to accept the plain and obvious fact of defeat, and remade reality in front of us. It was one of the most stirring pieces of sport I have ever witnessed.

Athletes are always talking about 'giving everything'. It is rare that you see this literally take place before you. At the close, Pinsent was a man empty, mind and spirit gone. Over the course of the next hour, his mind and spirit had slowly to reunite themselves with the big husk they had abandoned. And then Pinsent was embracing his Greek wife – no, not Penelope. Demetra, or Dee. She said that if he wanted to carry on for another sixteen years, she would be content. No doubt she would have got on with her weaving contentedly enough; but Pinsent retired, deciding that a mere four gold medals was sufficient.

The following day I was at the Panathinaiko Stadium, walking past a small house in which, many years ago, I had drunk prodigious quantities of ouzo. This was as an essential part of a wild schoolboy hitch-hiking adventure. But it was not my adventures I was writing about. It was Radcliffe's. Commentators say again and again: 'And now it's all about who wants it more.' Actually, the victory can often go to the one who wants it less: the one who can take the competition in their stride, with relaxed muscles and mind. The one who thinks it really is life and death can get consumed by the madness of the occasion. Ed Smith played three Tests for England and is currently with Middlesex. He also writes: 'It's the easiest criticism of all. "He lost concentration on that four-foot putt," people say, as though it's like forgetting to lock your car door. Just a lack of attention. Sometimes it is, but how much more often is failure the result of trying too hard, of tensing up, of over-revving. Most sportsmen try too hard, not too little.'

Nobody in the marathon wanted victory more than Radcliffe. That was precisely the problem. She failed to run away from her pursuers, and slowly, the exhaustion and the heat and the gut-ache and, above all, the fear ate away at her confidence, and she suffered the most desperate public breakdown. It was not decent to watch. It was a total collapse of will and personality: a terrible remorse at her failure, at her understanding that this had been her moment and she had failed to seize it.

Cruel, cruel: Britain bathed in the desperation of defeat. And I was able to counterpoint my tale of Radcliffe's defeat with that of Pinsent's victory the day before. An athlete who seized his time; an athlete who failed to seize hers.

Four years. A lifetime. And it comes to this.

24

She wept. She wept salt tears, and I could feel tears of my own prickle at the back of my eyes. All around me, I could see tough, hard hacks making casual little touches to the face – scratches, rubs, adjustments of spectacles – all moves designed to disguise the welling-up of tears.

Tell me, dear one, who died? It was I, Paula, who died. Me, the late Paula Radcliffe. This was a funeral at which the chief mourner and the deceased were the same person. She wept on television, and then she wept anew at the press conference, and all the while she was treated like a mother whose child had died: hushed, gentle voices, elaborate consideration, gentle gestures, pats on forearm, kind pressure on small of back.

It was as if Radcliffe believed that love would never again be hers, that only by means of victory could she deserve love. Much later, in her autobiography, she told the tale of her agony in the gutters of Papagou, and her rescue by friends who offered to contact her husband and coach, Gary Lough. Not that, she said. Anything but that. Some marriages are very curious arrangements, and certainly every marriage is a unique, incomprehensible civilisation, virtually impenetrable even to the most educated observer, sociologist, anthropologist, archaeologist. And it was for herself she was weeping; she made that quite plain: "No one was hurting inside like I was."

She deserved the pain, the misery, the anxiety. She brought it on herself. I would not wish such pain on her; I sympathised, to the point of clenched-fist, not-weeping-not-me eye-rubbing, with her sadness, her sense, not so much of defeat, but of loss, of bereavement. But she had deserved it all right: just as she deserved all the glory and praise for her queenly achievements in commercial marathons.

All the sacrifice! Sacrifice for what? If you sacrifice something for yourself, it is not really sacrifice, is it? I remember my wife asking me how some book or other was going. I replied, misquoting the God-struck church-cleaner in *The Commitments*: 'A lot of hard work. If you didn't do it for yourself, who would you do it for?'

Sport is a juggernaut. A huge vehicle with monstrous wheels, bearing a deity, rumbling its way across the world, perpetually surrounded by a seething mob of fervent worshippers. Frequently, the worshippers stumble, and are crushed between the pitiless wheels of the car. Sad enough: but the fallers are willing victims even if they didn't seek that end. It was only their adoration of the idol that made them vulnerable. And sport rumbles onward, the crushing of a victim failing to alter its course by as much as a centimetre.

Radcliffe has known disappointment. She has known triumph also; and in sport, all triumph is built on the disappointment of others. She had inflicted vast disappointment – vast pain – in her time. Now sport decreed that it was her turn. Sport is not only cruel. Sport is also dangerous. The more you devote yourself to the idol on the car, the more dangerous it is.

25

It was somehow reassuring to learn that the ancient story was still doing the rounds. Reassuring to know the contempt in which I am held by my colleagues. A youngish fellow, not been in the game – insofar as it is a game – for as long as I have, was heard asking if it was really true that I had been to a world heavyweight fight and hidden under the desk for its duration.

It is not. My objection to boxing is based on philosophical rather than squeamish grounds. But the untrue story sticks with me: it seems to possess a truth that no amount of fact can destroy. That sort of thing is true of many genuinely famous people, especially in sport. Fred Trueman, the great England fast bowler, was supposed, while touring the subcontinent, to have told an Indian prince: 'Pass us t'mustard, Gunga Din.' His denials only created new myths: 'It were t'bloody salt I were after.'

So in one sense I can never deny the story. Morally, if not actually, I watched Mike Tyson beat the bejasus out of Larry Holmes at Atlantic City in 1988 from beneath the desk. I accept that. No one wishes to listen to a rational destruction of a thing he loves: and many people in my profession love boxing.

And so I have had a myth created for me as a sort of immunisation against my rationally held beliefs. No one wishes to be infected by them. I should feel flattered.

Should I spoil the story with facts? Of course I should. Facts are just as interesting as myths. And I have some things to say about boxing, and I would wish you to understand them as things fully baked. So there I was in Atlantic City – white and reeling from a monstrous hallucinating flu which required me, that night and for two following nights, to remove the soaked sheets from my bed halfway towards morning. I was feeling pretty ghastly at the fight, but I reported it with competence. That required me to watch the savagery. I am not proud of doing so: nor apologetic. Facts, that's all.

My witty friend and colleague Roy Collins (now football correspondent for the *Sunday Telegraph*) remarked, mischievously, after I had staggered off to my as-yet-unsoaked bed, that I had watched the fight from beneath the desk. It was a joke: a sharp but affectionate one. It wasn't intended to be something people actually believed. But it was a joke that certain people needed to believe in. Alan Hubbard, columnist from the *Observer*, absurdly, tried to stand the joke up as fact, and failed – but he stuck it to me anyway, writing a piece that advised *The Times* to send out a proper boxing writer in future, and not 'a somewhat sensitive soul' like me. A somewhat insensitive soul, then.

Sport is a metaphor. Every sport. Football and rugby are

cod battles: tennis is a cod duel. Running races are about predator and prey. Cricket is a complex metaphor about life and death. Horseracing is a paradigm of evolution: only the fastest get to breed, get to become ancestors. That is the point of sport: it is pretend. Its metaphorical nature is what gives it meaning. Sport can be fast and dangerous and painful. People talk about killing the opposition off, the killer instinct, striking the deathblow, but no one dies. Instead, people score goals, take wickets reach the post before the rest.

Boxing is not a metaphor. Boxing is a death duel. The weapons are fists, padded so that a man can punch without breaking his hands. That makes these weapons potentially lethal, because the main target is the head. The point of hitting some one in the head is to cause damage to his brain. Fact: all brain damage is permanent. In short, the idea of boxing is to cause more permanent brain damage in your opponent than you yourself sustain. If it is cowardly to state that you believe that this is not a suitable entertainment for civilised people, then I am happy to be a coward.

I happen to think that concussion is a bad thing. I have personal experience here. I have concussed myself on two occasions doing sport, which makes me permanently brain-damaged. I did it once coming off a horse and once when struck by a cricket ball. Look, sport without risk is a bloody mary without Tabasco, and without the bloody vodka as well. People get injured in the horsey sports all the time – yes, and killed, too – but I don't want to see the horsey sports banned.

I want to see boxing banned. All right, it is perhaps

acceptable for two men to agree to try and cause each other brain damage. But that doesn't make it acceptable to watch. Still less to make money from people watching.

And there in Athens, quite by accident, I found myself at a table of boxing lovers getting all Paula-eyed on vinous sentimentality about Amir Khan – a conspiracy of men infinitely braver than myself, in that they enjoy vicarious violence. It was not an evening in which I could play much of a role, but inevitably, a few days on, I found myself asked to cover Khan's quarter-final bout. Of course, this is amateur boxing, which makes quite a point of being different from the professional game. The bouts are shorter and therefore, at least in theory, less brutal. Contestants wear headguards, which stop them getting cut so much. This is, in fact, purely cosmetic: headguards actually increase the chance of concussion by making the head a bigger target. What's more, the width of a headguard appreciably increases the torsional effect of a blow, making your head spin faster, and therefore making your brain hit the inside of your skull with more of a whump.

Your brain is the texture of lightly cooked scrambled egg: when it hits the inside of your skull, it gets scrambled a bit more. It's like kicking the crap out of your laptop, except that your laptop is far more robust. Your brain, as Woody Allen said, it's my second favourite organ. (I once quoted that line to a woman I deeply admired. She responded icily: 'It's *my* favourite.')

But that is by the by. I watched Khan, who was seventeen, defeat Baik Jong-Sub of South Korea in 93 seconds: combination punches of astonishing speed, each of which caused his opponent's guard to open, inviting the assault into a new gap, thereby making possible the next part of the combination: a process as remorseless and inevitable as chain of logic. It was brilliant, I accept that, and wrote as much. But it was not a metaphor. And it was not something that comes from the Olympic heartland. Not for me. I was not to know that less than twelve months further on, I was to write a piece thanking God, more or less explicitly, for Amir Khan.

26

I had a good view from my cell: I could see most of the Olympic complex and a fair bit of Athenian sky. And one morning I was drinking rooibos tea, made with my immersion heater, in the mug I had also brought with me, gazing over the Games from the heights of my personal Olympus. Soon, I would descend to the Unpleasant Café and eat Greek yogurt, a pleasant dish not at all unlike the traditional British dish that is called Greek-style yogurt. And I saw a bird.

Or rather, seven or eight of them. Swifts, yes, but not normal swifts. They flew with the same disdain for base earth, but they were bigger, burlier, more glidey. I had the bins focused on them soon enough, and observed the pale bellies, the chinstrap. Alpine swift, surely. I looked them up – for I had a birdbook between Kazantakis and Seferis – and I was right. Glorious, glorious flying beasts, masters of the air, creatures who know that gravity is for wimps.

And I thought of Danny McGrory, when we had dined together in Cadiz before the UEFA Cup Final the previous year. He was there for his love of Celtic, but he is also, unlike me, a real journalist. The conflicts he covers for *The Times* are real. No cods, no metaphors: Danny does death, life, war, destruction, disaster, famine, the four horsemen. And he was telling me what it was like – unimaginable for me, though I am not unadventurous – as we sat and drank before the cathedral. Iraq, yes, $100 a night to park his car, and sleep in it, and well worth it because the owner had a gun, and it was as near safe as you could get, and the British colonel knew about the gun, but was prepared to blind-eye it because at least that way he knew that the British journos were safe, and so he had one fewer thing to worry about.

I thought of that evening, and felt a decent flush of shame for my muttering about the inadequacies of my cell. And I recall Danny's curiosity – perhaps the mot juste here is irritation – at the way, in the midst of these splendid and humbling tales, my eyes kept stealing skywards. It was the swifts. Screaming their way about in a vesperal frenzy, one of my favourite sights in the world. I tried to explain not what but why, and asked him: when a young swift leaves the nest, how long do you think it is before he next perches on anything?

Dunno. Two weeks?

Two years, Danny. Or maybe three. They travel to Africa, come back to Europe the next year, then they do it all over again. They eat on the wing, and socialise on the wing, and sleep on the wing. In that third year – or maybe they wait for a fourth – they mate. And yes, they do that on the wing as well: screaming and tumbling through thousands of feet. A must, I said, for anybody's reincarnation wish-list. I raised my mug of tea to the alpine swifts, finished, and went off to yogurt and sport and stories.

27

Two or three years previously, I had challenged my colleague Alyson Rudd to a race: the first person to get the word chthonic into the paper is the winner. It was in Athens that I secured my victory. Appropriate, too, since Chthon is the Greek god of the earth. The creatures of the earth I celebrated with this fine word were the super-heavyweight weightlifters. This is one of the great events of the Games.

At super-heavyweight level there is no upper limit for weight. So these strange trolls strut out with huge full-moon faces and frank counter-weight bellies: no need here for last-minute fluid loss, for sweat-baths and dehydration. No necessity for a honed, perfectly rippled physique: at this level, you hide your six-pack under a cushion. These giants with their giant baby-faces emerge blinking into the light, dressed in baby romper suits, and each in turn lifts the weight of the world above his head. It is gloriously ugly, deeply visceral, and unapologetically sweaty. There is a stink of tortured bodies and heaving masculinity: men at one with the gross earth.

Try visiting this competition. Try watching as the huge men balance the huge weight on their chests and then, with desperation, with certainty, with prayerful might, raise it heavenwards. Go on! A cry escapes you, despite yourself, go on go on go on, and the weight is lifted it seems, by the will of the entire audience, for it is more than flesh and blood can stand to watch the lifter stress and strain without trying insanely to help.

And, as I watched the great and gigantic Reza Zadeh Hossein win the gold medal, to go with the one he won in Sydney, I reflected that he is my brother: just as we are both kin to the alpine swifts that flew across the Olympic site that morning. We are all three of us addicted to flight.

My mind went back to the World Gymnastics Championship in Birmingham many years ago, and the evening I spent with a former gymnast, then working as a journalist. I bought her dinner. And she talked about flight: 'I always wanted to fly. I used to dream of flying, I still do. And that's what I was doing, when I did gymnastics. I was flying.'

Well, we all have flying dreams. Freud says that flying dreams are really about sex, not a theory that has ever destroyed their pleasure for me. But it occurred to me that flight is a deep-seated human urge, a hunger that can never be satisfied. And we seek flight all the time, in thousands of different ways. All the non-confrontational sports are in fact about flight. Starting, of course, with gymnastics.

Out there at the athletics tracks, the great performers were showing how much ground they could cover between football and footfall, or how much height. I remember that glorious women's pole vault competition in Sydney, a series of ever more beautiful women leaping to ever more impossible heights: chicks on sticks, as the gold medal winner, Stacey Drugila, summed things up. I was supposed to be watching Jonathan Edwards at the time, but for some reason, I found his series of flights less enthralling than those of Stacey and the chicks.

If you can't fly yourself, there is still joy to be found in making other things fly: a javelin, a discus, a shot. Non-confrontational sport is nothing less than an all-out war on gravity. And, if it is a war we are doomed to lose, it is worth it for the striving, and still more for the glorious moments when the illusion is intact and we seem for a moment to fly.

I can fly. I fly on a daily basis when I'm at home, for I am a horseman. A horse lends us wings, gives us impossible speed, enables us to leap impossible obstacles and to move in a wild, extravagant never-quite-tameable fashion. I have ridden a grand prix dressage horse, and gasped at the athleticism, the power, the impossible distance the horse gets off the ground in every elevated gait. For every rider, every horse is Pegasus.

Diving is a flight, even if it is mostly downwards. It is still about controlling your passage through the air. And I went to the diving to watch a glorious victory from Guo Jingjing of China. All sports without a ball are about flying; and Hossein had just shown us the most monstrous defiance of gravity, and we who watched had responded with our guts.

A couple of days later, I was on a boat in the harbour following a load of other boats. I have never had much affinity for boats, but the sea was gratifyingly flat. It was explained that for a certain leg of the race, the yachts had the wind directly behind them, and yet they would all make the journey in a long double-zigzag. One of my land-loving colleagues asked the ultimately naive question: why? How? Surely it would be faster to be hooshed along with the wind blowing straight up your arse?

I answered for the yachties: 'A sail doesn't work by shoving. It's a wing.' A sail operates on pressure difference, like the wing of a glider or a jumbo jet, which is why you can sail faster than the wind. Counterintuitive, I know. And, surely, the fact that a sail is a wing makes this yet another flying sport. Find your sport, and you have found a wing.

Flight sports: thrilling to do, thrilling to watch. It is one of the greatest and deepest of all human urges, and yet it is something that we can never pull off. Explain that, if you can, in pure evolutionary terms. Why do we long to fly? What benefit do we get from our yearning for flight? What survival advantage is conveyed by our search for flight? A too-fervent desire to fly runs counter to the interests of the host body: and yet it is something that is inescapably human. A reaching beyond.

28

If you wish to understand sport, go to Greece. Better still, go to Greece and read the poems of George Seferis. It is not necessary to do this during the Olympic Games, but that certainly helps to concentrate the mind on the central problem of being Seferis. If you are a modern

Greek poet, you can either write as if Homer never existed, or as if he had completed the *Odyssey* a couple of days ago. I don't think there is much room for manoeuvre between these two options.

Seferis takes the second path. His poems are full of dry, rocky landscapes from which stray, broken columns emerge beneath an ageless Aegean sun. The past is always with us, wide awake, informing the present and paving the way for the future with cracked and broken marble slabs. The deep past made us what we are: the deep past is as much a part of the now as the Nike ads. I read Seferis as I refuelled daily at the Caracas café across the road from the Main Press Centre: an omelette, a salad, a beer, while I tried to deal with the man wounded by his own soil, and condemned by his own gods.

A couple of days before the Games began, I had paid a long cool visit to the archaeological museum, where infinity, of course, goes up on trial. I went there to see the sport, naturally. I watched the great marble horses with a horseman's eye, wondering if I would do better as a horse-tamer than this charioteer with his overly punitive approach, whether anyone could get more speed from a horse than this perfectly balanced boy jockey, and wishing it were possible to mount and ride away on this mare (for surely it was a mare, though seen only in bas-relief) with the kind eye. Later I would walk among the horses at the three-day event and think much the same things.

At the museum, I watched the clothes-less and nameless orange men wrestle and race and pummel each other around the coal black vases, and admired the heroes with names: especially Heracles, as we must call him in Athens. And for the following sixteen days, I had watched the same men: women too, praise the Lord, both only a fraction less naked than the vase-borne grapplers, but all fighting for the same invisible prize: the one called Glory. And I watched the tears of Matthew Pinsent and the tears of Paula Radcliffe: ancient Greek masks of triumph and disaster, and the two impostors looking, it must be said, exactly the same: two faces racked with anguish at the nature of their own deeds. In Homer, of course, most of the characters are in tears for most of the story: Odysseus himself is perpetually in floods as he longs to make his journey to his home: *nostos*, in the Greek, from which nostalgia, a condition I am myself not unfamiliar with.

But I would not return home before the Games were out, nor would I wish to, for the Games had, as ever, ravished me with their perfection. And so to contemplate a further pair of masks, this time the faces of Kelly Holmes, as she won two races. The first was the 800 metres on the track: in the moment of victory, her face registered a wild surmise, but it was at once eclipsed by self-doubt. Only when her name appeared on the screen, with the number one beyond all question alongside it, did she allow herself to believe what 100,000 people in the stadium and millions more around the world well knew. And after winning the 800 metres in disbelief, she won the 1,500 metres with a smiling certainty, queenlike, giving us a second and gloriously antithetical mask.

Two faces that left me writing the tale: the tale of Kelly nearly-but-not-quite, the tale of an athlete who was first class of the second class, the tale of one of life's silver medal winners, and how, at the last, all that changed. For once entering a major championship with a proper preparation, unspoiled by injuries and illness, Holmes was at the end able to show herself as she really was. A hero: heroine if you prefer. 'Tis all one.

This is a simple heroic tale, a simple piece of mythology. I saw the tale new-minted, and it is as old as humankind. Cinderella, Jack and the Beanstalk, Aladdin. Such tales have been told ever since humans began to tell each other stories. And that is what sport is: a living, breathing mythology. Sport creates archetypal situations of triumph and tragedy, and it does so bloodlessly, for at bottom, all is play. Nobody dies: Agamemnon is unmurdered, Oedipus unblinded, Troy unsacked and Penelope's suitors unslain. And yet the strong myths are created in front of us, and we respond to them with passion and delight. Some intellectuals (not of course AS Byatt) would speak of such delight as superficial, but it is the very reverse of superficial. It touches something in us that lies deep. Delight in sport touches some of the most basic things that make us human.

Marshall McLuhan, the man who foresaw the global village and the communications revolution, hated sport. Blast the sports pages, he wrote, creators of pickled gods and archetypes. McLuhan was enraptured by the new: a man obsessed by a nostalgia for the future. He missed the point that the modern human is nonetheless an ancient species, a species that has a profound need for pickled gods and archetypes. That is why a human responds to the foolish superficialities of sport from the very depths of its being.

29

I went to the supermarket to buy chocolates, but it seemed that they don't do chocolates in Greece. You can get bars of chocolate, but not big, extravagant, grateful, beribboned, thank-you-so-much-for-everything boxes. I wandered around the endless acres of this truly colossal supermarket (superagora?) and made a cultural assumption. Biscuits. The place was full of big fancy tins of biscuits. So I guessed that in Greece, you say thank you with biscuits, and bought four large tins. These I presented serially to the four student volunteers who had manned the desk that guarded the way to my cell, and with whom I had talked about Greece, laundry, breakfast, England, sport, studying, Seferis and life, and, they being female, kissed each one chastely but agreeably on the cheek.

I returned my CDs to their travelling wallet, put the library in the bag. The last piece had been written: a celebration of Games, medals, victories, tears, sex, pickled gods, archetypes, women, men, Paula, Kelly, Matt, Reza Zadeh, Jingjing, losers, winners, medals, tales, tales and tales.

Five Olympic Games. I have already covered five Olympic Games. How much longer can I carry on writing about sport? The Olympic Games make me think of the pleasures of body-surfing: the sweet catching of the salt wave, the long, brief thrill, the triumphant arrival, and the instant decision – just one more. Oscar Wilde said that there was nothing in life to compare with the pleasure of a cigarette: 'It is exquisite and it leaves you unsatisfied.'

In one sense, I left Athens profoundly satisfied: great sport, great men, great women, great tales. And yet I knew already that I wanted more. Not now, no, for God's sake not now. But I already knew as I left Athens that the exquisite pleasures of the last sixteen days of sport had not been enough. God knows I never want to leave my home again. But I could already taste the thrill of Beijing four years on. The myths that would unfold there, the tales I would tell there. What larks, Pip, what larks. Already, I could feel a faint pang of nostalgia for a time that lay four years ahead.

30

I had expected to have a full week at home, but they called and asked me to make that four days if Tim Henman reached the semi-finals at the US Open. So with quiet inevitability, Henman won his next match and I was on the plane to New York. To return to New York was another powerful exercise in nostalgia. In the late 80s and early 90s, I had conducted a passionate love affair with the United States in general and New York in particular. Being in New York summed up everything I loved about being a sportswriter: I was a swaggering adventurer at home in the world's coolest city. Bloody fool. But glorious fun all the same: for in New York, you are always the star in your own movie. I had sought reasons, even excuses to be there. I was in love with my own starring role in a movie never made. Bloody, as I think I said before, fool.

New York does odd things to you. There is a story told

among sports journos of one of our number, who, full to the brim on the heady feeling of arriving in New York – one that comes not only from being in a movie, but also from the fact that you generally arrive pissed, since flying East-West in the middle of the day gives you ample opportunity for relaxed sipping – was talking to his office from a taxi. He stuck his phone out of the window at the sound of a siren, and then shouted overexcitedly: 'You hear that? It's the sound of New York. I love New York – and New York loves me!'

I had the same taxi-siren experience on my way from JFK to Central Park. So I called my old friend Jim Lawton, chief sportswriter of the *Independent*, who had told me the tale. 'Hear that, Jim? It's the sound of New York. I love New York!' Jim asked politely: 'And does New York love you, Simon?' 'No. New York doesn't give a fuck.'

And feeling every bit as full of myself as the sportswriter in the story – though with a few more of the ironies intact, it must be said – I arrived at the Mayflower, where I 'always' – how I used to love that word – stay when I am in New York. Out of love with travel, with the United States, with my own movie, I still felt that treacherous lifting of the heart at being in this fabled place. Not immune, no. I rang my American publisher – savouring the joy of having such a thing – and we met for drinks and supper and talked soothingly about me, an authentic New York experience. With my head spinning in a fashion far from disagreeable, I went back to my hotel. The next day I had a date with Henman. That date, I noted, was September 11.

31

Tim Henman got slaughtered. Murdered. Reduced to a pulp. He was taken apart by Roger Federer, put to the sword. By the end of the first set he was a dead man. As Henman died the death out there, something in all of us died as well. After that, Henman talked. Federer was great, but there were a lot of positives he could take from this, etc etc. So I went back to Manhattan on the subway.

That morning I had taken the subway downtown, got off when I saw someone in a uniform do the same, someone who looked as if he might be a high-ranking fireman, and followed him at a polite distance. I was right: he went to Ground Zero, vanishing past the security. I hung about outside, looking at the two monstrous sockets from which the great incisors of the Manhattan skyline had been so shockingly extracted three years previously. And I listened.

Names. Just a list of names, read out by various voices, occasionally with a message attached. Miss you, always love you, never forget you. The names were the thing though, names that once meant a person, now a memory. As a boy, I had annually gone to church on All Soul's Day. The long list of the dead from the parish: the endless army of people I had never known, many of whom were no longer even memories, not for anyone. If death can be said to have a dignity, it is in this utter finality: in the, as it were, anonymity of a name.

Just to hear the names on that balmy New York morning was extraordinarily moving. I thought of all those answer-phone messages of love and farewell. I thought, too, of the absurdity of it all: killed, yes, but why? For the crime of going to work. For no reason whatsoever, save for the fun of the thing. I walked away after a while, and made my way to the A train for Queens and Henman: who did not, of course, die at all.

And no, it didn't put sport in perspective. Sport is already in perspective. I don't claim any privileged insight in saying this: everybody in the world who watches sport has sport in perspective. If sport wasn't in perspective it would be meaningless. Sport is not supposed to be real life: it is something quite different. And real life and sport don't sit well together. After September 11, 2001, sport was suspended in Britain for the weekend, and rightly. Not just as a tribute to the dead, for all that they cared, but because we just weren't in the mood for it. Real life was simply too pressing. But come the following weekend, sport was back and welcomed. We were now ready to be cheered up.

After September 11, 2001, they had postponed the Ryder Cup, the biennial golf match between Europe and the United States, for twelve months, so that it now happens in an even year. That meant I had to fly to Detroit, where I would see one of the greatest sights I have ever seen in my life. But golf: I was not, shall we say, in danger of taking that over-seriously. The difficulty was quite other, in finding some way of believing in it, if only for three days.

32

I made a promise to John Hopkins, the *Times* golf

correspondent. I said that if I wrote a single derogatory thing about golf in the course of the week ahead of us, I would buy him a bottle of wine of his choice. This had a useful effect on the mind, for John chooses wine by price rather than taste. I was then into my now-biennial exercise at the near-impossible job of taking golf seriously.

I can't do it. I can believe in a dozen impossible sports before breakfast, but not golf. I love gymnastics, as you know. More reprehensible still (at least for someone who wishes to be taken seriously as a macho no-nonsense sportswriter) I love ice skating, and have covered world championships twice. I have a genuine adoration for the sport of dressage, and words were spoken when I suggested that my time would be better spent covering the Olympic dressage prance-off than Amir Khan's boxing final. But golf: no. It can't be done.

I have tried to explain by means of jokes: nothing you do in pink polyester trousers can be a sport; golf is what you do if you are too old for sport; if you can smoke while you're doing it, it's not a sport. But, while being perfectly fair to golf and golfers, these jokes do not reveal a truth. What is the problem here? Partly, it comes from my media-pinko upbringing, and my parents' – aesthetic rather than political – dislike of suburban values, the more vivid since we lived in Streatham in south London. There was and is a snobbery attached to this. But it also involves a soul-deep loathing of the snobberies of the southern-England golf club: only the right sort of people allowed in places that were traditionally womanless, Jewless and clueless. And clubbability: no. Not my way. I'm in the chair, old boy, name your poison. No.

But there is far more to it than that. Sport depends on your ability to believe in it. You must believe that sport is important, while knowing all along that it is nothing of the kind. You must keep sport in perspective, yes, but you still have to believe in it. Or, more accurately, you have to suspend your disbelief. Coleridge wrote about this in *Biographia Literaria*, as all students of English know: about 'that willing suspension of disbelief for the moment, which constitutes poetic faith'.

I do not believe that Stephen Dedalus, Leopold and Molly Bloom are real: and yet I have been almost unbearably moved by them. That's poetic faith: disbelief suspended, willingly. By the same token, I do not believe that it matters one way or another whether Wayne Rooney kicks a bladder into a net or not, whether Matthew Pinsent's boat crosses a line before all the others or not, whether Roger Federer hits furry balls into a white oblong or just outside: but over the course of the summer, I had been deeply moved by all three occurrences. The willing suspension of disbelief for the moment, which constitutes sporting faith.

But with golf, I am unable to suspend by disbelief. I am like the sort of non-AS Byatt intellectual who refuses to see the point of sport. Why play golf, why watch golf, when you could be reading *Ulysses* or watching birds? But I am lost even in the asking of the question. If one sport is silly, then, all sports are silly. If none is silly, then golf is not silly. If football is not silly, then synchronised swimming is not silly, bog snorkelling is not silly, dressage is not silly. Golf is not silly. I was convinced of this matter intellectually, but I still could not deal with the Oakland Hills County Club, North Michigan, in any sort of comfort.

I coped by rushing from the press-tent, like a man starved of oxygen, whenever the oppression of unsuspended disbelief became too much. Occasionally I broke out in fits of hysterical yawning, or of mantraic repetition of the word fuck. But by a supreme effort of will, I wrote as if it mattered: re-reading carefully and pressing delete every time I came across even the hint of a sneer; knowing that on Saturday, I would escape from the hideously unreal green of the greens, and from the people shouting 'you the man' and 'in the hole'. I would go birdwatching.

33 I went out for the day with three retired ladies and it was beautiful beyond conception. They were from the Audubon Society, the American wildlife and conservation organisation. I contacted the local branch looking for information about a likely spot to find a few birds, learned that there was a field trip that Saturday, asked if I could join it, and was welcomed. And we saw sandhill crane and bald eagle, but that was only the appetiser.

Most birds of prey hate to fly over water. Most migrating birds of any kind fly over as little water as possible, on the reasonable grounds that water is a poor emergency-landing ground. So when an expanse of water opens in front of them, they funnel together over the nearest thing they can find to a landbridge. If you stand in the right place at the right time – at the Bosphorus, say, or Gibraltar in autumn with, crucially, the wind in the right direction – you are going to see a lot of birds. And we got beneath the flightpath on the Great Lakes. The wind was blowing firmly from the north: and the birds of prey were moving south, so that they might winter in balmier places than Canada.

We were there for two hours and saw 20,000 hawks fly over. It was a record day, and in all, 100,000 hawks flew over that one spot between dawn and dusk, most of them broadwinged hawks, with a good few sharp-shinned hawks, and a few exoticisms to excite the small group of experts that we met, leaning against the rails on the pier that stuck out into Lake Michigan. But it wasn't about identification, not for me: it was the numbers, the glorious and endless stream of hawk after hawk after hawk, gliding over with power and purpose, or rising in the thermals, circling together, 'kettling' the birders there called it, gaining height so that they might glide south some more. And barely a flap of wing among all 20,000: all masters of the airways. It was truly one of the most wondrous things I have ever seen, and I have seen some wonders. What's more, it gave me an understanding of golf.

People have tried to make me understand the joy of golf, and they talk about being out in the wild – Oliver Rackham, historian of the British countryside, once described golf courses as the airport lounges of the countryside – about the freemasonry that exists between golfers – no thanks – and about the best thing of all, hitting the ball. Hitting it true, hitting it sweet; when the amount of effort you put in is out of all proportion to the distance the ball travels; when, by some miracle of timing and coordination, you have made the ball fly. You have defied gravity, you have created, though you cannot share, a form of flight.

There is nobility in that, there must be, for all that I can't share it, for all that nothing on a golf course is capable of touching me. It is a lacking in me, I accept that. I am inclined to be censorious of those who 'just can't get on' with Joyce. Golfers have a right, then, to be censorious of me. And we share a common ground, or common sky, in the love of flight, that deeply human love of flight, for all that the shallow-arcing drive up the middle of the fairway does not stir me. In northern Michigan, beside the Great Lakes, with a sky full of hawks, I flew all right. My heart lifted and soared and took wing, and I knew I could face even one more day of golf with a good heart.

34

The Ryder Cup was done, Europe had won emphatically, and I was going home the next day. Back in my cell, final piece written, tooth-glass full of whisky, Hildegard whispering from the baby speakers, I felt as if I had had enough, on the whole. Sport might see its way to letting me off for a while. I read, lurked in my cell, ordered room service. It wasn't a bad cell, as these things go, spacious and light. The drawback was that the hotel was on a freeway intersection, and to get anywhere required a 20-minute car journey: that's far more typical of America than strolling round to the deli in Manhattan. It was a no-place, which was where I had been living for most of the summer. The realities were the phone and the laptop: far more solid than Lisbon and Athens and SW19 and Michigan: more solid even than the stories I had been telling. The phone: for professional and emotional needs. The laptop: my reason for being in all these no-places. My reason for existing. Hildegard, dear, sing on and keep me sane. Or sane-ish, anyway.

How odd it had been, to spend time in America again, watching one of America's very rare incursions into international sport. And to note how America has still not got the hang of it. In 1999, in a lather of patriotic fervour, America shattered one of golf's most sacred bits of etiquette, and was profoundly shocked by the way the world responded. Hideous triumphalism: the Ugly American in apotheosis. Five years on, and Americans were beginning to get the idea that not everybody in the world is prepared to offer them unconditional love. How, then, to react on the field of international sport? Should they be polite and hospitable and loveable? Or should they be their old unabashed unrepentant selves? How deeply should they care about losing at sport, in a new world? All these questions made for a strange few days of sport. The entire event was dominated by those moments of golfing shame, and by the memory of the events of September 11, for which the competition had been postponed three years ago. A strange mixture of the trivial and the momentous.

There were also mere sporting issues to wonder about: why Colin Montgomerie is unbeatable when playing for a team, but beset by saucy doubts and fears when he is on his own and in a major tournament; and why Tiger Woods is utterly dominant when he plays strokeplay golf, but when he is part of a team, he sulks, like me in my cell. The best moment of the tournament was Woods's face when Phil Mickelson, his partner, drove into the rough. It was an expression of bemused contempt, mixed with the thought: what the fuck am I doing here?

Some people like to be part of a team, others hate to be part of anything that involves other people. Years ago, I wrote a biography of the cricketer Phil Edmonds. The only reason he was in a team was so that he could be different from everybody else. All goalkeepers know that feeling, and I speak as a lapsed goalkeeper. Being a goalkeeper, you literally play by different rules to everybody else, and you even wear a different outfit to prove it.

Journalism is also a team game. There were half a dozen of us writing for *The Times* at the Ryder Cup, and we had to divide up the work between us, help each other with quotes and facts and practical problems, keep each other cheerful. Back at the office, there was another interlocking team of editors and sub-editors. And as I play for my team, I get to wear a different coloured jersey, at least in my own mind. 'Great team,' I told the sports editor, back at the Olympic Games. 'No big egos. Apart from mine, of course.'

But I had been away for nine weeks of the past fourteen: this is nothing, as cricket writers will tell you, accustomed to outings of three months at a time, but it felt like a lot to me. I sulked and sipped and listened to the murmurings of sweet Hildegard, and thought of sweet, sweet Suffolk. The long, long summer of sport was drawing to a close.

35 Everything that needed to be written had been written, my bags were half-packed, I was eating breakfast. The phone went. A new story had just broken – nothing to do with golf – would I supply 900 words in about an hour? Full of apologies. Egos have to be massaged, after all, especially mine. They knew what a dreadful imposition it was, they knew how hard I had been working, but all the same, they would deeply appreciate it if I could write something (i.e. do my job) and anyway it was a great subject. So I said of course, and no trouble, I was delighted, and I let a sigh fall into the conversation at just the right moment so that they would know just how tough it was for me, and they told me I was a hero and left me to get on with it. Finished breakfast, set off back to my cell to unpack my laptop and its various leads. On the way I bumped into Jim Lawton, who, with perfect irony, summed up my own feelings. 'Brian Clough's dead,' he said. 'Why does everything happen to me?'

36 It's not always like that. Those periods of high stress, high productivity, soul-wearying travel and unending quantities of live sport: that is not how a sportswriter lives, any more than a marriage is exclusively about furious arguments and frenzied making-up. The peak times are when we are busiest, when we are most read, when we are most under examination. But perhaps it is in the troughs that our real work is done. When we work with the excitement of the great occasions, there are many times when a story is so self-evident and we respond to it so extravagantly, that it seems that we are not composing but taking dictation. My colleague at *The Times*, Martin Samuel, once suggested that, when it comes to annual dishing-out of journalistic awards, sportswriters should be judged not on their pieces from the Olympic Games, or their reports of England's last match in a great tournament, but on the 0-0 draws. The person who writes the finest and most rewarding evocation of a 0-0 draw is unequivocally the master of our profession.

Away from the great events, our most frequent assignment is to write about the trivial parts of sport: to find from them some kind of wisdom, some kind of meaning. We are not to pretend that small things are – even in sporting terms – great things. To pretend that small events have a major sporting importance when they clearly have no such thing is a trick that readers soon weary of.

No: what we have to do is to take the stuff of everyday sporting life, and, without pretending that it is something which it is not, turn it into a piece of writing that means something, at least for the day in which it was written. We have to take the stuff of everyday life and find the epic that lies within. Every sportswriter is James Joyce, seeking each day to write a brief and unforgettable *Ulysses*.

37

Home. Not a place; or not just a place. Home had not been part of my routine for a long three months, for a quarter of a year. But it was still there, and, far more to the point, it was still happening. It was still the more-than-place to which I always return. It was there to return to, not because I had been making money to pay the bills, but because the will of my wife kept it together. This is not an insignificant matter. Hers is the tough job, the real job, the job that matters.

Not just my opinion, as it happens, but also the opinion of anthropologists. Women created humanity, and maintain humanity. This thought came up in response to a conference at the University of Chicago in 1966, which had the chest-beating title of 'Man the Hunter'. It was hunting, and the quest for meat, so the conferrers maintained, that made us truly human. It was hunting that made hominids co-operate, that gave hominids the need for language, that brought out all the dexterity of the hominid hand and that used all that residual power of the great brain that is the humans' most prized asset today (unless they like boxing).

This thesis was contradicted in the 1970s, as you would expect, by a feminist take, and the 'Woman the Gatherer' hypothesis. It was not men and hunting that made us truly human: it was women, and the quintessentially female skills of gathering food, inventing technology, raising children and keeping together the family unit. Without which we are not human at all.

I find this notion seductive, and not least because I am

reluctant to give meat-eating the central role in human development. I know, not from nutrition charts but as something I have experienced for 30 years, that survival does not depend on large quantities of dead animals. What is more, I have been shown the ways of the gatherer in the Kalahari Desert, by Cobra Kepile, of the Suakhwe or Salt People; and what he showed me was not a desert but a world filled with food.

Gathering was enough to ensure survival, and to keep family together, in pre-agricultural times, and women did most of it. That makes a deep, intuitive sense, certainly to me. So what, then, was hunting all about? Why did people do it, if it wasn't necessary for survival? And I recall a time spent in the Matopos Hills in Zimbabwe, a wonderful landscape of steep cliffs and dramatic crags, overflown by glorious black eagles: huge birds of prey which, so anecdotal evidence suggests, hunt co-operatively, in pairs, one to hoosh and one to pounce.

The area is full of ancient paintings, images laid onto rock walls thousands of years ago, and I was filled with a heady love for them all. Most of them were known and mapped, and the local guides took visitors to the main sites, and very fine they were too. But I recall most vividly a chance find: walking along the side of a rock wall in pursuit of some beast or bird, and spotting a declivity, a small sheltered place at the foot of the wall, and saying: surely there ought to be paintings here. And finding them, and wondering when they had last been inspected, and who knew about them.

That moment of discovery joined me to them for a time.

Fine things: a forest of small images, a deep red earth colour on a background of yellowish, chalky cream. Men – mostly men, often with an exaggerated stroke of paint to point out how truly male they were – in enigmatic poses, some clearly dancing, some of them with exploding heads. These, it is suggested, represent trance or hallucination, a state of spiritual exaltation that came, no doubt, from rhythm, dance, self-hypnosis, starvation, and Lord knows what infusions of herbs.

And all around them, animals, painted with a fluency of line that would make Picasso's nose bleed from envy: elephant, rhinoceros, deer, zebra. The pictures were full of reverence. They seemed to be about a search for deep meaning, the meaning of the animals, the meaning of their pursuit. Hunting was not, then, a matter of mere protein: it was far more. It was a search for meaning. The wall, as I looked at it in the finest hour of the African day, the hour that follows the dawn, seemed to me to be filled with pickled gods and archetypes.

I was looking at the sports pages. There may well have been enough to eat in the society nourished by woman the gatherer, but there was, it seems, a hunger for something more. And so the men sought this by means of adventure, an adventure justified by the occasional mountain of protein. Hunting was not reliable; it was perhaps not even necessary to the business of staying alive. But it supplied a need for a certain kind of adventure.

The adventure was sanctified by the occasional glorious success: an excuse – no, better, a reason – for a high day, a day of feasting, a holiday or, to spell that term out fully, a holy day. And in the act of hunting, the hunters and the hunted were joined together in a complex tissue of myth. Hunting did not matter, in the sense that gathering mattered. But hunting enriched everybody's life with glamour and excitement and peril and rich reward. Hunting satisfied something very deep in human nature: the hunger for stories, for stories with meaning, for myth. Hunting supplied heroes, it supplied tales of good fortune and of bad, it showed fate, gods, God – call it what you will – in benevolent and in hostile moods. And the heroes were all the more heroic, because their hunting was not entirely necessary. And it was so wonderful when they won.

Modern sport follows on from the myth of man the hunter in a cleansed and organised form, far safer for its participants than driving a spear-maddened elephant over a cliff. Sport doesn't recreate the age-old need for the hunt: I am inclined to think that hunting was a response to a primordial thing in human nature. It was the promptings of the sporting spirit. Hunting was nothing less than the anticipation of sport as we know it today. The urge for sport goes deep; and it is an urge, not to hunt, but to create tales of adventure and glorious failure and still-more-glorious victory. It is the tales, not the meat, that make us human.

Sport was always a male thing: but it has, over the course of the previous century, become a female thing as well. And women have since taken it much further than mere men, as I was to see at first-hand in due course.

38

Affection, and gratitude. That was the prevailing tone of all the Brian Clough pieces. Even mine and Lawton's. I never actually met him myself, but that had nothing to do with it. I remembered my favourite Clough line, on his signing of David Nish, the first £100,000 defender: 'He's a nice boy. But now he's come to Derby he's going to have to learn how to play football.' What a line; and all of us who saw him deliver such lines know exactly how he delivered this one: glazed eyes on the camera, chin tilted almost to nose level, voice filled with profound personal satisfaction at the fact that he was not like the rest of the world.

It needed the success, of course, and we all paid due deference to success. It all had to be grounded in extraordinary ability. He took one second division club to the top of the first division (then the top division) and then he did it again with a different club. With his second club, Nottingham Forest, he followed the trick by winning the European Cup the following season, and then doing it again. It is probably the finest feat of football management ever seen in this country.

But that was not the reason for the love: that was the justification for the love. All journalists love Clough, at least in retrospect, because he was always copy. A story is the better for a strong lead character, and Clough revelled in the role.

He did so quite consciously. He was an actor who spent his life overplaying the part of himself. He fully embraced the narrative-driven nature of sport, and forced himself to the top of the cast-list. He loved the story-making process, not as teller but as self-created hero.

This is not an uncommon type. They are generally referred to as 'characters': where would the game be without characters? There just aren't the characters any more, and so forth. Anyone can be a character, and it is generally the hallmark of inferior performance. To be a character requires some kind of superstructure built onto a personality: as compensation for the inadequacies of the original personality. You find them in football as managers of third-tier sides, with their well-rehearsed aphorisms, or as attention-seeking, haircut-ridden footballers who can't get the glory they yearn for by mere talent – Robbie Savage being the type specimen here.

But Clough combined his determined attention-seeking with the most extraordinary level of ability. Self-promotion was not his pleasure but his method. He used the role-playing of himself not just for self-gratification, but also for success. He used his self-created persona to deal with his players: as an inspiration, or to deal out histrionic bollockings. He was best at the making of young players and the rehabilitation of old ones and he did so by the most remarkable use of his stage personality. He was a star in the movie of himself, he was the prince in his own *Hamlet*, the artist-young-man in his own portrait.

He wrote the stories, we took dictation. Not just in the things he said, the quotes, but the narrative itself. One of a kind, we all wrote, we will not see his like again. And we were all wrong.

39 You know that someone is going to be a part of your life for some considerable time, and yet you have no idea what the relationship will be like: happy or sad, fulfilling or damaging, rewarding or the reverse. It happens in the first cautious, sizing handshakes on taking up a new job, with the first moment that a slight acquaintance laughs at your joke and, most thrillingly of all, in the fizzing unexpected eye-contact between yourself and another.

This awareness that a relationship will be a long-term business happens even with people you do not actually know, or rather, with a person that you will know increasingly well, but who in their turn will never, at any time, have the least idea of your existence. That is one of the extraordinary things about modern communications: you can have a long-term and significant relationship with all kinds of people who are totally unaware that you have ever taken a breath. Nor does this make the relationship meaningless, at least, to you.

David Beckham has some kind of meaning in the eyes of almost everybody in the country. He has a relationship with us all, even with those to whom he represents nothing but futility. For that matter, I have a deeply important relationship with James Joyce, and he's dead – died before I was born. And for that matter, with Odysseus, and he, perhaps, never existed.

The football season was gathering pace again. It was time to respond to its futilities as if they carried meaning; or rather to try and perceive the meaning in the futilities.

Time, then, to start to hammer out some kind of relation-ship with Wayne Rooney. And I was smitten. Not with what he was, but for what he might be. That was the thrilling thing: just turned eighteen, and the most exciting foot-baller on the planet. Not for what he has done, but for what he might do.

We have already touched on the idea of the fearlessness of youth. I remember youth as a time absolutely hag-ridden by fears of every kind: of failure, of success, of responsibil-ity, of adulthood, of childhood, of past, of present, of future. Insofar as I have confidence now, I acquired it from experience, not lack of experience.

If the notion of fear seems never to have touched Rooney's mind, it is because of something more significant than mere age; and I suspect that it is something to do with being a prodigy. The infant Mozart was never touched by self-doubt when asked to produce a piece of perfect music; I suspect that the only thing that troubled his mind was a vague curiosity as to why everybody else couldn't do it as well. Rooney had rampaged through Portugal while I read Pessoa, and it seemed that England might very well win the European Championship until he got injured.

He was a Manchester United player by the time I was picking up the rhythm of football again – he had joined the club at the beginning of the season – and he was already rich beyond easy understanding. It was time for everybody in the country to work out the beginnings of a relationship with him: after all, it was clear now that it was going to be one that lasted. It was a time when journalists wrote reams of advice on how the boy should be 'handled', as a kind of fumbling beginning to what would surely become a serious relationship for us all.

But Rooney is no Clough, no actor. He does not work on his own persona, he does not play a conscious part in the creation of his own story, his own myth. Rather, he seemed then to be the personification of some kind of natural force, leaping fully formed into our lives: an explosion of exuberant life, like Blake's *Glad Day*. I was surprised at this thought: it was one at odds with Rooney's face, which is like a King Edward – the potato rather than the monarch.

When Rooney played football as the season began, you could not help but feel a fizz of life: and all linked with the most dangerous possible kind of sentimentality, that is to say, sentimentality about the future. Living in the past is a trap that some people fall into; living in the future is the trap we all fall into. Tomorrow; it will be all right tomorrow; tomorrow, something will happen, something will turn up, someone will come along and then everything will be easier, everything will be ever so slightly wonderful. We all know that feeling, and there was real delight, real recognition when that feeling was embodied in the thundering form of Rooney. With Rooney, we might find some real joys in football. With Rooney, perhaps even the ultimate prize was within our grasp. And, whatever happened, we could at least relish the feeling of hope. Rooney could make it happen, and no one could say now that it was impossible. That's always the most prudent way to enjoy the future: before it gets here.

40

My grandfather was inordinately proud of his ability with a knife. He kept his ancient carving knife honed like a razor, and after breakfast, which he cooked for us himself, despising men who affected culinary helplessness, he would cut ham into large near-transparent slices, which he would then make into sandwiches. He would next create two perfect parcels of them, each with the ends of the paper mitred and tucked in, and place them in a small leather valise. We would then set off. Just the two of us, catching a bus at the top of Vicarage Road, and getting off at Edgbaston. We would enter as members – membership was a retirement gift from his two daughters – but we never sat in the pavilion, because my grandfather was never one to push himself forward.

And we would watch the cricket all day. Warwickshire, against whoever was in town that week. Norman Horner, Billy Ibadulla, Big Jim Stewart, MJK Smith. At lunch, we would have lunch, unwrapping our parcels. Afterwards, we would go to the bar, where my grandfather drank a half-pint of Mitchell and Butler's mild, while I had lemonade. At tea, we had tea, purchased in the tea-room, with a slice of Dundee cake. After that, the final session, and the bus home.

These outings were a deep pleasure to us both. I don't ever recall being bored. I was fascinated by the events that unfolded before us, enraptured by the extraordinary beings, these giants in white who did such wonderful things. There was a mystery at its heart, that was clear.

These outings were part of my summer. We would spend an annual week, me, my mother and my two sisters, in King's Heath, Birmingham, where my grandparents lived until their death. Most days, my grandfather and I went to the cricket. We made these trips even when I was comparatively grownup, grownup enough to change my lemonade for shandy, anyway.

I didn't find sport by doing it. I didn't move into sportswriting because I was good at sport, but not good enough to do it for a living. Far from it. At a school reunion, the constant theme of my meetings with the curiously bald and stout half-strangers-half-intimates I encountered was of wonder: how had someone so poor at sport, so little interested in the great world of school sport, ended up writing about sport for a living?

The answer was not in the awful chill and mud of Blagdon's playing fields in Raynes Park, but in the ham sandwiches and the buses and the crisscrossing white figures on the Edgbaston turf. Whenever I cover a match in Birmingham, I make a silent pilgrimage with my eyes: to the stand that lies just to one side of the pavilion, the concrete steps, which we would climb to halfway, for the finest possible view. I look at the place where we would sit, where my grandfather would place the valise and its lunch, and where he would rest his stick.

I played sport, of course I did, and enjoyed it very much, cricket on the common, football in the playground, football on the common, too, which I liked better, because on the grass I could dive about and make saves. I loved being a goalie, not because I was no good at kicking but because keeping goal was a kind of completion, a right and fitting conclusion to it all. The shot is nothing without its save: the dive, the hand-tingling contact, the deflection.

That was fun. But it wasn't something that filled me with wonder, or with reverence, or with a feeling that this had a deep and powerful meaning. That was something I acquired at Edgbaston. In a sense, I have been writing about Edgbaston ever since, in every piece I ever write. I can still see sudden, vivid moments: a cover drive from MJK Smith, his name so gloriously asterisked on the scorecard; a run-out from the boundary, Big Jim the victim, though he was still first to a thousand runs that summer; a leaping one-handed catch from a strapping boy with red hair whose name I have long forgotten; a stump cartwheeling across the grass, Fred Trueman then returning to his mark, re-rolling the right sleeve of his shirt, which unfurled, as John Arlott remarked, with every delivery of his life. Even the sandwiches were perfect. I can't remember that it ever rained.

41

In mid-October I attended a rally in Trafalgar Square to celebrate all those British medals at the Olympic Games. It was also an exercise in boosting the London bid for the 2012 Olympics. It was far too long after the Games to catch the wave, of course; the organisers had rather missed the moment. But it was still pretty well attended, and Kelly Holmes made the front of all the newspapers, cupping her ear to the crowd and smiling that glorious winner's smile, all the more lovely for being acquired so late in life.

I was reminded, inevitably, of the open-topped bus parade the previous year, to celebrate England's victory in the rugby World Cup. That was an extraordinary business. I had ridden in the third of the three buses, neither cheering nor cheered, but observing the cheerers and the cheered. And it struck me then that I had no understanding of the event I had just covered, not until that bus-ride. I had been in the wrong place, in Australia, in the stadium, when it all happened.

So many. I had not thought sport had undone so many. They reckoned that there were three-quarters of a million lining the brief route through the West End – ten deep at the pavements, shinning up lamp-posts, balanced on litter-bins, hanging from windows, crowding onto balconies: and cheering and cheering. How could I have understood how much it mattered, when I was stranded out there in Sydney watching Jonny Wilkinson make the winning drop-goal?

The real event happened in England, on television, where everybody had a better view than me and everybody surfed the wave of rising hope as a shared thing, as a common experience, as something that united stranger and stranger. Now, back home and scarcely unjetlagged, I was at last able to understand what I had been seeing and what I had been writing about. They were the people to whom I had been telling the tale: it was their love of the unfolding tale and their growing love for the characters in the story that made the telling worthwhile. No one had a moment for the tellers, of course: the third bus was mostly ignored, though once or twice greeted with a brief chant of 'Who are yer?' Who are we? Nous? We are the tellers of the great tales, the greatest of all tellers of tales, we are Anon. Nothing less. So cheer the heroes, then, and rightly; for it is the heroes, the characters, the players who matter. And a pretty girl was jumping up and down with a banner that read 'I won't have sex unless it's with Jonny.'

I suspect that the players themselves only truly understood what they had done – or rather, how much people cared about what they had done – when they travelled those two or three cacophonous miles. Sport unites. A great event and a national team, or a national hero, a national heroine, becomes a great shared experience, something that affects practically everybody. There are fewer such things than there once were. Once, major television programmes emptied pubs and dominated conversations the following day: people watched Tony Hancock and the *Morecambe and Wise Christmas Show* in now-incomprehensible millions. These days, television is a fragmented affair, with each household having a thousand choices.

Sport is one of the few things that can unite a nation. And the sharing of the delight in the rugby team's epic victory was a crucial aspect of everybody's joy. You acquire a certain carapace of professional cynicism, to protect yourself from the daily buffetings of the sporting life, and as a result, you can you find yourself totally out of touch with the people you are writing for. A short supply of naiveté is a damaging thing for a writer of sport. Perhaps for most kinds of writer.

42

Another moral maze: and the sporting world rejoices. Where would sport be without its extraordinary notions of morality? We would have nothing to write about, nothing to talk about. Sport would lose its point. We already have an England football coach who was sacked for heresy; now there were calls to sack the England football captain for immorality.

Beckham got himself booked against Wales for a rather intemperate encounter with Ben Thatcher, and then claimed that he had done so deliberately, to get a suspension out of the way at a convenient moment. His boasting about this piece of cleverness triggered a wave of shock and indignation across the country.

An equivalent manipulation of regulations would be ignored in business or political life, very much accepted as the way of the world. But for an England football captain to admit to such deviousness of the rules was somehow unacceptable. Morally reprehensible.

The only conclusion we can draw from this is that we expect a higher standard of morality from a footballer than we do from a businessman or a politician. Most particularly from a player representing England – most particularly from the England captain.

This is because sport and morality have a special relationship. The origins of this relationship lie deep in sporting history, and they are something over which we seem to have very little control. A race memory of virtuousness lies behind all modern professional sport. An atavistic and puritanical morality is therefore perpetually in wait, always ready to ambush the modern professional athlete – as if a Victorian sense of propriety were used to make judgments on the doings of 21st-century rock stars.

This race memory of morality exists because sport was originally codified and played quite specifically to teach morality. Boys who played sport were decent types. They learned to sink self in common cause, they learned to take setbacks in their stride, they learned about loyalty and authority, they learned, above all, about devotion to a code of conduct. As a result, they grew up to become manly, beloved word of Victorian educationists, and it was sport that made them so. Games produced the types that were essential in maintaining and extending the Empire. Sport was not an end in itself, but a way of inculcating a certain decency in sporty boys. Sport was not real life: sport was a moral preparation for real life.

Why are 'Games' so moral? Partly, at least, because by the time you had completed all these manly activities, you were in no fit state to masturbate once you got to bed, still less to go in for more gaudy experiments. The headmaster, a godly figure, in Kipling's *Stalky & Co*, explains the secret of his success: 'It's shameful to admit, but I loved every one of you. The rest was only sending you to bed dead tired.'

Kipling is the only genius to have written a book of school stories. (Admittedly, PG Wodehouse wrote school stories, but he did so before the flowering of his genius.) As a result, his take on schoolboy sport and adult morality is deeply revealing. It is shown best in the story called 'Regulus'. In this story, a dull, hard-working boy called

'Pater' Winton, commits a small crime – releasing a mouse in the drawing class – and is given 500 Latin lines as punishment. In order to complete these lines on time, he must miss Games, and missing Games, for all boys not in possession of first XV colours, is punishable by a beating from the head boy – who is Winton's study-mate and best friend. There is no appeal. Winton, massively distressed, does his lines, with the support and dictation of his house-master, Mr King, is involved in a vicious punch-up which his classmates hush up, and then takes his punishment like a man. After that, his first XV colours arrive, and he is promoted to sub-prefect by Mr King. All well and good, you might think. But Kipling is never obvious.

After these salutary lessons, the schoolmasters discuss Winton: 'A first-class type. Absolutely first-class,' says Mr King. But the school chaplain, a wiser man, says: 'Ha-ardly. First class of the second class, I admit. The very best type of second class. But... Pater'll never be anything more than a colonel of engineers.'

These things take place in counterpoint to the doings of Stalky, Turkey and Beetle. The inseparable trio are disruptive, subversive and highly creative: and what they create is mayhem. The original of Stalky went on to be Major-General Lionel Dunsterville; Beetle went on to be Kipling. Each, in his way, was first class of the first class. Neither set much store by Games: Beetle was let off cricket because he had his gig-lamps – his glasses – smashed in the nets too many times. Stalky 'affected to despise football' and significantly, only played conscientiously when the Old Boys – real soldiers – came to school for a match. He didn't need sport's lessons in small moralities. At the end of the book, we get a glimpse of his early career. He is already a soldier of brilliance; and still with his ferocious independence and his deeply subversive streak.

The moral lessons from sport, then, are important but pretty humdrum. Camus thought much the same thing. They will make decent muscular Christians of decent hard-working boys, people who will do a thoroughly decent job wherever they are posted. But they won't produce a Stalky, still less a Kipling. Kipling explicitly praises the legions of men of little showing, whose work continueth – broad and deep continueth – great beyond their knowing. But implicitly, the book celebrates the exceptional. Those beyond the reach of the nursery morality of sport.

43

The great story of that autumn, 2004, was soup. Pizza and soup. After Arsenal played Manchester United at Old Trafford, a story emerged that pizza had been thrown at the Manchester United manager, Sir Alex Ferguson, during a post-match supper. Also soup. The story, dubbed 'The Battle of the Buffet', dominated all serious discussion of just about anything for days. And they say sport is trivial.

I was, of course, in the wrong place, that is to say the Old Trafford press box, and I was writing about the wrong subject, that is to say football. But even if you were concerned with these irrelevancies, there was a tale to tell. Arsenal had gone through the previous season unbeaten:

Manchester United's hegemony had been shattered. This was a side more thrilling than they were, more effective than they were. Arsenal had stolen their trophy and, far worse, stolen their identity. Manchester United were anxious – desperate – to redress the balance. And more importantly, or at least, more humanly, to take Arsenal down a peg or two.

I was correct, at least, in identifying this match as turning-point, a changing of eras, not a hard conclusion to reach, it must be said. And when the facts about the school-dinner rumpus came out, it was clear that the business of the soup was only football's way of showing that this was the case.

Both sides attempted to show their moral superiority over the other, just as they had done a year before after an outbreak of unseemly jostling that was called 'The Battle of Old Trafford'. (Football aggrandises its little spats, just as it aggrandises its triumphs. It is all part of the same thing: football's out-of-control sense of its own importance.)

Each side claimed to be the more moral in an atmosphere thick with soup: a further and interesting gloss on the subject of sport and morality. Stalky & Co, great feasters when they could raise the money (by such expedients as pawning Beetle's watch) would have found the debate piffling, being above such small moralities. Added moral problems were raised by the manner of the victory: a dive from Wayne Rooney winning the home town decision of a penalty from the referee, Mike Riley, from which Ruud van Nistelrooy scored. This was a serious piece of revenge: he had missed a penalty in the same fixture the previous season, a miss that had allowed Arsenal to continue unbeaten. For that miss, van Nistelrooy was abused and shoved a bit by the Arsenal players, hence the 'battle'.

A year on, it was Campbell's tomato for Manchester United and defeat for Arsenal. Two matters emerged from this passionate and soup-drenched occasion. The first was the extreme vulnerability of the victor. Arsenal had swaggered past everybody for the space of twelve months, and had been praised, rightly, as one of the greatest teams ever seen in English football. This record, you might think, put them in a position of quite extraordinary power, but it did not. It made them exquisitely vulnerable.

By winning so many matches, they had lost the ability to deal with defeat. Defeat, when it came, was therefore traumatic. The greatness of the side vanished, as if it were a dream. Suddenly, players who had been – rightly – convinced of their own brilliance, were forced to go slumming for points, to go digging into the deep and dirty parts of themselves. And they couldn't do it. The side never recovered from that October Sunday. One of the great truisms of football is that a good side does not become a bad side overnight. But this was literally what happened to Arsenal: or, to be more finicky about terms, a great side became a comparatively ordinary one. Certainly, that great Arsenal team was never the same again.

The second thing that emerged is the nature of feuds. A rivalry is one thing, a feud quite another. A rivalry enriches each side, lifts each person to greater heights, stimulates each half of the rivalry to find something more. Bjorn Borg and John McEnroe; Chris Evert and Martina Navratilova;

all four know and will admit that they owed something of their own greatness to their rival, to their antithesis, to the opponent they feared and more than half loved.

But a feud is something quite different. A feud is characterised by the fact that both sides lose. And that was the case here: Manchester United 2, Arsenal 0. Result: both were defeated. The losers lost everything, and the winners lost far more than they gained. In that afternoon of self-destructive hating, it was decided then and there that neither would win the things they wanted that season. It was a lesson in the self-destructive nature of hating. And the pizza flew like arrows of vengeance and the soup fell as rain.

44

When I was in Japan for the World Cup of 2002, I had an affair with a Japanese woman. Her name is Sei Shonagon, and she was 1,000 years dead, but *The Pillow Book of Sei Shonagon* is one of the world's treasures. And she loved a list. Her narrative of journeys and affairs and snobberies and irritations and joys is punctuated by lists: Shameful Things, Awkward Things, Annoying Things, Pleasing Things, Times When One Should Be On One's Guard.

That year, I had been 30 years in journalism. Journalism, bloody hell. It was 30 years since I had joined the *Surrey Mirror*, with my hair insufficiently cut and my confidence insufficiently high. *The Times* was looking for an excuse to run a week-long series – an inflection of the circulation war, and the recent decision to go tabloid – and so I was asked to make a list. The 50 greatest sporting events of my life.

Kipling's poem 'The Ladies' ends each verse with 'An' I learned about women from 'er!' Each event of my list should be concluded: 'An' I learned about sport from that!' The list covers 21 sports: eight entries are football, six athletics, five cricket, four rugby, horse-racing and tennis. Six events involve horses, eight and a half involve women, 14 are from the Olympic Games with two more Olympians in non-Olympic events. I was physically present at 32 of these events. The piece ran over six days, and included a fat paragraph for each entry explaining the reason for my selection. It would be otiose to repeat all that now, but here is the list, from which you may draw your own conclusions, in the manner of Sei Shonagon:

50. Redhill v Fulham, 1976
49. Michael Johnson, Olympic Games, Atlanta, 1996
48. Scotland v England, Murrayfield, 1990
47. Ellen MacArthur, Vendee Globe, 2001
46. USA v Colombia, World Cup, 1994
45. Roger Federer v Andy Roddick, Wimbledon, 2003
44. Michael Jordan, NBA finals, Chicago, 1993
43. Mike Tyson v Larry Holmes, Atlantic City, 1988
42. Istabraq, Champion Hurdle, Cheltenham, 1998, 1999, 2000
41. Torvill and Dean, Winter Olympics, Sarajevo, 1984
40. Lance Armstrong, Tour de France, 2004

39. Joe Montana, Super Bowl, 1989

38. Kelly Holmes, Olympic Games, Athens, 2004

37. Katarina Witt, Winter Olympics, Lake Placid, 2004

36. Colin Cowdrey, batting against Lillee and Thomson in Australia 1974

35. Tim Henman v Yevgeny Kafelnikov, Wimbledon, 1996

34. Linford Christie, Olympic Games, Barcelona, 1992

33. Andre Chemerkin, weightlifting, Olympic Games, Atlanta, 1996

32. Florence Griffith-Joyner, Olympic Games, Seoul, 1988

31. India v West Indies, cricket World Cup, Lord's, 1983

30. Holland v Bulgaria, World Cup, 1974

29. Sebastian Coe, Olympic Games, Moscow, 1980

28. Ian Thorpe, Commonwealth Games, Manchester, 2002

27. Cameroon v Argentina, World Cup, 1990

26. Great Britain v Australia, hockey, Olympic Games, Seoul, 1988

25. St Louis Cardinals v Minnesota Twins, World Series, 1987

24. Svetlana Khorkina, gymnastics, Olympic Games, Sydney, 2000

23. Bonfire v Gigolo, dressage, Olympic Games, Sydney, 2000

22. England v Argentina, World Cup, 2002

21. Shergar, the Derby, 1981

20. Martina Navratilova v Zina Garrison-Jackson, Wimbledon, 1990

19. Fiji v New Zealand, Hongkong Sevens, 1984

18. Pakistan v England, third Test, Karachi, 2000

17. South Africa v New Zealand, rugby World Cup Final, 1995

16. King Edward VII Stakes, Royal Ascot, 1987

15. England v West Germany, World Cup, 1990

14. England v Australia, sixth Test, 1985

13. Liverpool v Juventus, Heysel Stadium, 1985

12. Men's coxless four final, Olympic Games, Athens, 2004

11. Muhammad Ali v George Foreman, 1974

10. Dancing Brave, Prix de l'Arc de Triomphe, 1986

9. Fu Mingxia, diving, Olympic Games, Sydney, 2000

8. Australia v England, rugby World Cup, 2003

7. Peter Schmeichel, Manchester United v Arsenal, 1999

6. Pete Sampras v Andre Agassi, Wimbledon, 1999

5. San Marino Grand Prix, Imola, 1994

4. Horton Point and Mark Todd, Badminton, 1994

3. England v Australia, Headingley, 1981

2. Ben Johnson, Olympic Games, Seoul, 1988

1. Men's coxless four final, Olympic Games, Sydney, 2000

45 I was seriously tempted to put Ben Johnson at the top of my list. Partly from perversity: every journo, no matter how highfalutin his style, retains the love of shocking the reader. But also, partly from a genuine admiration for Johnson: he was the fastest man in the world. He even *looked* like a human bullet. He made himself into the person – the thing – he wanted to be, and was prepared to pay every price. Except, presumably, disqualification. That run, the electrifying run, it still affects me, with its awful perfection. Awful even at the time, without the benefit of hindsight. The most perfect single piece of sport I have ever seen.

The only problem with it all, that I can see, was the destruction of both the sportsman and his sport. It was brutally and beautifully climactic. In a sense, it was the end of sport: the final achievement of sportingkind. It was not that innocence had been destroyed. Sport is never pure and rarely simple; all of modern sporting journalism depends on that fact. But when Johnson failed that drugs test, the illusion of innocence had gone. Gone forever. Not from track and field, but from all sport.

It is not precisely that all sports are filled with drugs, though there is certainly far more use of drugs than we assume. Rather, it is that no champion gets there by simple means, by easy, unspoiled, natural talent. To be a champion can only ever be a hard and bitter journey. It must involve a willingness not only to express a natural talent, but also to leave all the rest heartbroken. Above all, it is the realisation that every champion must pay for his medals with his life. At least, that is to say, by the manner in which he lives. In modern professional sport, to be a champion requires a hideous totality of commitment. In one sense, every champion is Ben Johnson: not because every champion cheats, but because every champion must be prepared to go the distance.

A champion must be unstinting of himself. We admire a man who gives his heart to his sport: Johnson gave his liver. For that crime, he will be forever hated. That is his role, but there is no such thing as a villain who lacks all sympathetic qualities. In all villains, as in all heroes, one always finds a touch of oneself. Be the best. Be the best ever. All it takes is everything.

And then I thought: if I considered making Johnson number one, why not Flo-Jo? Florence Griffith-Joyner won the 100 metres and 200 metres at the Olympic Games in Seoul that same year, 1988. And she certainly gave more even than Johnson. The records she set that year still stand and that in itself is as close to a condemnation as you can get. No one is even close*: and the drugs-testing technology has advanced by miles. Hardly coincidence, let us be frank.

But she was never caught. The reason I can be so free with this implicit accusation is because she is dead, and you can't libel the dead. But even her autopsy showed no unambiguous evidence of drug-taking.

I met her, a few months after her victories, at the Four Seasons, in Orange County, just north of LA. There was a glorious unselfconscious silliness about her, and I made no attempt to resist it. She was, in a sense, a comic-book character, every bit as much as Berry Bambam, in the children's stories she was writing. And I asked her the overwhelming question, intrepid journo that I am.

'Come on Florence,' I said. 'We all know you were taking something. You can tell me, I won't tell any one. What was it? Essence of panther?'

She laughed, a deep, husky laugh. She spoke in a kind of baritone whisper, in a way that rather reminded me of Margaret Thatcher. Thatcher was told to use a silly voice because her natural tendency to a shrill bullying rant rather alienated people; Florence, I suspect, used the same trick because if she relaxed her control and slipped into her natural voice she would be singing 'Old Man River'.

'Ohhh noooo,' she husked, lowering her eyes shyly – for like many show-offs, she was a naturally shy person. 'Ohhh nooo, I just gave it my ahhhlll.'

And that was the secret to life. Whether you were designing one-legged catsuits, or giving motivational speeches, or painting your nails – we caught a lift or elevator together, and she operated the buttons by means of a knuckle, so crippling was the affectation of her three-inch nails – or writing Berry Bambam, or running in the Olympic Games, you just have to give it your ahhhlll. And if you give it your ahhhlll, then how can you fail?

Florence Griffith-Joyner was preposterous. Self-deluding, self-serving and corrupt. And yet there was a strange innocence about her: she was not really of this world at all. I heard of her death when I was researching a piece about the Pony Club mounted games, and felt the most unexpected sense of loss. It was all for this, then. And I recalled the words of Janis Joplin: 'I love being a star more than life itself.' The ultimate athlete, then.

* Griffith-Joyner's records are 10.49 for the 100 metres and 21.34 for the 200 metres in 1988. The fastest times set in 2004 were 10.77 from Ivet Lalova of Bulgaria and 22.11 from Veronica Campbell of Jamaica. Flo-Jo still wins by a distance.

46

But if there is something of Ben Johnson in every great champion, in terms of the readiness to go the full route, then there is rather more of Steve Redgrave. I was there for the final race: the one in Sydney when he and the coxless four won the gold medal, and Redgrave collected his fifth gold at his fifth Olympic Games. I remember the dreadful shaft of pain I felt when I was convinced that the Italians had beaten them to the line, the incomprehension I felt at the eruption of British cheers, and the extraordinary joy when I realised my error.

This was patriotism all right. I have always been a patriot for the land of the uncompromisingly excellent, even if I lack citizenship for that nation myself. But as a sportswriter (not to mention a reader of books and a listener to whispering masterpieces) I have a tourist's visa to this country, and I go there as often as immigration will let me. And I wanted to write the tale of the fifth gold medal, the final perfect chapter in that 16-year-long quest for perfection. It was a finely achieved thing, but it was achieved. It was right that Redgrave won. More: it was necessary.

I remember also the curious professional schedule of that fine Australian morning. Let me explain. To preclude confusion, daily-paper journalists often talk of writing Thursday-for-Friday or Friday-for-Saturday. To talk about a Friday piece is ambiguous: are you filing on Friday, or are you writing it for Friday's paper? Well, that Sydney morning, I was required to file Saturday-for-Saturday, a thing made – just – possible by the prodigious time difference. I was required to press the Send button just 20 minutes after the race. It is not physically possible to write 800 fully baked and correctly typed words in that time, so I had to cheat. I pre-wrote, something I never do at football matches, regarding the practice as cheating. I wrote about 400 words of praise for Redgrave before the race, words that would stand up, win, lose or draw (that's another piece of professional jargon, I fear). The race run, I made a prop forward's run to the press-room and hammered out the additional 400. I pressed Send, and it Sent. Joy.

A day later, I was able to tell the story all over again, and at greater leisure Sunday for Monday. After all, my last gasp piece only made the London edition. And so I let myself go a little: it was an epic, I wrote, it was the fifth book of the *Redgraviad*, and it was an extraordinary privilege to be allowed to write it. It was not the greatest piece of sport I had ever seen. It was the greatest piece of sport that anybody had seen.

Greatness, then, requires an aspect of longevity. It is not about one perfect performance or one perfect tournament, a single masterpiece. No: it is about the accumulation of an oeuvre. A life. A CV. A biography. An epic, yes, I like that term very much.

Redgrave is not only a person. Redgrave is also a quality. You look for someone who might achieve great things in sport. Napoleon would ask of his generals: 'Has he luck?' I ask of athletes: 'has he Redgrave?' Redgrave is the ability to go beyond yourself. It is the ability to go the full distance, Johnson-like, and more. It is the ability to commit, day after day, to the one goal of winning. It is the ability to achieve the ultimate goal: and to be unsatisfied. To want more. To demand more, to seek more, and to get more.

Redgrave constantly sought security, and he found it in the knowledge that he had done more than anyone else who opposed him. He had rowed more miles, lifted more weights, erged more ergos. He had suffered more. He had cared more. He had overcome more setbacks. When Redgrave went into battle, he knew that all the others had had the choice to work just as hard as he had done, and that they had chosen not to do so. From this comes the tiniest scruple of contempt. These people had stinted themselves in their desire to be the best. Redgrave knew he had not done so. And so, as he approached the final stages in 1996 with everything as it should be, his constantly repeated instruction to Matthew Pinsent was: 'Let's not fuck it up.' That same year, I was at the press conference before the final. Pinsent was full of good cheer and good lines. Redgrave was silent, distant, staring ahead, eyes focused on some spot half an infinity away. And my colleague, Alan Fraser of the *Daily Mail*, broke press conference protocol with a surprising outburst: 'Steve, are you all right? Are you pissed off with us or something?' Redgrave refocused with a start. 'No,' he said. 'I'm all right. Mind's on the race, that's all.' An infinitesimal pause. 'Sorry.' It was a little vignette – about the most that Redgrave ever allowed – into the matter of possessing the quality of Redgrave. For in that press-er, Redgrave the man was almost entirely absent. All his strength, all his self, was already committed to the events that would unfold over 2,000 metres of water.

At every great moment in sport, the athlete who faces that moment must locate the Redgrave within. Do I choose to win, or do I choose not to win? That quality of Redgrave is the part of yourself that holds no compromise: that part that drags you over the line first, when you have already given all you thought you had. You find the quality of Redgrave at the end of 2,000 metres of water, after 26 miles and 385 yards of Athenian tarmac, in the final showjumping round at Badminton, or as you prepare to throw the last dart of the night at the double-top. It is not something to do with body, it is something to do with mind.

When any athlete anywhere in the world wins anything at any sport, he should give Redgrave royalties. Or she should. Redgrave is the quintessence. That is to say, the fifth essence – which originally meant the essence that is beyond the four elements of earth, water, fire and air. It is the substance of which the heavenly bodies themselves were composed. The idea of the quintessence is both Platonic and alchemical. And no, Redgrave is not the quintessence of sport. Redgrave is the quintessence of victory. After that race in Sydney, the one that put me through such agonies, Redgrave explained everything. Absolutely everything. He said: 'It was never in doubt from 250 metres.'

47 It was a strange thing, Steve Redgrave's press conference after he won that fifth gold medal. Like the

rest of us, I rather wanted to give Redgrave a hearty round of applause when he walked in. But we journalists are diffident about applause, and no one gave the lead, which would surely have been followed. So it began in the usual way: 'Questions for the gold medal-winning crew?'

After the ritual had been completed, the questions asked and answered, Redgrave half got up. He then bent to the microphone and said a strange thing. 'Thanks for making it all worthwhile.' And that broke the dam. No one was required to give the lead: we all gave the lead all at the same time. We gave him a storm of applause, and clapped him every step of the way out of the tent.

In the middle of the applause we all did a rather belated double-take. Surely, that wasn't thank you, as in thank you. That was thank you, as in fuck off. It was a bitter, and rather gracelessly timed remark, one that was intended to shame all those who had doubted him, all those who had dared to suggest, in the troubled months that preceded the race, that this final victory was a miracle too far. So, rather than bask in glory, he chose to leave his sport in an atmosphere of bitter confrontation. It was rather pleasant that we threw it back at him in genuine warmth and admiration. But it was an instructive moment. Even Redgrave, garlanded with praise more than most athletes could ever dream of, could not bear to finish his sporting career without expressing his contempt for those who had chronicled it so admiringly.

48 One of the great experiences of the sporting life is to be in the Olympic Stadium when a world record is broken. The place fizzes with a wild joy: to be there, to see it, to share it, to be part of the moment when a man runs faster than a man has ever run before, that is a very wonderful thing. The air is filled with an extraordinary infection of delight, as if the world itself had been made new. I was there when Michael Johnson ran the 200 metres in Atlanta in 1996. He did so in 19.32 seconds – the record still stands – with the most remarkable power and purpose. And, like everyone else in the afterglow of greatness, I was on my feet, and looking for someone to share it with. Feeling exactly the same thing was Colin Hart, then boxing writer for the *Sun*. He is a man who has in the past made his dislike for me uncompromisingly clear. The matter of boxing divides us, as do other matters of taste and background and temperament. And our eyes met, and we both grinned hugely, and Colin said: 'Makes it all fuckin' worthwhile, don't it?' I expressed whole-hearted agreement. It was a good moment.

I set off back to my cell, and on the way encountered my *Times* colleague John Goodbody. I told him about the record, he asked about the atmosphere in the stadium. 'It was so extraordinarily beautiful that Colin Hart smiled at me. And he hates me.'

'No, Simon, Colin doesn't hate you. He despises you.'

49

Clive Woodward, when head coach of the England rugby team, once told the assembled journos at a press conference: 'I have the greatest respect for what you do.' The response was an instant, instinctive belly-laugh, as spontaneous as the Redgrave round of applause. It's like mice saying that they have the greatest respect for cats, or stomachs speaking of their admiration for nematode worms.

But not because they are prey and we are predators; or that they are hosts and we are parasites. It is because we are completely different life-forms. We look for different things in life: we define our lives in different ways. There is almost no common ground at all. We certainly don't have sport in common. For the two groups, sport is a very different thing. Sport is our subject: sport is their object.

Our lives are led in the knowledge that the people we write about despise us, and despise what we do. Frequently, professional athletes join the media. Some of them even join the written press. It happens quite often in cricket, sometimes in rugby, occasionally in football. It is not a difficult transition, because it happens so quickly. One moment you despise the press, next moment, you are the press, and are despised in your turn. It is an instant metamorphosis.

The autumn was enlivened by two routine, almost ritualised spats between athlete and press. The first involved Tim Henman, who said that the tennis press knew nothing of the technicalities of tennis. He said he had talked tactics with a few of the boys in the press-room, and 'it was embarrassing' how little they knew. But tennis technicalities is how Henman makes a living. It is not how journalists make a living. Our job is not to count forehands and backhands – but you can't expect a practising athlete to understand that. Newspapers don't usually need close analysis of Leyton Hewitt's shot selection, or of Roger Federer's use of the backhand slice. And, if they ever did, a tennis correspondent would know exactly which respected big-name to ring for the most illuminating or sensational quote on that very subject. What a newspaper needs in a tennis correspondent is someone who can tell the tale of a match, put together a nice preview, and pick up a news story as it breaks, or better still, before. An ability to analyse the first serve percentage to the backhand in the deuce court is a bonus: but no more than that.

Then Jason Robinson, the captain of the England rugby team, decided to boycott all press conferences at the autumn internationals. This was because the *Daily Mail* had run a piece about his unsavoury past. An added layer of irony was that Robinson was paid to 'write' a column for the *Mail*. He felt this was all frightfully unfair, and he chose to sulk. To deprive the despised press of what they wanted.

The point that Robinson missed here is that newspapers have readers. This is a connection very few professional sportspeople make. You do not talk to the press in isolation. The press is your portal to the world. Robinson was not depriving the press of copy: he was depriving the world of a part of their pleasure in anticipating the England rugby matches of the autumn.

Meanwhile, Sir Alex Ferguson continued his policy of boycotting his own post-match press conferences. He refuses to do them, because he despises us. He only does them for the Champions League, for which press conferences are, by UEFA edict, mandatory. Me, I wish he would boycott all press conferences: and that all managers would follow suit and boycott all press conferences, and all players as well. The demand for 'quotes' is one of the manias of modern journalism: no match report is complete until the manager has added his own warped views and leaden clichés to the mix.

All right, I exaggerate. But only a little. Most press conferences and interviews tell us very little. The sportspeople themselves are too good at them. They speak fully and say nothing. It is a skill they deliberately cultivate, and they cultivate it because they despise us. Accept it, then: and don't, whatever you do, despise them back.

We need each other. Professional sport needs a paying audience. Without the media no one would know they were there. What sound does a falling tree make in a deserted forest? How popular is an athlete who has never been on television or been written about in newspapers? And we, quite obviously, need them, to write about, to pay the mortgage, to sell the newspaper, to provide the tale. This is not a predator-prey situation: it is a symbiosis. They use us and we use them. We, at least, should have the grace to admit that.

50

Eunuchs in the harem. That's how athletes see writers, no doubt about that. People who would do it if they could, but they can't. So we write as a second-best. No doubt the hunters in the Matopos Hills thought the same of the people who recorded their hunts so beautifully on the rock wall: and it is the paintings that remain.

Well, so I say in my pride as a 21st-century rock-painter... but, of course, the hunting also remains. The danger, the importance, the epic nature of the hunt, the beauty of the quarry, the reverence for the animals themselves: these we still have. We have them by means of the paintings. The artists would not have had these things to paint had it not been for the hunters. Without hunting, there would be no painting. And now the hunters have all gone, but the tale of the hunts survives, there on the rock walls.

Many people in the press-box were and are decent performers at sport. Others have only imagined themselves as such. This does not reflect a difference in abilities as a writer; rather, it is a difference in method. Some of our number had wanted to write about sport ever since their imagination was captured by sport at an early age. Their own daydreams of sporting greatness were games of the imagination, rather than plans with any serious hope of realisation.

There are some who went into sportswriting as a second-best: because they couldn't make the grade as professional athletes, or because their sporting career had run its course. Practising athletes like to see such people as perpetually gnashing their teeth that they can no longer, or could never, bowl at 90 miles an hour, hit a screamer to the top corner, burst the tackle and touch down. But writing is a dangerous thing; and it comes out to claim even those who approach it with resignation. Those who were athletes first and writers second cannot help but be affected – transformed – by what they are doing. By easy stages, they find they have become writers first, ex-players an increasingly distant second. Writing is not a thing that can be done half-heartedly: that is true whether you are writing *A La Recherche du Temps Perdu*, or 600 words on Blackburn v Aston Villa, to be filed on the whistle.

Me, I had no intention of ever becoming a sportswriter. I got a job on a local weekly paper because writing was the only thing I could do. I started well, and was much encouraged. 'Simon is good at features.' Then there was a change of personnel, a new chief reporter. 'Simon must never write features.' The office was re-organised: the chief reporter and her five favourites sat at one desk, the three arseholes sat at another desk some distance away, writing the arseholes' stories. I know. I was the least of those arseholes. She wanted me gone, and so I was moved. I was No Good.

I began a peripatetic period: every time there was a temporary vacancy at any office in the group, I was despatched to fill it. No Good. Don't let him write features. This went on for eight or nine months, in which time I read *A La Recherche du Temps Perdu* three times. Then they remembered that they were supposed to be training me, and they decided that Something Needed to be Done. So I was sent to yet another office where the editor, who cultivated his reputation as a Hard Man, was told to knock me into shape. He took this as a license for a personal mission to break me. No, not paranoia. The real thing. Years later, my sister met him at some Fleet Street do, and introduced herself. Startled into frankness, he said: 'Good God! Of all the reporters I've ever had under me, he was the one I hated the most.' This from a nature richly endowed for hating. An honour, I suppose.

So no features, for a start. Only bad stories. At least two night jobs every week, more often three. I shall never forget the faces of the Merton Borough Council Allotments sub-committee when they discovered that they had a reporter present. I don't think I ever got a story above the fold in the newspaper: always the dross. And always, total contempt from editor, and his sycophantic chief reporter.

It was not nice, no, and as you will readily understand, the memory is still uncomfortable. The personal animosity of that editor was a devastating thing to live with, and here was the catch. I couldn't leave. Not without breaking indentures. And to break indentures was to abandon the profession. God knows I hated journalism enough then, but what could I do, if I couldn't write for my living? He had me just where a bully wants a victim to be.

I resolved to take whatever vacancy turned up next in the group. No matter what, no matter where. I had to get it. The misery of getting up each morning to spend a day being despised was rather getting to me.

A vacancy turned up. It was on the sports desk at Redhill. Not quite what I had in mind. Sport? Sport was for idiots. Sport was for arseholes. Sport wasn't real reporting, was it? It wasn't real journalism. But I had to get out of that office. So I went to Bill Woodhatch, sports editor of the *Surrey Mirror*, and lied through my teeth.

'Bill, I've always wanted to be a sportswriter.'

'Then I'd love to have you.'

Destiny.

51

In November, Paula Radcliffe took part in the New York Marathon. She didn't run away with it. I watched it on television in Suffolk rather than New York, and listened to the assertions of the BBC commentator, Brendan Foster repeated at least once during every one of the 26 miles: 'Paula's not a quitter.' Hm. Interesting semantic or philosophical (insofar as they can be separated) point. In Athens, Radcliffe quit. But that apparently doesn't make her a quitter, merely someone who quit. Not a serial quitter, but someone who quit in extremis.

And in New York she ran shoulder to shoulder with Susan Chepkemei of Kenya over the last grinding miles. She did not get away from her until the last few hundred yards on the uphill finish in Central Park, and she did not quit. In fact, she was clearly and decisively the stronger. Physically stronger, mentally stronger, spiritually stronger. It was an inspiring performance. The Redgrave in her was stronger. Is Radcliffe, then, a great athlete? Her staggering world records, her epic fight with Chepkemei: do these things make her great? Or does her experience in Athens remove her from the company of the great, and make her merely a great story?

Greatness is a great word in sport, a great concept. In a sense, sport is all about greatness: the search for greatness, the falling short from greatness, the rare, rare achievement of greatness. Greatness is elusive of definition, but unmistakable when viewed plain. We use the adjective often and without much meaning. A nice cover drive: *great* shot. A well-struck volley: *great* goal. And yet we are mean and begrudging when it comes to the noun. Greatness? As I began the round of year-end pieces, assessments of the state of the sporting nation and so forth, I pondered on greatness. Who has it?

Not Henman (too late), not Rooney (too soon), not Radcliffe, not Beckham. Matthew Pinsent, yes, great by all standards save his own, or at least, the standard set by his former partner, Steve Redgrave, five gold medals against four. The Olympic Games is the greatest of all sporting events, and therefore it is profoundly involved in the search for greatness. Carolina Kluft, I thought, remembering Athens, Hicham El Guerrouj, Reza Zadeh, Hossein, Svetlana Khorkina, Guo Jingjing.

What is greatness? Can an objective definition exist? These are not straightforward questions. The process of growing up might be described as the retreat from perfectionism, or as an enforced peace-making process between the warring factions of dream and reality, of ambition and talent.

I had to accept, in my early teens, that I was not going to

be David Attenborough and Peter Scott. At 21, I had to accept that I was no poet. Later, I had to accept that I was not going to be James Joyce or Marcel Proust either, though I tried. I have had three novels published. Read them, make your own judgment. I think two of them are really not bad. But I have not established myself as a great novelist.

This is a process that just about all of us go through: a realisation, a reluctant acceptance of the fact that life is difficult and that our wildest dream will always be both wild and dreamy. No shame attaches to this adjustment: it is a common experience. Many use disappointment as a spur, something that drives a person to reach the most ferocious levels of second-best: to become, unquestionably, uncompromisingly, first class of the second class.

Perhaps the great thing about people who have real greatness in them is that they have never had to make these little adjustments. No setback has ever set them back. Their own talent, their own mental powers were always adequate to the task in front of them. Their dream never needed to be compromised, perfectionism was never retreated from. Perfection was in their grasp all along.

One of the most important indicators of greatness is a certain ability to change reality. To force reality to conform with your own desires. To believe so strongly in your own destiny that no person can bring himself to stop you. I witnessed that first-hand at the final of the race for coxless fours in Athens. The British crew had given everything, and it was still not enough. They had put in the final, brilliant, decisive effort, and they were still behind. This was not what was supposed to happen. And Pinsent, with that extraordinary outpouring of his personality, swamped both crews with his own inner force, somehow picked up his own boat and hurled it like a javelin at the line.

Pinsent refused to accept reality. He forced his own dream into actuality instead. It was perhaps the most remarkable explosion of one man's spiritual powers I have ever seen. No wonder he was off his head afterwards.

All this explains, perhaps, why there is always something difficult about dealing with people who have achieved greatness. They are not like the rest of us. They have never had to go through that process of compromise that is at the heart of growing up. It is not that they refuse to grow up, in the Peter Pan sense. It is more that they have never been presented with the opportunity to do so.

Sport is cruel, not only to the losers, but also to the winners. Sport is cruel, even to the genuinely great. Sport gives such people everything, and then takes it away. Sport allows the great people to express their genuine greatness. Sport tells them there is no need for compromise, no need to deal with the real world, no need to grow up. And then sport takes it all away again. Leaving them with the shell of greatness, the memory of it, and the instruction to get a life.

A life? What's that?

52

The Olympic Games do not only demand the best you are capable of giving. They demand that you produce it now. Today. Not any other day but now. The

Olympic Games say: this is your moment. Seize it, then. Your choice. If you miss it, you won't have another chance for four years. If ever. That is the whole point of what we are doing: the seizing and the now. And this ability to do the seizing on the day of days is an ineluctable aspect of greatness. Which makes Steve Redgrave and Matthew Pinsent both great, which makes Paula Radcliffe not great. If she somehow lasts, and does some seizing in Beijing in 2008, then we must reassess, and it is a story I would love to tell. But at the end of the year 2004, she had had her tilt at greatness – and discovered that it was not for her.

It's all about who wants it most, say the commentators. In the case of the women's Olympic marathon of 2004, it was all about who wanted it less. Call that Smith's Law, for Ed Smith. Radcliffe wanted it too much and the wanting destroyed her. Gary Lough, her husband and coach, said in her autobiography: 'She looked drained and broken-hearted. The worst thing that could have happened to her had happened. I put my arms around her. There was nothing I could say, all emotion had gone. She was numb now. It was like a part of us had died.' It reads more like the story of a woman suffering a bereavment, than someone failing to finish a race. The worst thing that could have happened? Get a life. Get a death.

Henman, too, failed to seize his moment, which came during those rain-washed three days in SW19, when he played his eternally delayed semi-final against Goran Ivanisevic. That was his moment and the seizing, alas, never happened. Greatness is a hard thing; but compromise is still harder.

Certainly, most practising athletes believe that all sportswriters are disappointed athletes. Perhaps that is true: but then so are most athletes.

53

Freedom. That was the first and most glorious feeling, when I joined Bill Woodhatch on the sports desk of the *Surrey Mirror*. But it was not freedom from the chief reporter at Redhill and the editor at Wimbledon. It was another, and more profound freedom that had me intoxicated.

I was free of news. I was free of politics. I was free of all the routine structures of the news story. I was writing about something else entirely. The politician, whether he is prime minister or chairman of the planning committee of the Reigate and Banstead Borough Council, is adept in the art of covering up. The people you speak to, on any important story, are similarly seeking to manipulate, conceal and evade. As a news reporter, you are dealing with concealment every second of your life.

But an athlete in competition is emotionally stark naked in front of you. He creates his tale, and you are there to do the telling. Once the match has begun, no word or posture or attitude matters any more. It is all in the doing. The result: you can talk all you like, but a 1-0 defeat is still the loss of two points in the Athenian League.

A novelist writes of love and enmity. There is not so much love for a sportswriter: enmity is there as his daily subject. It is there, unconcealed, unambiguous, and available. All you have to do is catch it and write it. A sportswriter, then, has something of the novelist's freedom. It was a wonderful discovery. I was Barnes Unbound. I owe Bill more than I can repay.

54

Free, too, from the macho culture of the news desk: a culture embodied by the Redhill chief reporter, who, unbuttoning her blouse dashingly to the level of her sternum and flirting with her favourites, was a slave to her own understanding of the macho nature of newspapers. I still find it uncomfortable working with the news desk at *The Times*. I ring the sports desk for the routine of queries/questions from the sub-editor in the piece I have filed. Say it's a live match, we're right on edition.

'Hello, sport?'

'Evening, Phil, it's Simon. How are you doing?'

'Great thanks, yourself?'

'Good. Any queries?'

'I think Pikey's ready for you. I'll put you over. Pikey?'

I call the news desk: 'Yes?'

'Simon Barnes, any queries?'

'No.'

The sports desk is one of the least macho places on the paper. But not, I should point out, because the work is easier. I recall the night of the Soho pub bombing, which took place just on first edition. The paper was remade more or less from top to bottom. The sports editor loaned a couple of his top subs to the news desk. Afterwards, speeches were made: you've all done wonders tonight, you've made journalistic history, heartfelt thanks for a remarkable effort from each and every one of you.

The sports subs went back to the sports desk to collect their jackets. 'What was it like?'

'Bit like a European football night.'

This extraordinary level of professional skill is something that news saves for special events. It is a matter of routine for sport. But instead of getting all macho about it, there is always an air, almost of gentleness. Personal ties are acknowledged, voices are low, and quiet competence is appreciated far more than loud posturing. All these things I learned from Bill Woodhatch, and I found his way of working perfectly familiar when I started to work for *The Times*.

The sports desk never gets above itself. We know that the world won't stop if we fail to get Arsenal v West Brom in the second edition. That is not a charter for sloppiness; rather, it creates an atmosphere that is less strident than elsewhere. It's only sport, it's only newspapers, and a gentle sense of humour and a touch of amiability works better than hysteria when you get near deadline. Sports journalism tends to create an essentially female working method.

55 Fearful things took place at the end of the

year 2004. Change. Keith Blackmore, head of sport, went whizzing up to the giddy heights of executive editor, that is to say, number three on the paper; David Chappell, sports editor, became deputy managing editor. Time, then, for an adjustment.

There is an extraordinary intimacy between a newspaper writer and the person with whom he works most closely. In some ways, the relationship is closer than a friendship; certainly, it partakes of satisfactions and shared experiences unavailable to people who meet and share each other's company in the usual ways.

Writing for a newspaper, for an editor, is less lonely than writing a book or a poem. You have a single person to please, which adds a certain tension to proceedings: But at least he is there. And having pleased that person, you have succeeded in what you set out to do. Provided that person is right, of course. You have to do a fair bit of trusting in each other's instinct, in each other's competence.

With Keith in charge of the sports pages, I had enjoyed myself for many years as the flaky winger. I had revelled in a period when I was gently steered into a backwater: a very pleasant and remunerative backwater it was, too, writing about horses and televised sport. But the far greater intimacy began in 2002, when the then chief sportswriter Oliver Holt went to join the *Daily Mirror*. I had a lunch with Keith – hot and sour soup, bean curd with chillies, Tsing-tao – in which I sought to persuade him that a new chief sportswriter was surplus to requirements. He disagreed, and asked me to do the job. The flaky winger was now centre forward.

The best of the relationship before then had centred around my weekly column. Keith would frequently come up with a half-baked notion: my task was to complete the process of baking. The finished piece often turned out quite differently to anything either of us expected and that was a great satisfaction to both, when it came off. But after I had taken the chief's job, the heart of the matter was a new kind of freedom. I had to do the chief's job, to tackle the chief's natural subjects, but I could only do so – was encouraged to do so, was expected to do so – with a freedom of approach that is not a traditional part of sportswriting. What I learned when I first began to cover Redhill's matches in the Athenian League I was now putting into practice at the Olympic Games. Free: well, use that thrilling and frightening freedom as best you can.

Because writing for a newspaper is not like writing a novel. It is a team game. For a writer, at least, it is rather like cricket: a team game based on individual performance. You can't write unless you are asked to: you can't get the damn thing in the paper without it being touched by many hands. The writer does not plan the page, select the picture, write the headline, decide how large his by-line should be.

Another analogy is American football. This sport is based around the idea that each team is at heart two teams: offense and defense. In a newspaper, the defense is the subs, who produce the paper. The offense is the writers, who give them stuff to put in it and who take all the glory. Editors are like coaches, wandering about with a clipboard and a pair of cans, thinking they are actually doing something. Which they are, in a way, I suppose. They are preparing to take the blame.

At *The Times*, I have worked under a series of seriously good sports editors. In the course of their succession, they had established a tradition. Each had left his mark, though only someone who has spent as long as I have working for the same department – that makes three of us – would appreciate the huge contribution made by Norman Fox more than 20 years ago. I was sorry that Keith was moving, greatly disorientated by the prospect of change, optimistic that the promotion would come from within this tradition, readying myself to make the most of what came next. It would be a strange thing to get used to, for Keith was more than a friend. A colleague.

56

A succession. A handing-over. A tradition, a culture intact. The temptation to bring in a genius from outside to bugger everything up was resisted. Tim Hallissey rose from deputy sports editor to sports editor, to great relief all round. That meant he had to eat an awful lot of lunch. I had hot and sour soup, bean curd with chillies, Tsing-tao.

Tim had advice, all of it useless. A new year starting: and the great thing was that it was an odd-numbered year, so no Olympic Games, no Ryder Cup, no European Football Championship, no World Cup. 'It's an easy year,' I said. 'The perfect year to find your feet.' Before autumn came, the year was to bring us three of the greatest sports stories ever told.

57

It was the Christmas party that swayed the editor's mind. So the story goes, anyway. Robert Thomson rather sportingly came along. The *Daily Telegraph* sports department has an annual and strictly hierarchical formal sit-down lunch, in which you gauge your year according to your proximity to the sports editor's table, as Simon Hughes explained in *Morning Everyone*, his own cheerful account of a sportswriter's life. *The Times* has a hugger-mugger democratic free-for-all: vertical drinking, and a chance to chat to everyone. The do is traditionally financed by the leading writers, and the subs come as our guests: a very right and proper thing. It is always a matey and merry affair, with lots of handshakes, kisses and even male-to-male hugs. Robert found the ungrudging camaraderie a very pleasing thing and was able to appreciate the fact that all this talk of a tradition and culture actually had some kind of truth in it. It was, then, the softer side of the sports department that reached him: the, as it were, feminine side. That's as it should be. Me, I kissed my old friend Jenny MacArthur, the equestrian correspondent, and we gossiped like mad about horses.

58

On then, to the first moral dilemma of the New Year. Roy Carroll, the Manchester United goalkeeper, dropped the ball over the goal-line, and no goal was given. Naturally, this sparked a great debate: should the technology to judge such issues be introduced? Was Geoff Hurst's goal in the World Cup Final of 1966 really a goal? (Actually, there should be no debate on the matter. Look at the still picture of the moment. Not at the ball crossing the line, at the forward in attendance. Of course it was a goal. Roger Hunt was there, perfectly positioned to put away the rebound, but he didn't do anything of the kind. He turned away to celebrate. Instantly, spontaneously, instinctively. It would have been a tap-in, but he turned it down. A goal-scorer only refuses a goal when he knows, knows in the very deepest parts of his being, that the goal has already been scored.)

The one question of the non-goal against Manchester United that remained undebated was whether or not Carroll should have owned up. No, ref, that was a goal, I let it cross the line. Carroll's right to cheat went more or less unquestioned. In matters of conduct, especially violence and illegal drugs, as I've said, we require professional athletes to have rather higher standards of behaviour than everybody else, on the strange grounds that they are 'role models'. But it seems on these issues of how a game is actually played, we accept the prevailing morality of the players themselves. This was perfectly expressed by CB Fry in 1911: 'In football, it is widely acknowledged that if both sides agree to cheat, cheating is fair.' This view, put over by the players and managers themselves in a thousand television interviews and backed up by ex-players who become media pundits, has seeped into the consciousness of the rest of us who merely watch. We identify with these professionals, these real footballers. Therefore, we accept their view on footballing morality.

That is true in all professional sports. Cricketers don't walk when they give a catch behind: they wait for the umpire to make a decision. We who watch now accept the fairness of that. When Michael Atherton gloved a ball from Allan Donald to the wicket-keeper in that famous joust in 1998, he didn't walk; and the nation celebrated not his immorality but his unyielding spirit. Perhaps we were right to do so. In football, both sides routinely claim every corner, goal-kick and throw-in; both sides hold and grapple at every set-piece; both sides obstruct each other. All this is cheating: all this is considered fair by referees, by players, by commentators, by pundits, by spectators. The morality of such acts goes unquestioned.

Sports are governed not by their rules, but by a vague consensus of players and officials as to what is and what is not acceptable. Late tackles, in which the ball is completely missed, are routinely punished, and even the guilty player seldom objects when the referee has got the decision absolutely right. Deliberate assault with an elbow, and two-footed and over-the-top tackles are regarded as not only illegal but immoral. In cricket, intimidatory bowling is acceptable (though technically illegal, if you take law 42.6.a literally) but a beamer – a fast, head-high full toss – is considered immoral.

I remember my old friend Eddy Pratt, with whom I played a lot of cricket. 'I would die rather than cheat at golf,' he told me. 'In cricket, I used to cheat sometimes. For example, if a batsman was annoying me, I would sometimes throw one at him from eighteen yards. And when I played football, I cheated all the time.' It is not that Eddy's moral worth depended on the size of the ball he was playing with. Rather, he was inclined to conform to the conventions of whatever sport he found himself playing.

Do the rules of a game have a moral force to them? Is it, for example, immoral to be offside? The offside law exists in order to prevent a player from taking an 'unfair' advantage of a defender. It is an attacker's job to get ahead of a defender: it is an attacker's lot to be penalised unjustly and frequently. Is it immoral to try and steal a yard when there is an opportunity?

Or, on the contrary, is such a theft a deeply moral act, designed as it is to please colleagues and supporters? Cheating of a certain kind is not only uncensured: sometimes it is praised unambiguously. 'He used all his experience and went down under the challenge,' say television commentators. That is to say, he won a free-kick, or a penalty, by cheating: this is a skill, and is therefore worthy of praise. And we who watch do not approve of this, no, we do not approve at all... unless, for example, it is Michael Owen playing for England at the World Cup in 1998, when he won a penalty against Argentina by going down in the box 'after the faintest of touches' from Roberto Ayala. Morality, it seems, depends on the side you support. Not a sporting truth, that: a universal truth. War would be impossible without it.

Me, I approve of moral behaviour, disapprove of immoral behaviour, just like everyone else. But given a choice between the self-righteous rule-worshippers of golf, and the spiky give-and-take (and then get him back when he isn't expecting it) of football, give me football every time. Freedom: a freedom, perhaps to create your own morality on the fly. A truer morality than one that is imposed on you by a man in a blazer.

59

Sports stars are 'role models'. That means that whenever a sports star does something wrong, he is wrong twice over. He is not only a human being who has failed, he also failed all the other human beings who copy him. This is an idea that goes unchallenged throughout sport: that young people base their own behaviour on that of their favourite sports stars. Sports stars show young people how to hold their arms when they take a corner, how to cut their hair, how to walk, what clothes to wear, how to behave with women, how to drink, what drugs to take.

Young people also admire rock stars. Many rock stars make their money by explicitly setting themselves up to be imitated. They express a style of appearance, they embody a particular way of living: and these matters are often as important as the beauty of their music and the profundity of their lyrics. Their flamboyant use of drugs and gladiatorial sex lives are reported in the papers. Many young people do, indeed, dress like these people. Yet a musician in trouble is never supposed to be a 'role model'. He is just a musician; and in interviews, he will speak out about his freedom to behave exactly as he pleases.

That freedom is denied to sports stars. Sports stars must be better, not worse than the rest of us. It all goes back to the Victorian notion of sport: that sport teaches you to be a better person. Breaking the thing down to its basics, more is expected of a sports star than a rock star, because 150 years ago, sport was supposed to stop boys masturbating.

Charles Barkley, the American basketball player, whom I saw as a Dream Team member at the Barcelona Olympics and also in the NBA finals when he rashly attempted to defeat Michael Jordan and the Chicago Bulls, is one of the few people in sport to have thought about this role model business. 'Just because I dunk a basketball doesn't mean I should raise your kids,' Barkley said. Responding to the objection, 'But you're paid to act like a professional,' he said: 'I'm paid to kick ass on a basketball court.'

Parents are role models, not sports stars. There is statistical and anecdotal evidence to demonstrate that children from violent homes become violent in their turn, that children from broken homes become home-breakers, that children from criminal backgrounds break the law. There are no statistics whatsoever to show that when the country's most popular sports star drinks and drives, an epidemic of drink-driving follows; that when a sports star takes drugs, a million children go out and score.

That doesn't stop many sports stars playing the part of

role model. Some do so out of genuine conviction. But all – especially in America – are doing it for the money. The pseudo-role-models are the ones that get the big endorsements. Jordan, not Mike Tyson. Virtue – or its appearance – rewarded.

I admired MJK Smith of Warwickshire and England, but did not grow up to be an amiable, geekish middle-Englander. I admired George Best, but failed to become a womanising pisscart. My father was in television, my mother was a writer. I bear their mark: not the mark of MJK and Bestie.

60
It was a huge sporting achievement, the nation was beside itself with delight, a new world record was set, there was a wonderful person to write about and an absolutely terrific story. So why did no sportswriter write it? I was one of the very few sportswriters who went down to Falmouth. The event got plenty of coverage in the papers, mainly on the news pages. Why were the sportswriters not interested? Because, if this wasn't sport, I don't know what it was.

The event was Ellen MacArthur beating the single-handed, non-stop, round-the-world sailing record. A race, then. Which is sport, is it not? I was out on Pendennis Point as she came into harbour, and there on the quayside as she leapt onto the land for the first time in 72 days, there as she did her press conference, there as she addressed the public.

It was an astonishing achievement. Bernard Joyon had set a new record twelve months earlier, beating the old record by an extraordinary 21 days: a Beamonesque leap, nothing less. MacArthur set off in pursuit, in a brutal, pared-down, ugly great tank of a trimaran, poetically named B & Q. And she hammered the new record into submission.

It was a tale of infinite hardship and endless sleep deprivation. But she didn't suffer in order to survive: she suffered in order to win. You don't have to worry about sailing a boat all the time you are out on the water. You can park if you like, even in the Southern Ocean – heaving-to, it's called. You can heave to and have a good old kip and catch up and be right as rain next day. Or you can drive the boat relentlessly, constantly adjusting sails and course, always making the last additional effort to squeeze the last desperate half-knot of boat-speed. MacArthur is absolutely pitiless on herself: that's how she managed it.

I spent an evening with her once, in Cherbourg, where she was preparing for another jaunt. The questions I asked were absolutely incomprehensible to her. I asked about fear. 'What's the choice?' she asked, giving me the Paddington Bear stare from beneath the crew cut. 'You're out there. You made the choice to be out there. So deal with it.' People who see the world like that simply frighten the life out of me.

This is a rare person, a very rare person. Terrifying, and deeply impressive. Yes, she has plenty of that quality of Redgrave about her, along with all that means, for good and for bad. She is hard, as well as soft, vulnerable, emotional.

Sailing, winning, winning, sailing: it's all one.

I, apparently alone among my tribe, found all this fascinating. Why so? Was it a question of categories, then? Is round-the-world sailing not really a sport, but more like climbing a mountain or flying a balloon round the earth? Or was it because she's female? Did MacArthur's gender – and the consequent sentimentalising of her – make this a soft, human interest (Simon mustn't write features) story?

It was a story that also unleashed a gathering of sneerers, who called her Bridget Jones on a boat, the great whinger, and so forth. Sneerers: life-deniers. Yes, yes, yes, Bach was wasting his time with all his silly music, van Gogh should have stuck to being a preacher instead of using all those crazy colours, and Joyce was just messing about with words. Sneer, sneer – and miss the life.

But perhaps the fact that it was a woman who had done this thing did not make the story unacceptably soft. Perhaps it made the story unacceptably hard. For it is a matter of fact that extreme records tend to be held by women. Alison Streeter had by then swum the channel 43 times. The unrelated Tanya Streeter has dived to 112 metres, 400 feet, on a single lungful of air. At the time that MacArthur landed, Rosie Swale-Pope was halfway round the world, running all the way, having been at various times held up at knife-point and hit by a bus.

Women. Bless 'em. Fragile things. Visit the poorest places on earth and time and again, you find women holding the family together: women making some kind of go of things. In Zambia, later that year, I was to meet a group of nine illiterate women who had founded an orphanage for children whose parents had been carried off by AIDS. They sang, played drums, scrounged mealie-meal around the community, started a school as well, saved lives. Woman the gatherer. The female capacity for extremes is the story of humanity. Women hold life together while the men goof off playing sport. An old story: as old as humanity. Amusing and ironical of MacArthur to remake that point in the sort of dramatic fashion that only sport can provide.

If you find women's ability to deal with hardship a hard thing to believe, then you are not a parent. Sleep deprivation is the stuff of parenthood: and women do it better. MacArthur's triumph was a great piece of sport: and it also told us things about the nature of human history, the nature of human life. That when things are at their hardest, only women will take the job on. It was a story not many of my colleagues wanted to tell.

The weekend football was more important.

61

I learned how to write about sport while travelling by boat between Yung Shue Wan and Central. I used to make that journey three or four times a week, to get from my home on Lamma Island to various places of business in Hong Kong. When I set off for the east, mad for adventure after my spell on local papers, my then girlfriend's sister's husband did a very kind thing, and bought us a subscription to the *Guardian Weekly*. It arrived, a beautiful thing to the touch, and made entirely from cigarette papers. (Years later, I became friends with a great African bird expert who did, indeed, roll his own cigarettes with the *Guardian Weekly*.)

I had never been a *Guardian* reader, but I enjoyed the weekly fagpapers very much. Especially, I enjoyed the sport. For they had a man who wrote about sport in a way that sport had never been written about before. And I was entranced.

I remember the first piece that caught my eye. It was a hymn to the genius of the three-day eventer, Lucinda Prior-Palmer, who won Badminton six times. It celebrated her Jaeger scarf, her flawless skin, her beautiful vowels, her extraordinary mixture of reticence, self-deprecation and courage, her perfect, unalloyed, archetypal Englishness. As the big double-decker ferry chugged past the container ships and the junks – still occasionally seen with a sail – Lucinda lived. And I thought, a little like Corporal Jones: I would like to volunteer to be that man what writes that prose, sir. Frank Keating. *The* sportswriter.

He did jokes. He did time and place. He did weakness as well as strength. He did hero-worship, but his heroes were always humans, with their foibles and their fears and their fallibilities. Above all, he did people.

The tradition of sportswriting had always been writer-as-expert. Writer as the man in the power-seat. Wiser than the reader; wiser, too, than the men and women who merely played the games. Players were seen in utterly uncompromising terms. But Frank softened the edges, blurred the distinctions. He frequently used a sweetly engaging persona: of a chaotic, rather ignorant, distinctly humble person, overwhelmed by the beauty and the glory before him: and so the words came tumbling out, born of sheer enthusiasm, out of sheer love for the day, the game, the people.

Even then, as a writer myself, I could see that Frank was, of course, disciplined, knowledgeable, hard-working, rightly proud of what he did, and the most frightful swot. The persona reflected another, equally valid side of himself, and he employed it as a master.

I understood, even then, the trick that Frank was pulling off. He was working like a reporter but writing like a novelist: with a novelist's eye and a novelist's freedom, and about a subject that suited such freedoms as none other — or at least, none other in daily newspaper journalism. That man, I thought, is a genius. He has reinvented the way we write about sport, and therefore the way we see sport and the way we understand sport. Sport is played, not by invulnerable superheroes, but fallible humans, battling against fear. Frank saw the Clark Kent beneath the cape.

The truth about sportswriting, and by extension, the truth about sport, is not to be found in the caricatured masculinity of many of the athletes of either sex. The truth is much wider than that. To be fully human, a view of anything, even sport, must be soft as well as hard, female as well as male, weak as well as strong. There is fear and weakness in Mike Tyson: there is unyielding strength in the tears of Ellen MacArthur. The devil is in not seeing whole.

Years later, Lucinda was to tell me how much she hated the piece. And Frank has told me many times that he hates it when I go on about him like this.

If you're a genius, you have to take that sort of thing.

62 Sports do not build character. They reveal it. Words of Heywood Brown, 1888-1939, an American humorist and writer, and quoted in Frank Keating's *Sporting Century.*

63 That spring, the sporting nation was in the process of coming to terms with a new reality. The England rugby union side was losing. The culture of excellence had been broken. Sir Clive Woodward, the head coach, had resigned, the captain, Martin Johnson, had retired from international rugby; the nonpareil, Jonny Wilkinson was injured. Again, or still, I forget which.

The soft side of Johnson? The gentle side? Absurd even to doubt it. When I was in Australia for the rugby World Cup of 2003, the press and the players were accommodated in the same hotel in Brisbane for a week. This used to be the regular arrangement in most sports; now it is no longer the case. Players blame the press for this change: no longer discreet, no longer keeping secrets, no longer prepared to hush things up. In fact, the problem lies with sport. It is just too popular. There is endless television coverage, and the newspapers fill page after page with big events. Where newspapers once sent a single writer to an event, they now send gangs. And reporters have got to report something.

There is a huge demand for sport, and it makes the

athletes themselves rich and famous. There have been gains, there have been losses. There always are, in everything, as times change and the world moves on. Trust has gone, friendship between athletes and journos is virtually unknown, so is obscurity, so is poverty. Being a professional journalist has become a different game; being a professional player of games has become a different game. I recall getting pissed with the England cricketers at the Hilton in Port of Spain, Trinidad, where the journos and players were both staying, and that in 1986.

But even at the time, the relationship was all falling apart. The fame and the notoriety of Ian Botham required coverage from beyond the traditional pure-cricket school of journalism. It was the beginning of the end. And yet, if you happened to look at *Barclay's World of Cricket*, published that same year, you would find a picture from that same tour, that same hotel. The caption reads: 'Press conferences and interviews are an important part of the modern cricket-writer's job. Here David Gower, England's captain, talks to the Press during England's tour to the West Indies in 1985-6.'

Gower is sitting by the pool beneath an umbrella, and around the same round table, eleven journalists are writing on notebooks. I'm one of them. It's a despatch from the lost world. These days, there would be closer to one hundred, plus half a dozen or more television cameras, and it would take place in one of the hotel conference rooms, with the captain miked up, and with an ECB press man to take the questions, advise the captain, keep order and try and maintain some kind of tenuous control.

Everything has changed. So out in Brisbane, it was uncomfortable for both press and players to be sharing the same hotel. A nod, a smile, a greeting, and the journo walks on, not breaking stride, not wishing to be presumptuous or intrusive. And I found myself sitting with my colleague Alison Kervin, having a swift lunch, while at the next table, Johnson sat with Molly, his daughter of about six months. She had a comely version of his own ferocious brow. Alison smiled and greeted and averted eyes politely. I nodded, not having been introduced, also averted.

'Don't you know him?' Alison asked, out of earshot.

'No, and I am always too frightened to introduce myself, in case he knows that I once called him the man with the Cro-Magnon brow-ridge.'

'Oh, he knows all right,' Alison said reassuringly. 'He rang me up so that he could quote it accurately in his auto-biography.' And meanwhile, Johnson cooed, and pulled silly faces and held Molly high above his head, while she cooed back and waited for the dizzy, swooping descent into another daddyhug. Is it possible to reconcile the gentle Johnson with his girl, and the ferocious Johnson playing rugby with his boys? Of course it is. In both cases, it is just a man looking after his own.

64

That had been one hell of a tale, that World Cup, and Martin Johnson had been at the heart of it. Johnson, the man who never took a backward step, had taken England to their victory. Johnson, a man who possesses that quality known as Redgrave, had simply insisted on victory. A fitful performance against Wales in the quarter-finals, a masterly demolition of the French in the semis, and finally, that extraordinary match against Australia, when England came close to losing against a series of baffling decisions by the referee.

Most teams would have lost. They would have got angry, hit people, conceded penalties, lost tactical discipline, tried to play inappropriate catch-up. But no: under Johnson, England ground out the result they needed, refusing to be dismayed by the obstacles that they encountered. They won by means of Johnson's will. Finally, at the end, to Jonny Wilkinson the glory, and that was great and wonderful.

But the triumph was all Johnson's. Out there, on the field, the team were Martin Johnson.

Leadership is a remarkable thing. Johnson always said that he never set himself up as a leader. We must accept that, just as he accepted that he happens to be the sort of man that people follow. They follow because they know they'll be all right. He looks after his own. The gift of leadership lies in the ability to inspire in others the gift of followership. So Johnson led, England followed. The stuttering and the self-doubting were conquered by means of one extraordinary mind.

It was wonderful, indeed. But it made the Six Nations tournament of 2005 rather uninspiring stuff. Not purely for patriotic reasons – though for a London-based newspaper, England is the story to write – but also because the tournament itself was short of greatness. A decent Welsh side won it against opposition that wouldn't last half an hour against the southern hemisphere sides.

But at least I had been there and written the story of the time England won a World Cup: and I told the tale with a full heart. And now, the ordinary, straightforward odd-numbered year was proceeding according to plan. I heard a great piece of news: my old friend Jess was getting married. I had spent much time with Jess in Zambia, when she was running the catering at a bush-camp in the Luangwa Valley where I made a two-month stay to research a novel. I was delighted, and vowed to come out to the wedding, which was, of course, in the Luangwa Valley. I then discovered that the wedding was to take place on May 25, the day of the European Cup Final. 'Of course you can go,' Tim Hallissey said. 'So long as there isn't an English team in the final, of course.'

Of course.

65 The deepest and most elusive process within ourselves is, roughly speaking, sport. But it's normally called dreaming. I'm not talking about the it's-always-been-my-dream-to-win-an-Olympic-gold-medal sort of dream. Those are daydreams, fantasies, that some people are able to force upon reality. But that is a quite different process to the one I am talking about here – the real nightdream experience of the spectator. Sport is such stuff as daydreams are made of, for sure; but it's also the stuff of real dreams: the dreams that happen to us when we are asleep, the dreams that thrill, alarm, concern and baffle every one of us.

When we enter the dream state, the aroused state of rapid eye movement sleep, we take all sorts of odd things and weave them together into some kind of story. A dream is a narrative of heightened reality, in which we take extraordinary things for granted: a dear friend with a completely different face, wild sexual romps with the most unusual partners, the ability to fly.

What is sport but a narrative of hyper-reality? A place where the normal rules do not apply, where the usual sort of reality has been temporarily suspended? Like dreams, sport can bring us the most ecstatic and profoundly felt pleasures, and can also bring us matters so complex and confusing that we don't know how to react to them. Sport can deliver those moments we thought only possible in fiction or daydream, but with a visceral intensity that no amount of private musing can rival.

But perhaps the dream state that sport brings us most frequently is the anxiety-dream. That is to say, the dream in which you have an important exam to take, but you can't find the room where it's taking place, and as you search with increasing desperation, it gradually becomes clear that you haven't read the books you are to be examined on. My own most regular anxiety-dream is a reflection of professional life: it takes place at an airport and I can't find the check-in desk, and then the plane is leaving and I must run, and my legs become bound together, as if I were suffering from the leg-locker curse in Harry Potter, and I can move neither one way nor the other. It's not the sort of dream that gives sleep its good name.

But sport brings us anxiety-dreams on a regular basis, and many of us actively seek sport all the time, as something that enhances our lives. The greatest example of sport as a real anxiety-dream is the match between England and Poland in 1973. England had to win to qualify for the World Cup and failed to do so, thanks to the inspiration of the Polish goalkeeper, the immortal Jan Tomascewski. Watching this match was a hard and bitter agony; and yet I would not have wished to miss it. It was an evening of prolonged anxiety. The hyper-reality of sport created a mood that was almost unbearable, and yet had for some reason to be borne.

Sport brings us these anxieties again and again. They come most often to those who believe that the best way to follow sport is by means of partiality. My friend and colleague John Goodbody has reached a stage where he cares so much about Arsenal that he can't watch them play football. He can no longer deal with his own anxiety levels. He watches them when he knows the result, and then only if they have won. I have also heard of a supporter so committed to his side that for him, the worst thing of all was to see his own side score: 'Oh God, now we've riled them!'

Do passionate supporters put up with their anxiety because the taste of triumph is so wonderful? Or is there an addictive quality in the anxiety itself? Either way, the sporting experience is a way of engaging with hyper-reality, and that is a necessary part of the human condition. Particularly when we can wake up from them. Dreams end in waking: sometimes to tear you from the girl whose beauty has touched your soul, sometimes to lift the burden of murder from your shoulders, and sometimes to free you from the plane you will never catch and the leg-locker curse that has bound you forever. Likewise, sport ends: the whistle blows, the umpire announces game, set and match, England or Arsenal traipse sadly to the tunnel, Tim Henman walks | stiff-shouldered to the locker-rooms for the last time that summer – and we, we who watch, we who have the dreamer's experience, why, we get on with our waking lives. Unencumbered. Why should we not? We know, all of us, that the confusion of the dream and the waking state is stepbrother to madness.

66 In Atlanta, at the Olympic Games of 1996, there were a number of pairs that dreamed they could beat Steve Redgrave and Matthew Pinsent. They believed they saw vulnerabilities, and they dreamed that these could be exploited. They dreamt of gold. At the final, the two British oarsmen slid machine-like on their seats for the first stroke, for the brutal explosion of power with which they would butcher the unoffending water. And Redgrave, the bowman, leaned forward a little and growled into Pinsent's ear. 'Let's crush some dreams.'

67 Loyalty. What are football fans loyal to? A club, they would say, a football club. How can you be loyal to a club of which you are not even a member? But for many people, and perhaps for the majority of those who would call themselves lovers of sport, it is essential that the sporting experience be connected with partiality, with loyalty. It has to matter who wins.

It is a question of raising the stakes. There was a time in my life when I used to bet on the horses. I had a bet more or less daily. It was when I worked in an office, so I had to find something to get one through the day. The perusal of the *Sporting Life* – first the news and the results, then the day's racecards, and at last a good hard stare at the mystical inscriptions of form – was an essential part of the day, followed as it was by a wager, and subsequent visits to the bookies next door throughout the day to follow its course.

I worked for a few months for the *Stratford Express*, and my dominant memory of that time is of nonchalant, shirt-sleeved, as-if-to-the-lav strolls from the main office, followed by mad freezing sprints through the winter weather to check on the course of the day's investment. And I made the obvious discovery that the more money you stake, the more exciting it is. The art of a good, enjoyable bet is to stake perhaps ten per cent more than you can lose without a qualm. It is the same thing with emotional investment in sport. You don't want to care too much, but you want to care enough. Otherwise the spectacle has no savour.

I remember reading a book called *Only the Goalkeeper to Beat*, by Francis Hodgson, a suitably eccentric work from a man who described himself as 'a good bad goalkeeper'. In this glorious tribute to 'the most important member of the team', he has an aside on the phenomenon of fanship. He sees no point in it, reflecting that there is as much logic in supporting a football club as there is in supporting the English National Opera and in consequence refusing to visit Covent Garden.

I have always felt something of this, at least so far as club football is concerned, for all that I have never cared for opera. I wasn't brought up to the notion of supporting a football club. My father (who loves opera) supports the Wigan rugby league side (he never refers to them by the modern appellation Wigan Warriors, no doubt feeling that when he was young, such a name would have been considered a tautology) and Lancashire County Cricket Club, also England at cricket and rugby union. Football came to me by a circuitous route: not straight through the genes, and certainly not through parental guidance. Perhaps fanship is like acquiring language: it has to be done at a certain, and very young age, or it simply doesn't happen. Perhaps you reach a moment when your sporting-bias receptors atrophy.

I was to learn plenty of things about the nature of partiality, my own and other people's, over the coming months. But, as I caught the plane to Liverpool from London City airport, I couldn't begin to imagine what it must be like to kill for a football team, though I certainly tried.

Liverpool were to play Juventus in the quarter-finals of the European Cup. It was, of course, Juventus they played in 1985, at Heysel Stadium in Brussels, when Liverpool supporters charged the Juventus end, a wall collapsed and 37 people died. Liverpool, as a city, marked the occasion with rather theatrical contrition. The *Liverpool Echo* led the front page for the match of 2005 with the headline 'We're Sorry', followed by a list of the names of the dead. Before the match there were ceremonies of reconciliation, and the Kop End held up cards to spell out the word '*Amicata*'. Friendship.

The hard-core Juventus fans turned their backs, not willing to play their part of forgivers in this game of sentimentality. It was a shocking thing to witness: brutal. No *amicata*, we're Italian. Still, I wonder how many supporters of English clubs would have missed the chance to claim the moral high ground and look tough and mean at the same time.

The extraordinary tensions of the game allowed the Liverpool players to find something deep within themselves. They played with a kind of passionate certainty. Football is the most emotional of all games, and matches turn on very small things. And this really rather ordinary Premiership team found themselves, much to their surprise, playing like champions. How do these things happen, these strange infections of brilliance that can run through an entire side? Football can produce this bizarre effect more often than any other sport, partly, I think, because the value of the currency – the goal – is so extraordinarily high. Liverpool won the match 2-1, and went on to a goalless draw in the second leg.

This was a remarkable achievement, but I must say that I was rather cast down by it. Liverpool were drawn to play

Chelsea in the semi-final: no matter how much I meditated on the possible permutations, it seemed that there was going to be an English club in the European Cup Final. So much for my promise to Jess: so much for the bush wedding in the Luangwa Valley of Zambia. I wanted to be there. As a supporter.

68 My friend Tone – he insists on this truncated appellation in all his social and professional dealings – is a psychotherapist, and he has a theory about the reason people support football clubs. It is, he has told me over glasses of Laphroaig (the whisky of which he is loyal supporter), 'a bearable way of facing the fact that God doesn't love me'. You desire a certain result, but inevitably, there are times when you are thwarted. The act of fanship, then, is a way of seeking out and finding disappointment. It follows that there must be something deeply attractive about disappointment.

Being a football supporter is a way of finding a container for disappointment, Tone argues. A list of names and numbers, the classified football results, has a personal meaning for you, and often a disappointing one. You have to care enough to feel a very real disappointment, or the therapeutic process doesn't work. You go to work brooding on the disappointment that Chelsea failed to make the European Cup Final, and feel genuinely downcast – but that is far better than brooding on the disappointments of marriage, career, children, life. The football business protects you from all these other more meaningful, less bearable disappointments.

I like this, but I am not wholly convinced. I tend to counter-argue: after all, I put water in my whisky (unlocking the flavours), while Tone does not (not wishing to drown it). For there are many other things we do willingly, even though they lead almost inevitably to pain. My mother used to say that to buy an animal was to make a long-term investment in sadness. That didn't stop her loving the dogs in her life. We do many other things that are highly likely to lead to sadness. One of these is to stay in touch with our parents after we have left home. This is foolish, if you want to avoid sadness: the chances are that they will die before you. But most people stay in touch with their parents: not to make a long-term investment in sadness, but because of love.

Falling in love is also something that gives you a very a high chance of disappointment. Having children brings you a certainty of anxiety. A lifelong marriage gives you a 50-50 chance of bereavement. It seems to me that the human condition is based around things that give you a very high chance of pain, misery, distress, anxiety. We do not seek to avoid them at all: on the contrary. We seek them out, avidly, voraciously, incontinently. We do this in the name of nothing less than love. We all know that the joys of loving make pain inevitable; but we do not ever seek to avoid love. And, after all, there is only one truly efficient way of avoiding love, and that is dying.

Football, then, must be seen as an aspect of love. And

when love becomes twisted it is the most terrible thing on earth, as anyone who has been divorced will tell you. Perhaps the events at Heysel in 1985 can be classified as a love, fatally contorted.

69 There was an American gambler who summed up not just gambling, but all sport, for all time. He said: 'The most exciting thing in life is winning. And the second most exciting thing is losing.'

70 It is always odd to be part of a crowd yet not part of a crowd: and that is the lot of the sportswriter. Travelling to and from matches is a trial, and covering matches is a tricky business, and mainly because you are surrounded by people enjoying themselves. I find this very unhelpful. I want to go up to them and say: do I come and shout and sing when you are on your way to work? Do I get drunk and go to your workplace and make a terrible racket while you are doing the most difficult and stressful part of your job? Well then.

Sports fans seem sometimes almost deliberately unhelp-ful to the sportswriter. They make concentration on tale-telling difficult and trying. You leave a football match with your mind ringing with the effort of trying to keep your head while all around are losing theirs. In the days before laptops, we used to dictate copy over the telephone. Try spelling out complex and unfamiliar names while 50,000 people are singing 'You'll never walk alone': it is a nerve-racking experience. England versus Poland never made for a happy evening.

But when I went to Anfield to watch Liverpool take on Chelsea in the European Cup semi-final, I was over-whelmed, as not often before, by the passionate – loving, if you like – response of the crowd. It was extraordinary to be a part of it. Normally, I write off the cheering as so much din, so much distraction, so much white noise to edit out of my experience. That night, the din itself took centre stage. The audience was the star of the play.

It was a corporate reaching-out for the impossible. Chelsea were so much better, so much stronger, so much more confident. True, Liverpool had held them to a goalless draw in the first leg, but that was surely just a one-night aberration. Chelsea had been performing brilliantly: it was obvious that they would win in some comfort. Liverpool were really nothing much: a team that had been trading for too long on past achievements. This was a match of ambi-tion versus tradition, of new money against old, of brash success against dignified failure. But shockingly, it was tradition that won. A strange thing happened: the players became an extension of the ancient and undying passion in the crowd. It was as if the side that had the greater, the deeper love carried the day.

There have been comparisons between sport and reli-gion since time and sport began. There are many semi-facetious terms that acknowledge this. They began as jokes, at least, but by degrees they have become accepted terms, from which most of the humour and irony has been removed. A stadium is a 'cathedral'; a new manager is a 'messiah'; the crowd are always 'the faithful'. The club itself is always 'beloved': when not inspiring the nation, Alastair Campbell can be found watching his 'beloved' Burnley. And there was a religious fervour that night in Liverpool, and with the fervour came an immense power. Liverpool's victory was a triumph of faith, a triumph of love. The emotion of the crowd turned the better-beloved side into the better side. Chelsea played as if they feared that victory would offend some divine law: as if victory were forbidden, taboo, physically, perhaps even morally, impossible.

It was extraordinary to see the extent to which so many people cared about something they knew did not matter in the least. The wrong result would have had very little effect on their lives: and yet they sang, cheered and wept as if life itself was dependent on the victory. They willingly set themselves up for a colossal disappointment. The emotional investment was absolutely massive. They took the risk of caring to a stupendously high level; and in the end, that was the difference between defeat and victory.

Tone hasn't got it quite right, no. Supporting a football team is not entirely – or not only – a seeking-out of disappointment. It is more a willingness to risk being disappointed.

But even this is not a straightforward thing. The deal is not that you are happy to risk being disappointed, because it is so agreeable when the team wins. It is rather the acceptance that both pain and pleasure are integral to the key matter.

And that is love. You don't love anything or anyone for the pain or for the pleasure: you love for the love of loving. And that is an inextricable aspect of the passionate and committed support of a football team.

We. Not them. We won 1-0 over two legs. And I was powerfully moved by it, for all that there was no we in it for me, only them and it. So it was time to go to Istanbul for the European Cup final. AC Milan would murder them, obviously. It was a strange inspired fluke getting so far. All the way to Istanbul, for what would surely be a horribly one-sided match. But at least I could read Orhan Pamuk, visit my friend Suna, and send my love to Jess and Ade in the Luangwa Valley, hoping that their own love would enrich the rest of their lives.

71

I have a taste for perfection. And it seems to me that perfection is best looked for among the minimal: in the reduced, the distilled, the pared-down. You can apply Occam's razor not only to questions of philosophy but to everything else as well. And sport is part of everything else. It follows then, that my taste for the lasered, ultimately reduced essence of things means that, unlike my father, I have no time for the opulence and din of opera. Instead, I find supreme musical satisfaction in the voice of a single instrument whispering its essential truth without show or decoration or excuse. If you must have an example, take Yo-yo Ma playing the cello suites of Bach: all music – all time, all truth, all meaning – is boiled down to its Zen-like essence.

Zen, yes. When I covered the World Cup in Japan in 2002, I had a renewed love affair with the gardens of the Zen temples: three rocks, sand, a rake, and a reserved, austere perfection. A guide-book described one such as 'the most profound garden in Japan'. The profoundly unEnglish notion that a garden can in itself be profound was in itself profoundly revealing. And as I travelled across Japan, I read the haiku of Basho, and I read *The Narrow Road to the Deep North*, and I found something that sustained me through the most physically and spiritually draining task in a sports-writer's life.

I recall, too, a trip to the Namibian desert and instead of finding the gorgeous plenty of the wooded savannahs of the Luangwa Valley that I know so well, I found a land in which life itself had been reduced to Zen-garden essentials: a drive of many hours and then, in a landscape of stone and sand, or raked gravel, a lone oryx, white, equine, and in perfect profile so that its twin horns merged and I was looking at the last unicorn.

I was reminded of all this when the *Times* tennis correspondent, Neil Harman secured that rare thing, an interview with Pete Sampras, by then retired with fourteen Grand Slam titles to his name. In its course, Sampras said that he had always felt unappreciated: as if nobody had ever got the point of him. Then one day at Wimbledon he had read come words in *The Times*, and read some words that seemed to him to be him. The words made him briefly weep. I wrote them, though the point of the story is not the boast, but the meaning of Sampras: and through it, another groping lunge towards the meaning of sport itself.

Along with Neil's interview, *The Times* reprinted a piece I had written on Sampras, but I am pretty sure it was the wrong one. Certain tedious facts at my disposal make that quite clear. No serious error: it was still the same mood. The piece that I suspect moistened the Sampras eye was the one when I outed him as a Zen master.

Let us go back to the Wimbledon final of 1999, when Sampras played Andre Agassi. Agassi was then at the very peak of his powers. That day Sampras countered Agassi in the only way possible: by moving beyond perfection. He won the match in the manner of a champion – with a second-serve ace. In the post-match press conference, he was asked what was going through his mind at the time. There was a pause and then Sampras said, apologetically, a little baffled: 'There was absolutely nothing going through my mind.'

And in a flash I was enlightened. This is a man who can raise himself so far beyond fear and self-doubt that his mind is a perfect void, his only reality the ball, and the square inch of turf where he will put it. Pared down. All extraneous items removed. Read all about it; read about this state of enlightened perfection in DT Suzuki, *The Zen Doctrine of No Mind*, read it in the finest book on sports psychology ever written, Eugene Herrigel's *Zen in the Art of Archery*.

Perhaps you find this fanciful. Perhaps you think I am talking through my hat. You are entitled to your opinion.

But shortly after the piece appeared in the paper, I received an email: 'I do so agree with your understanding of Pete Sampras as a Zen master. I am a Zen master myself...'

72

Boring. People still tell me that Sampras was boring. And I answer, hotly, that if you find excellence a tedious thing, then what the hell are you doing watching sport? Go and find something smaller. But though I am sincere, I am also being disingenuous. We watch sport not only for the striving for perfection, but also for the drama. For most people, the finest Wimbledon final of recent years was Goran Ivanisevic versus Pat Rafter. And of course, yes, it was wonderful: a great drama, a wonderful narrative, an un-look-away-able lead character.

You may recall that it was the year of the three Gorans. This wonderfully wild notion came up after Ivanisevic had in a previous round talked about two Gorans: Good Goran and Bad Goran. Asked which of these Gorans had come to his rescue, he said it was neither. 'It was the third Goran. He is real emergency situation. He is the 911 guy. Ace, ace, thank you very much.'

And in the final, he kept shouting and praying and kissing tennis balls and double-faulting on match-point. No second-serve ace here. And he got there and it was indeed wonderful: the wild man with the wild card had his great day at last, and who could not rejoice? But I also know a still finer pleasure: the delighted awe that comes from the pared-down essence of sport, as embodied in Sampras, in Steve Redgrave.

Sport is many things but, if you wield Occam's razor with the ferocity of a Glasgow street-fighter, you find that sport is about winning. As in Sampras, as in the quality of Redgrave. You find sport reduced to a single thing: essence of victory. Quintessence of Redgrave. Everything – even, it sometimes seems, humanity itself – has been pared away. The greatest of all athletes celebrate the human condition by going beyond it.

73 On, then, to that wild night in Istanbul. It was an occasion in which, you might say, drama was in the ascendant over austerity and perfection. I wrote a sad piece about the way Liverpool were defeated by AC Milan in the European Cup Final within 50 seconds, and I must say, it was going really rather well. But alas, there came a moment, a little more than an hour later, when it began to become inexorably plain that my piece was not an adequate reflection of the events taking place before me.

AC Milan 3, Liverpool 0. A pretty final sort of score-line. But in a brief and extraordinary period, all logic went flying out of the window – the sort of thing, as I have said, that football brings us more often than any other team sport and one man's will changed everything. One man refused to accept the things that were happening before him. Steven Gerrard didn't like reality: so, in the manner of Matthew

Pinsent, he changed it. With quite exceptional inner force, he set about the match and took it over. This burly lad, with his plain and ordinary face, somehow transformed himself into an avenging angel, and it was a wondrous thing to behold.

I had always congratulated myself that I had missed Manchester United's European Cup final in 1999, in which they turned victory into defeat in the last moments of the match. Instead, I had England–France in Portugal, followed by England–Portugal; and now this. And I still had absolutely no idea as to which way the match would go.

Remorselessly, inevitably, it went to 3-all, and to extra time and to penalties. At the conclusion of the shoot-out, I added a final wild 200 words in a nanosecond or two and pressed Send. Nothing whatsoever happened. A dozen failures followed. The Turkish organisers had failed to supply *The Times* with the landline requested, and the mobile phone network was jammed solid as 20,000 Scousers reached simultaneously for their phones. However, Martin Lipton of the *Daily Mail* kindly gave me a lend of his landline, for we co-operate, on the whole, we help each other out, if only because of the high statistical chance you will be the needy one next time. My piece made the edition and I told the story on the back page.

Everyone else then went in for a top-to-bottom re-write for the next edition. I alone did not, and only partly from my ingrained loathing of re-writing. I wanted the piece raw and impetuous and excited and flawed: like the match itself. I don't know if this was the right decision, only that it felt so. Admittedly, I was pretty well off my head at the time: stoned blind with the drama of it all, and the extraordinary journalistic contortions required to keep up.

And by ones and twos the England press contingent gathered at the bus that would take us back to our hotel. A case of warm beers was discovered. These we drank in the car park, making football-bloody-hell and journalism-bloody-hell noises. It had been the best of times, it had been the worst of times. It was the sort of night you're in the profession for: it is the sort of night you dread.

Back to the hotel by five in the morning: coach leaving for the airport at six. I took the any-sleep-is-better-than-none option. I wrote a piece at the airport, and when it was late enough to speak to Tim Hallissey, he told me that we were doing a huge supplement – second in three days – and so another piece was required. I wrote it on the plane, read a bit of Orhan Pamuk and then slept. The night was to be called 'the miracle of Istanbul', but it was really the miracle of Steve Gerrard. It is only in sport that you can witness the impossible taking place before your eyes, and do so on a regular basis. I did not know then that it was to be a summer full of miracles.

74

Cricket has become the great disappearing game. Once we had timeless Tests: now even one-day cricket is too solemn and serious for some tastes. So the Ashes summer began with a Twenty-20 international. It was the first time I had covered a game played in this format. I found it difficult to concentrate, because I found myself operating to the pace of traditional cricket, in which the fall of a wicket is something of serious significance: serious enough, at any rate, to take a note about.

This dramatic devaluing of a wicket was not entirely sympathetic to me: and yet the format for winning at Twenty-20 is the same as for winning at a timeless Test. Build partnerships; take wickets. It is just that the wickets come one on top of the other, cheap as pennies, and a partnership of 30 is something to wonder at. This loss of gravitas made the sport seem a little silly, I thought, but by an effort of will, I could accept that the law of golf still applies: either all sports are silly or none is. I relaxed my frenzied note-taking to write a piece.

And what a tale I had: England winning by 100 runs, Australia reduced to 31 for seven. Outplayed, not because they took things with insufficient seriousness, but because England bowled to a plan, and it came off. England played hardball and Australia were not quite ready for it, certainly not from England.

It was a daft night, and yet it was to have a significance far beyond its own context. Naturally, everyone on either side played it down: just a bit of fun, doesn't really mean anything. But it showed the England players – and did so with pedantic clarity – that the Australian side was composed exclusively of human beings. The sort of people who bleed when you prick them. The wine they drink is made of grapes. They ache, they err, they worry, they defecate, they get tired, they get homesick. And they could, conceivably and occasionally, be beaten. Intriguing thought.

It's all very well knowing such a thing in theory. It's understanding the thing in the gut that matters. Briefly, over the course of an hour or two on a silly evening in Southampton, the most fearsome side in the history of cricket were made to look like a rabble. And it was England that made this come about. It was the right way to start: no doubt about that.

It was a pleasant evening, despite the fierce deadline and the excitements of trying to catch the train afterwards. I had been planning to improve the trip back with a modest sip of Scotch, first drink of the day, on the London-bound train, but was unable to. My homeopathic dose was confiscated at the bag-search on the way in. I did not take this in good part, mainly because as soon as I entered the ground, I was beset on all sides by bars. It has been one of the few tangible achievements of terrorism: we now graciously permit security personnel to invade our privacy, entirely for the profit of the catering trade.

But even this setback did not destroy the evening. England won. It was like the sighting of the first swallow, the one that doesn't mean a summer, but which certainly carries a strong hint that more swallows and a serious summer cannot be far behind. And I felt the stirrings of a known excitement. Or rather two excitements. The first was the feeling that there just might be a bit of story to tell, and me there to do the telling.

The second was a little different. England might even make a game of it, when it came to the Test series. And for all my talk about lack of partisanship, I felt a serous fizz of anticipation. Could it happen? Wonderful thought. But let us keep that sort of thing under control. Ahead was the near-certainty of a half-decent summer – so long, that is, as you bore in mind the second most exciting thing in life.

75 I always like to sit next to Richard Williams, chief sportswriter of the *Guardian*, former presenter of *The Old Grey Whistle Test*, former *Guardian* film critic, and so forth. This is not just for his wide-ranging intelligence and wit, but also because I love watching him taking notes. He keeps a very thick dictation pad, and writes everything in beautiful italic script. He always transcribes the teams from both sides, not content with a duplicated team-sheet. He takes elaborate and copious notes, and his pages look like the field notebooks of a serious birdwatcher. Watching Richard at a football match is like watching the scribes creating the *Book of Kells*. He keeps all his notebooks – he was deeply upset recently when he lost one and broke the sequence – and he must have thousands, because he gets through them at a terrific rate.

Me, I use a small, slim, stiff-covered spiral-bound notebook, A6, 192 pages. I make notes with a fountain pen, because I like writing with a fountain pen and also, because with such an impediment to my natural speed, I can very often read back what I have written. But I take very few notes: I had plenty of pages left at the Twenty-20, in a notebook I started at the Tim Henman match in New York ten months ago: and it would last me the full summer before it need replacing.

It's all the way these things take you. Jeff Powell of the *Daily Mail* covers any old piece of paper with copious Jackson Pollock biroings. Matt Dickinson, football correspondent of *The Times*, fills book after book with exquisite shorthand. Matthew Engel, now of the *Financial Times*, also editor of *Wisden*, uses a black Biro and a red, stapled, soft-covered notebook, and he writes wise things in it with an ungovernable air of self-satisfaction. 'Put that hateful notebook away,' I tell him.

I have a kind of ritual response to the notebook currently in use, for all that I don't keep them once I have filled them. I need to know where the current one is: and that the pen is in the bag alongside it. It's my system, it's not supposed to be anybody else's system. 'You a monk or what?' someone asked me at a football match.

I use a Lamy Safari pen with a fine italic nib, and have done for 20-odd years. My handwriting is not especially beautiful, but the act of writing, even the act of taking notes, seems to me to require some kind of dignity: some kind of seriousness from the person doing the writing. It's only sport, it's only journalism, but the uncertain dignity of my italic script seeks to clothe the futile process in a little meaning. There were plenty of pages left for Wimbledon. And after that: what should I do about the summer of cricket?

76

There are some women who are not gold-diggers, and yet are inordinately attracted to men with money. It's not that they want the money for themselves. They just like to be where money is. Well, one of the great things about writing about sport is that alarmingly often, you get to be where greatness is.

The kind of greatness that sport offers, anyway. A great champion is not a saint or a sage, an artist, a statesman or scientist. A great champion doesn't do great things, in the sense that, say, Mahatma Gandhi or Leonardo da Vinci did great things. Rather, their task is to show us what greatness is. That, after all, is what myths are for: and why we treasure them. And Wimbledon of that year was to become a showcase for greatness: a two-week celebration of genius.

Insofar as such a term can be used of sport. But the vivid and serene perfection of Roger Federer's tennis that fortnight was something to treasure. Before the fortnight began, I had had a serious talk with Tim Hallissey about whether or not to go to New Zealand for the Lions tour. Frankly, I didn't fancy it, and not only because New Zealand is an awfully long way away.

I was tempted by the birdwatching, obviously – who could resist the thought of New Zealand's unique avifauna? – but I didn't think much of the story.

I had a bad feeling about the tour before it started. It also seemed to me to be a trip that offered a total of zero days of live sport, the three internationals all being played early Saturday morning, British time, perfect for a Sunday paper, but not for *The Times*. This was a story for rugby buffs, I thought. Wimbledon would attract far more readers, especially women. But at the heart of it was the fact that I didn't want to watch the British Lions fail. I wanted to watch Roger Federer succeed.

I remember bumping into Hugh McIllvaney in Japan during the World Cup of 2002, and, not for the first time, as you will have noticed, he made a remark that rather got to me. I had expressed some sort of pleasure in the unpredictable nature of the tournament. 'Yes, you like giant-killers,' he said. 'I like giants.'

But to be accurate, both enthral me. I like to see greatness: I like to see pretension pricked. I don't care much for bluster: I care a lot about the achievers. Anyway, on this occasion, I picked the giant over the giant-killer: I chose to follow the great one rather than the underdog. Federer, not the Lions.

I was present at one of the great underdog wins in sporting history, when India beat West Indies in the cricket World Cup final at Lord's in 1983. It was one of the last sporting events that I went to as a punter. I wore a shirt I had bought in India. Though I admired profoundly the great West Indian side, the decision of partisanship was made easy by the romance of the underdog and the love I bear for India. But it was obviously a decision to cheer for the losing side; I had to accept that.

I hoped that West Indies would bat first, so that we would at least see a decent day's cricket. After all, this really was an absurd mismatch. And, had that happened, I am certain that West Indies would have won by a distance. I arrived a little late, to find India batting and Sunil Gavaskar,

India's alpha male, already out. We would be home by tea. It was hopeless: a procession. I remember vividly a shot played by Krish Srikanth: a square drive for four on one knee. And the ignition of a feeble, incredulous hope: they might even do this, you know.

And they did. West Indies bowled India out for a poor total of 183, and then swaggered out to knock off the runs. They were practically locking shoulders in the doorway in the rush to come out and take the glory. Thus it was that they found themselves undone by their own hubris. It was an extraordinary revelation of weakness from the strongest cricket team the world had ever seen. It was a perfectly enthralling occasion, whether you prefer giants or giant-killers.

A love of greatness, a love of seeing the pretensions to greatness found out. These are equal and opposite things: complementary things that any one who likes sport can encompass.

It is not a contradiction to enjoy both; it is not even a contradiction to go to a match in order to purr of the greatness of the French football team, and to leave it celebrating the impudence of the team from Senegal, which happened in the opening match of the World Cup Finals of 2002.

Or better still, that extraordinary night in 1990, when Argentina, the world champions were beaten by Cameroon. That was a night of infinite possibilities.

Well, Perhaps I would have relished an unknown boy who rose from nowhere to expose the weakness in the heart of Federer. But I didn't get the chance to write Jack the Giant-Killer: instead, I wrote Giant the Jack-Killer. Once, and then again, and then once more to make thrice.

77 Wimbledon 2005 was the perfect celebration of the illusion of complicity: the way that the opponent, a man who is trying with all his might to win, seems somehow to be collaborating with the victor. And Roger Federer created this illusion again and again.

I covered his last three rounds. This is not usual: normally, we would try and mix things up a bit, try and keep one's powder dry for later rounds and so forth. But I covered Federer's matches against Fernando Gonzalez, Lleyton Hewitt and Andy Roddick, and the cumulative power of all three was a deep and powerful sporting experience – though not, of course, if you are fixated on the notion of the underdog. Gonzalez: huge ground-strokes, clay-courter's patience. Hewitt: intensity, hustle, never gives up on a point or a match. Roddick: power-serve, all-court hurry-up game, unstemmable aggression.

Three hugely different natures, creating three hugely different styles of tennis. And each one seemed perfectly tailored for Federer. Each one seemed to dove-tail perfectly into Federer's own style. Each seemed to be custom-built to showcase Federer's talents. Federer played each match with an air of quiet serenity; and didn't drop a set. All opponents seek to raise their games when they are playing Federer. Federer has the extraordinary knack of playing that little bit better than his opponent. Any opponent. The game is raised: Federer raises his. Raised again: Federer finds another raise. He can do this again and again, as the great Sergei Bubka did when he set world record after world record in the pole vault. Bubka did this 35 times, seventeen outdoors, eighteen indoors: Federer seems sometimes to be capable of doing it forever in the course of a single match.

After the final, Roddick spoke about the problems of playing the man who might be the greatest tennis player ever to pick up a racket. He paid just tribute to Federer, and then spoke about the way he goes out to play him. He goes out thinking that he can win: that Federer is not the greatest tennis player ever to pick up a racket. 'I'm in denial the whole time I'm out there.'

And I wondered: is complicity really an illusion? Does the opponent himself get sucked into the inevitability of defeat? Is there something about playing against a talent such as Federer's that compels a kind of obedience, compels a subservience, compels a complicity? Does a player find himself doing what Federer wants, despite his own determination to do the exact contrary?

This was Federer's third successive Wimbledon championship. Pete Sampras managed two hat-tricks, Fred Perry one, Bjorn Borg got five in a row. It is in this kind of company we must consider Federer now. The story of Federer's greatness is unfolding before us, and it was a glorious thing to be a part of this. What's more, I took a morning off on the day of the women's semi-finals, getting back in time for the tennis, naturally, and went to see a pair of peregrine falcons from a site in Regent's Park: hunched-shouldered, menacing shapes, birds I am used to seeing on wild Cornish cliffs with the wrinkled sea far below: now using sky-scrapers as cliffs and city pigeons as lunch. It was a wild and heart-lifting sight, and an important part of a fortnight filled with greatness. But now to get home: I had promised to take my older boy Joe to the excellent animal park a few miles north of us. I was looking forward to it very much. Especially the lemurs.

78

I had planned it all properly: there was plenty of time to get home and write. It was only when the call came, as Joe and I were watching the ring-tailed lemurs on their island performing a series of ring-tailed acrobatics, that I realised that I had prepared myself for everything except for what actually happened.

'Are you sitting down?' always a worrying first line.

'No, I'm watching the lemurs while standing up.'

'Well, hold on to the fence or something. London's got it.'

'Fuck.'

In that syllable, overused and inadequate, I wished to convey amazement and delight, and at the same time to pay just and proper tribute to the work-load I would now be required to carry towards first edition. It was only as I uttered it that I realised I had not expected London to get the decision. Such an idea had scarcely crossed my mind. I had been a supporter of the bid throughout, never having much time for the begrudgers of this life, but just for the form of it. I had written a number of pieces saying that a London Games would be a good idea and here's why. I hadn't seriously supposed that I would be writing about a successful bid. I realised then that I had prepared myself mentally – adequately and well – to the writing of 800 words on disappointment, adding cheerfully that it was well worth the effort, and hearty handshakes all round.

I hadn't given a moment's thought to what I would write in the event of a successful bid. It was time to have that moment.

We said farewell to the lemurs and went home, and a further phone call informed me that I would be required to write 1,500 words on pages two and three, which would be the first read in the paper, because the front and back would be wraparound pictures of the celebrations. And then, please, 1,000 words on Seb Coe, leader of the bid.

There is something wonderfully refreshing about writing a piece for which you have done no preparation whatsoever. Your mind is beautifully cleansed. All you can do is write what happens to be in your heart and mind at the time. Shorn of clever ideas, you have no option but to write what you really think.

So I wrote that I was in a very good position to explain why a successful bid was a good thing: and it was nothing to do with urban renewal, national prestige and future profit. Rather, it was all about the shared civic and national joy at being part of the greatest party the world has ever seen. In an attempt to communicate this, I recalled my five previous summer Olympic Games, all the time explaining how such experiences would translate to London in 2012: how seven years of whingeing, rows, backstabbing, infighting, begrudging, misery, politicking, scandal, spin and claptrap would be followed by the greatest seventeen-day celebration in the history of the human race.

It was a piece about joy. Unashamed, unadulterated joy: 1988 and Great Britain's hockey victory, the dreadful wonder of Ben Johnson, and my own status as newly deflowered Olympic virgin. And then in 1992, a special Games even by the standards of the Games: for I was out of my head with grief at the time, my mother ill from a series of strokes. My own sadness, the hysteria of the Games and the splendid city of Barcelona combined to create a time when normal rules seemed no longer to apply, so that night after night I found myself pissed on the Ramblas at three in the morning, finding life and renewal in the fierce professional demands and the unendingly majestic sport that only the Olympics can bring. I left, two or three days before the end of the Games, when the call came to say that my mother was dying. As a result, my memories of this and every other Games are full of emotional complexity, and death and life.

In 1996 in Atlanta, we had the so-called Bad Games, when, sure enough, I got rather fed up with the red-necks on security – the kind of people whose family tree does not fork – but once you got to the venues – and you could indeed get to the venues if you won your battle with the appalling transport system – you could not help but revel in the glorious quadrennial, once-in-a-lifetime splendours: especially the world record 200 metres run by the great

Michael Johnson. Colin Hart and I still remember that one.

After that, the ecstatic Games of Sydney, where, in a nation en fete, Britain won a stack of medals and Steve Redgrave won his famous fifth. And then Athens: which I believe I have already mentioned. And all this fizz, excitement and joy would now be coming to London. It would be a time when it would be a joy to be alive: when the city and the nation would light up. Life: yes; greatness: yes: and beach volleyball on Horseguard's Parade as well.

79

Bill Shankley continues to get a bad press for one of the most profound remarks in sporting history. 'Football's not a matter of life and death,' he said. 'It's much more important than that.' Let us, please, give Shankley the credit for irony. His famous remark needs to be understood as an acknowledgement of the irrationality and innocence that is required for taking part in sport at the highest level.

Naïveté in short supply is a serious disadvantage if you wish to enjoy sport, or if you wish to write about sport, for that matter. I suspect a shortage of naiveté is a disadvantage when practising the arts, too. In fiction, a constant world-weary cynicism does not lend a sympathetic tone, certainly not over the long haul. You can be cynical in a short story: you need a certain amount of naiveté for the more lengthy and profound forms of story-telling. *Ulysses* ends with a long crescendo of affirmation, yes, and the end of *Finnegans Wake* is gloriously and unabashedly sentimental.

Sport requires from us a quantum of innocence. Without innocence, sport can't exist. Every sporting experience, then, demands from us an acceptance of the truly ludicrous idea that children's games have some kind of importance.

When it comes to sport, almost as a conscious act, we divest ourselves of the protective carapace of cynicism that governs our dealings with politicians, celebrities, journalists and businessmen. We allow some part of ourselves to become childish: or if you prefer, we bring out the childishness in our natures, something that we are at pains to suppress in our normal adult dealings with the world. Without such childishness, we would find no joy in the fact that England won a football match, or a cricket match. Those who watch sport behind the hedge of cynicism say: yes, yes, overpaid poseurs, doing it for the money, sordid little people elevated to an importance far beyond their worth, breaking the rules of their sport and all in order to kick a bladder through a pair of sticks. That is a perfectly reasonable view, but it prevents you from getting any fun out of football. To enjoy football, you must suspend your cynicism, at least for the duration of the match, and allow a quantum of innocence to come through.

And that is why the whole thing was doubly appalling.

Living in the country, working from home, writing about sport, it is perfectly possible to insulate yourself from public affairs, especially when politics and business hold no great interest for you. And so I was pottering along, the day after the announcement that London was to stage the Olympic Games of 2012, writing a further piece on What The Olympics Really Mean. And a phone call. With it, a gentle suggestion that I turn on the television and watch for an hour or so before reconsidering the subject of my weekly column.

London devastated. London blown up. For it was the day of the bombings. A day when people were, like the victims of 9/11, killed and maimed for the crime of going to work. Perhaps, as they did so, they were reading about how wonderfully jolly it was for London to have the Games, and what a party we would all be having in seven years' time. Perhaps they had run into a friend and were talking about it: I've got to get tickets. I want to see the gymnastics. No, it's the hundred metres for me, got to be. God, it's going to be good.

To celebrate these anticipated moments of sporting delight, we naturally assumed the quantum of innocence, and that made us horribly vulnerable. It made us, emotionally, the softest of targets. The day of London's rejoicing was followed by the day of London's horror: and this quirk of timing made the whole business unforgettably cruel. It was like biting into the loveliest, ripest peach you ever saw and finding your mouth closing on a scorpion.

The meeting of sport and death is deeply and stirringly vivid. We remember sporting deaths far longer than we remember many other incidents of horror, because the deaths came in innocence and in pursuit of frivolity – Munich, Heysel, Bradford, Hillsborough: others I shall tell you about. We need only the names of these places, most of them sporting venues, to feel that touch of despair, and with it, a sense of hopeless anger at the sheer bloody unfairness of it all. That is also a childish reaction, a naïve reaction. But it is also a correct reaction: coming as it does from the bottom of our souls.

80

I have hitch-hiked a few miles in my time. In my second summer at university, I hitched to Greece, and then back by way of Vienna, where the girl I was travelling with was studying. One morning, during the few days I hung around in Vienna, I resolved to do a bit of studying myself. That kind of travelling is full of austerity: travel by thumb, sleep out every night, eat cheap. But the great advantage of austerity is that it is easy to have a treat. That morning, as something completely exceptional, a real splurge, I decided to buy myself an airmail copy of the *Daily Mirror* and a cigar – the *Mirror* was, at that time, a serious sort of newspaper.

Coyly, I folded the newspaper up under my arm as soon as I bought it, so that I wouldn't be tempted to have a sneaky look at the front or the back page. I found a nice bench in the park, and lit the cigar, a special kind of cigar smoked by the Viennese. Once it was going nicely, and I was savouring its pungent smoke, I sat back in the sun and unfolded my newspaper. Let the treat begin. And the cigar turned to ashes in my mouth and horror unfolded before me.

This was September 1972, and the *Daily Mirror* told me that a group of Palestinians from the Black September Movement had broken into the Olympic village in Munich, shot some members of the Israeli delegation and were holding others hostage at gunpoint. It was a moment that put a match to my moment of innocence, and to the world's moment of innocence. It was not just the deaths that disturbed me. It was also the vandalism, the invasion, the deliberate decision to assault the world at precisely the time when the world had made itself emotionally vulnerable. When the word was having a treat. When it had assumed a seventeen-day period of innocence.

That hideous conjunction of death and sport is something I can never get used to, and nor can anybody else. The context of frivolity made the deaths seem far more terrible: the context of death made sport seem quite ludicrously unimportant, and at the same time, more important than ever before. We yearned for our innocence even in the losing of it.

Much later, I was to see the great documentary, *One Day In September*, which told the tale of those terrible events. When the terrorists were climbing the fence to get in, they met a bunch of Americans, who had sneaked out of the village for a few beers. Laughing companionably, the two groups helped each other over and parted, one to boozy slumbers, the other to murder.

I've never been able to forget that little detail, when the actual numbers of the dead is something I need to look up. In fact, they killed two Israelis in the village, and in a gun battle at the airport, nine hostages, five terrorists and a policemen were killed.

Why did the terrorists kill the Israelis? To make them dead, I suppose. What else did they achieve? They robbed the sporting world of another layer of innocence. These days, at major sporting events, especially at the Olympic Games, you must pass through many levels of security before you are allowed in anywhere. The old days of walking in and out of the athletes' village have long gone, and so have easy relationships between the story-makers and the story-tellers.

But what else was achieved? Absolutely nothing. What, for that matter, do the London bombers hope to achieve in the long run? Again, nothing. They have already achieved what they set out to. Terrorism is not about achieving things. Terrorism has no wider agenda. The only aim of terrorism is terror. Set that against a sporting context, when the world has its guard down, and the terrorist is all the more terrifying. Or at least horrifying.

81

After the horror of the July 7 bombings came the added horror: the knowledge that this was home-grown terror. Not the work of outsiders, but of British Muslims. It was an attack from inside the walls. This was not a happy thing to learn: every Londoner of every shade of skin colour began, on every tube and train and bus, to look at every brown face with misgivings.

It was shortly after these revelations that Amir Khan came out to fight again. Since his silver medal at the Olympic Games, he had become a professional boxer, and he was going through the traditional series of progressively tougher opponents over progressively longer bouts. And he was doing it in style: the speed of thought and mind undimmed, the hands, if anything, hitting harder than ever.

And he was doing it all with modesty and charm: and what is more, he spoke up, humbly and sincererly, when he felt it necessary. The crux of the business was that, so far as he was concerned, the phrase British Muslim implied no contradiction. That mixture was the boy, or man. His father, obviously enough a Muslim himself, still attended his son's fights in his Union-Jack waistcoat. And British people of all types and races and cultures carried on liking Khan and wishing him well: because of his talent and his transparent decency. Who would wish to live in a society that rejected such a person?

In troubled times, the sight of Khan plying his trade was a deeply cheering one – even to me, not an enthusiast for professional boxing. It was a sight that mattered to an awful lot of British people. I don't wish to exaggerate the significance of this, but I don't want to minimise it, either. Most people, asked to name a British Muslim, would immediately give the name of Amir Khan. Certainly not the name of a politician, however worthy, however confrontational. We have politicians out of necessity: we have sports stars out of love.

Through sport, a hefty part of the non-Muslim part of Britain had acquired a liking, an understanding, and an admiration for a British Muslim: for good old Amir. In the same way, there are increasing numbers of British Muslims coming into first-class cricket, and for that matter, playing for England. Amir Khan, Nasser Hussain, Sajid Mahmood: Our Boys. That's the best weapon against the tensions of division that has ever been devised.

The emergence of black British footballers made a huge difference to black–white racial tensions in this country. How can you hate all black people when a black man is scoring goal after goal for the football club you love? When he is embraced lovingly by his colleagues of all colours after each triumph? When Ian Wright was doing just that for Arsenal, many, if not most Arsenal fans wore an Arsenal shirt bearing his name; though a few preferred his number 8 and 'GOD'. Not many years ago, football fans made monkey noises and threw bananas at black players. Now we primitive people have made some advances towards civilisation; and the first step, obviously, is to worship the superior man as a god.

Sport is one of the very few things in life that are strictly quantifiable. You can believe in white supremacy all you like, but you can't claim that white men ran faster than Jesse Owens, winner of four gold medals in the 1936 Berlin Olympic Games. That is why sport has always been the hope of the no-hoper: you can be as prejudiced as you like, but you can't deny that a certain black man scores goals, or that another runs the hundred in 10-flat. Deprived groups have always been attracted to professional sport. If many middle-class children of promise are told to keep clear of sport – too chancey – this is not true of the less wealthy. Sport has a phenomenally high wastage rate, but that is not going to put off children who have no other hope for serious prosperity.

The result is that people from disadvantaged minorities are drawn to sport in disproportionate numbers: and those that succeed become cherished by the majority. Sport, then, has an extraordinary success at making the excluded groups more greatly included, so that they become a more easily accepted part of the national life than would otherwise have been the case. Sport, in its essential simplicity, cuts across all cultures: a goal for your side is still a goal for your side, and you rejoice in the same way whether you worship a single god, a triune god, many gods or none. And no matter which of these godly ways you follow, you give thanks for the scorer from the bottom of your heart.

82

I saw Michael Jordan play basketball. I saw him at his best, playing for Chicago Bulls in the NBA finals against Phoenix Suns in 1993. There is something particularly instructive about watching greatness in an unfamiliar medium, like reading a Japanese haiku or a Russian novel. You get closer to the pure essence of greatness, undistracted by peripheral concerns. Perhaps it is because all these matters depend so little on my subjectivity.

The British have never really got the hang of basketball. We don't see very much of it, and in a football-dominated culture, we find the lack of midfield off-putting. But as you seek to learn the rhythms of a different game, you also come to see with uncommon clarity the things that unite the unfamiliar game with all the games you know far too well. You get a glimpse of the essence of sport, or the quintessence. Sport is always sport, winning is always winning and greatness is – very often, more often than we have a right to expect – greatness.

Except that Jordan didn't play all that well in the first game I saw, which the Suns won. In Chicago, too: 'We are destined to win it,' said 'Sir' Charles Barkley of the Suns. 'Charles giving you that shit?' asked Jordan wearily. The suggestion was that Jordan was 'trying too hard'. He had, unusually for a man whose career had been ominously free of scandal, been going through a rough patch: his taste for high-stakes golf had been getting a lot of coverage. Small deal: except that Jordan's millions were built not only on his athletic excellence, but also on his ability to be 'a role model'. Exactly the sort of thing that Barkley has spoken against so eloquently, in fact.

So Jordan came out in the second game I saw and gave, as it were, a master-class in greatness. He scored 55 points, and the Suns coach, Paul Westphal, said two things that have stayed with me: two things that get somewhere close to an understanding of the notion of greatness, as the term is used in the field of sport. 'Were you surprised by what Michael did tonight, Paul?'

'No. I'm amazed, but I'm not surprised.' Perfect. The greats constantly amaze us: but there is a sense of inevitability about what they do. There is an utterly unstoppable quality about them.

And then Westphal summed up his night, Jordan's night, and with it, the whole notion of playing against an athlete who has something of greatness. 'He inflicted his will on us.' No: not just a matter of physical ability. It was his ability to seize an occasion and to do what he wanted with it that was so perfectly devastating.

The Test match series was starting very soon. Australia had been used to inflicting their will on all their opponents, especially England, and had done so for a decade and more. England had not beaten Australia in a Test series for eighteen years. Australia had at least one player of undeniable greatness: Shane Warne, a man who did things that amazed, without ever once surprising. I agreed with Tim Hallissey that I would cover the first match of the series, and after that, we would take a view.

83

Peter Roebuck called me 'a nationalist'. I found this a strange judgment. But it was worth thinking about: what Roebuck says about anything, particularly if it is cricket-related, is always worth listening to. Roebuck, now working as a journalist, is a former England cricket captain (he captained England in two one-day matches against Holland) who has turned his back on England and become Australian. Australia, he has pointed out frequently, shows us everything that is bad about England. (Perhaps, but it also works the other way round.) Roebuck sees England as the old bitch gone in the teeth, a botched civilisation. A lot of this is inevitably tied up with his own life, achievements and disappointments. Roebuck is an extremely intelligent man and one of the best cricket writers currently operating.

So his judgment on Barnes as nationalist was at least worth a moment's consideration.

The reason for the remark was that I wanted England to beat Australia in the Test series, and thereby win back the Ashes. Roebuck, for a complex suite of personal, emotional and intellectual reasons, preferred an opposite result. He told me that he believed a national sporting team was a reflection of the nation itself, and therefore, it was important to him that Australian superiority was demonstrated in the results of the five Test matches of the summer.

So did my desire for a certain result make me a nationalist? The *Shorter Oxford* is unemotional on the subject: a nationalist is 'an adherent or supporter of nationalism', and nationalism is 'devotion to one's nation'. *Longman* was closer to the nub of the thing: nationalism is 'loyalty and devotion to a nation, esp the exalting of one nation above all others'.

Disregarding the fact that this definition makes Roebuck more of a nationalist than I am, in his exaltation of Australia, I must say that I wanted England to win without wishing to go in for any serious exalting. I am happy with England as the home of Shakespeare and Darwin: less happy with England's history of war-mongering and slavery – but it is surely possible to cheer for England without offering England a complete and uncritical devotion.

England till I die, I'm England till I die. I am not merely English – I *am* England. So sing the football supporters, who take on the whole country as an aspect of themselves, much as Cathy declared 'I *am* Heathcliff'. Me, I'd rather die than make such a declaration, about Heathcliff or England.

Inger-lund, Inger-lund, Inger-lund. I don't know such a place, or if I do, I walk away from it at every opportunity. Inger-lund is another country: they do things differently there. All the same, I knew then that I would be hoping that England won the World Cup in Germany the following summer, and not only because it would be such a great tale to tell.

You can belong to a nation without exalting that nation above all others. Most of us do. We can identify with certain laudable traits, cringe at others less laudable. The obstinate courage with which Londoners responded to the bombs on that post-Olympic day, just a few weeks before the Ashes began, was a wonderfully edifying thing; England football supporters drunk and on the rampage inspires a less cheerful reaction.

I lived abroad for four years, and it was great. I never wanted to go home. I choose to live in England now: in fact, I own a few acres of England. And that's great, too. That doesn't mean that I think England is better than France, the United States, India or Zambia. It's just rather more English. It doesn't mean that I approve of the British policy of toadying to America and taking part in gratuitous warfare.

But I also wanted England to beat Australia. It would have given my grandfather a lot of pleasure. It would give my father a lot of pleasure. It would give me a lot of pleasure. I have Australians among my dearest friends: Al and I would exchange emails and texts and phone calls to discuss the progress of things throughout the summer.

Years ago, Al and I were neighbours on the island of

Lamma, outside Hong Kong. One evening, during which beer had been taken, we struck a bet on the outcome of the Ashes series of that year. At the time, England were 1-0 down with three to play and the captain had just been sacked. I bet 80 dollars to 150 that England would win. The year was 1981. Ian Botham's year, should you need to be told. Laugh? I almost paid my bar bill.

But this partisanship doesn't affect my admiration of the great Australian cricket side, nor my love of Australia and of – carefully selected – Australians. After the Sydney Olympics, a number of people who went to Australia on Olympic accreditations simply stayed, lost in the maw of God's Own. The mystery to me was why so many people went back to England. I occasionally have a fantasy: that instead of going to Asia in my 20s – a chance decision – I went to Australia. The need for an adventure would still have been there, so perhaps I would have stayed. And perhaps I would have got involved in the horsey life there: perhaps even in a professional capacity, since adventures are always the means for personal reinvention. Would I have done it? Could I have done it? Would I have been good enough? I shall never know. Had Pyrrhus not fallen by a beldam's hand in Argos, if Julius Caesar had not been knifed to death? They are not to be thought away. Time has branded them and fettered they are lodged in the room of infinite possibilities they have ousted.

But this overweening sense of opportunity: that is the thrilling thing about Australia, the feeling that, even now, the country is in the process of inventing itself – not reinventing, doing it for the first time, establishing a national culture. When I was in Australia for the Rugby World Cup in 2003, I read Patrick White's great Australian novel, *Voss*. White is a difficult man for the Australians to live with, because he was a plummy-voiced Pommy poofter – admittedly one who had worked as a jackaroo – but in *Voss*, he writes the heart of Australia. 'But in this disturbing country, so far as I have become acquainted with it, it is possible more easily to discard the inessential and to attempt the infinite.'

It was the English cricketers that I wanted to see attempting the infinite that summer. For the joy of writing the narrative, yes, certainly: but more, for the delight the narrative would bring me.

84

Years ago, when the Soviet Empire was beginning to crumble at the edges, I spent an hour with a delegation from the Estonian Olympic Committee. Estonia was not then a nation: it was a geographical entity on the Baltic, part of the Soviet Union. And I had to look that up, too, before the appointment. We met outside Westminster tube, where they had been talking to MPs, poor things, in an attempt to further their cause. We went to a café by Westminster Bridge, and I bought the two of them some coffee. And they told me how important for them it was that the International Olympic Committee recognised their nation, how seriously it mattered that there would be competitors in Estonian vests at the next Olympic Games, and that at the parade during the opening ceremony, someone would be there carrying an Estonian flag. Not for fun and games: this wasn't trivial. It was a matter of the highest importance for the future of their nation.

It's only sport. It's only running and jumping and stuff. But the idea of having an Estonian competing at the Olympic Games in Estonian colours: that had the most colossal importance. No just in terms of politics, but in terms, it seemed, of the world knowing who Estonians are; and perhaps more than that, of Estonians knowing who Estonians are.

After we had done the official part of the meeting, we hung around for more coffee and a more free-ranging conversation, for they were sympathetic people. And I said that I had a vision of how the Olympic opening ceremony ought to be. Every athlete would march in, nation by nation, and one by one, each flag-bearer would pitch his nation's flag into the eternal Olympic flame. And after that, every competitor would move, and re-gather under the banner of his and her own sport. As such – stateless athletes standing for the pursuit of human excellence – they would then march out again.

The female half of the delegation smiled at this fancy. 'It is nice, yes, I understand. Your country has always been able to take part in the Olympic Games. You would not think like that if you were from a nation like Estonia.'

And I saw, then, that I wouldn't, no. If my nation, my nationality was denied, I would also be denied. In refusing an identity to my nation, you are refusing an identity to me. Perhaps you cannot rise beyond nationalism for as long as your nation goes unrecognised. You don't want your nation exalted above all others: you just want it exalted to the same level as everybody else's.

Sport can do that better than anything else. Sport has far more effect on the way we see and understand other nations than trade or cultural exchange or tourism. Try this: pick any nation in the world, and name its leading politicians, its leading artists, and its leading athletes. Most British people are unaware the Portuguese prime minister's name is Pedro Santana Lopes – well, it was when I was writing these words, but he had just resigned his government – yes, of course I had to look that up – and not many have read Fernando Pessoa. But a very large number could tell you that Cristiano Ronaldo plays on the right wing for Portugal and Manchester United.

That's why the Soviet Empire poured so much energy and money into sport, why China still does, why, in different ways, all nations still do. And for a small nation – most especially for a nation that wants to be recognised as a nation – a place in the hearts and minds of the world is most easily obtained by means of sport. Most especially if there is a half-decent athlete to carry the flag.

Without this need for national identity, the Olympic Games would not exist. The Games pretend to be a feast of pure human endeavour, but the athletes parade with flags and when someone wins, they play his national anthem. Nationalism and sport is like ham and eggs: or rather, chickens and eggs.

85 Despite my nationalism, the one thing I wanted from the Ashes series was competition. A series in which you weren't sure who was going to win. In short, a pleasing narrative: to tell, and to be told. By the end of the summer, that perspective was to shift somewhat – that's nationalism, or at least partisanship for you – but my first response was perhaps the sounder one.

Few teams in sport have been as effective as Australia when it comes to exploiting Bull Elephant Syndrome. They had done so majestically over the previous decade and a half. They had done it to every one (apart from India in India) but they had done it best to England. Again and again, England had backed down, not because the opposition was better tusked, but because it was Australia. Australia knew that England would back down: England knew that they were going to back down. The only part of the tale you did not know in advance was when and how.

It had been thrilling watching the establishment of the great Australian side. It helps with your strategy if you have a couple of the greatest bowlers that ever drew breath, of course. But Steve Waugh's extraordinary captaincy maximised every one of Australia's considerable advantages. He created a brand: Australian cricket as savage, ruthless, and totally uncompromising. Anything that smelt of funk was weeded out: no nightwatchman, no farming the strike, no playing for time. Under Waugh, Australia reinvented Test match cricket. Intimidatory bowling had long been a part of cricket: Waugh introduced intimidatory batting. To tell the truth, I was never much good at telling one Australian batsman from another – it was just a succession of grim, unshaven jaws, chewing gum as if it were the flesh of an enemy, glowering behind the grills of grim green helmets and belting the ball vindictively, knowing that if they failed, two more would spring up to take their place. After that, the bowlers would feast on the carcass. Every Test match had to be won. Waugh is one of the great figures in Test history, alongside Clive Lloyd, who invented the West Indies supreme team of the 80s. Both men are more Sampras than Federer, both are generously endowed with the quality that might be called Redgrave.

But Waugh had retired, and the supreme member of his intimidatory batting corps, Ricky Ponting, was now captain. The unravelling of Ponting was to become one of the great sub-plots to the great narrative of the summer.

That first morning at Lord's was one of extraordinary anticipation. It was a morning fizzing with hope and resignation in roughly equal quantities: the feeling that England really had a decent side at last, countered with the memories of a thousand capitulations of the painfully recent past. Australia won the toss, and expected to cruise away from the Poms at four and a half runs an over. Instead, second ball, Steve Harmison hit Justin Langer on the elbow, and we had a gratifyingly long delay for treatment. Right from the start, it seemed, we had competition. Most of the people who attend a Lord's Test match are patriots for the nation of excellence. Cricket has a long tradition of appreciation of the opposition. But with Harmison's vicious and purposeful first over, you felt a palpable raising of the stakes. 'I hope' was turning into 'I think' and maybe even 'I believe'.

I watched all this from the absurd media centre at the Nursery End: a superb view, certainly. The place is perfect for everything apart from reporting on cricket matches: horribly cramped with nowhere to put your bag. I sat on a chair with castors, one of them poised uneasily an inch from the edge of the stairs. It was a situation that encouraged a meditative calm. Le Corbusier described a house as a machine for living: this press-box is a machine for winning architectural awards.

But it was glorious to watch Australia being despatched in 40 overs, and from there, the Test match was full of oscillating advantage, punch and counter-punch. And then came that Sunday at Lord's, when it poured with rain all day. If there is nothing so glorious in sport as the English summer delivering in full measure, there is nothing so dismal as the English sporting summer when it rains. For the journalist, it is a woeful business: you can't even get drunk, in case they start playing sport again and you have to write.

Only 61 balls were possible that day. Alas, only 61 balls were required to take the remaining five wickets. The only people to score a run were Extras and Kevin Pietersen. Four ducks. It was the Same Old Poms: a little promise, a little hope, even a taste of belief, and then the meek, feeble capitulation. Oh Australia, great is your strength, great your mastery; we acknowledge your might and wish only to serve your greatness. Australia flapped their elephant ears and England, in prime position at the water-hole, surrendered all they had worked for without raising a trunk or waggling a tusk. That pattern, I was confident, would be repeated again and again for the rest of the summer. I would miss the second Test. The family was going down to Cornwall, to stay with my father. Good chance, then, of peregrine falcon.

86

The game's gone. So the older sports writers say, often enough. It's true, too: the profession of being a sportswriter for a national newspaper has changed. So it bloody well should, too: things that remain as they are tend to do so because they are dead. One of the many things that has changed about the profession is the drinking. When I first worked in Fleet Street, doing shifts on days off from local newspapers, serious drinking was de rigueur. After doing my Saturday stint on the *Sunday Telegraph*, three or four pints at the King and Keys was regarded as an essential part of the process. I then went home: others went back to work.

When I first started writing for *The Times*, a rain delay at Wimbledon generally meant a fair bit of drinking, despite the dangers of having to write. It was expected. It was part of the job. We even thought that a failure to be at the bar was a failure to keep up with the twist and turn of events. It was part of the creative process; part, too, of not getting left behind. In a sense, that was all true.

New technology has done for that. It is a sad fact that you can't operate a computer when half-pissed, even though you can dictate a story into the telephone in the same condition. I have seen a writer too drunk to use a typewriter, reach for the phone and dictate a few perfectly acceptable paragraphs to a copy-taker. He was in the news-paper building at the time.

These days, Perrier, coffee and Red Bull are the drinks of choice for the sportswriter at work, though many seek a balance with horrific bingeing when work is done. But we are a less colourful profession now, and we must live it without the 24-hour-a-day maintenance drinkers of the past. I recall a friend at the Barcelona Olympics pointing out – over a drink, naturally – what he described as 'gold, silver and bronze. Look in the next bar and see what I mean.' I did: the three champion drunks of what we still, for convenience, term Fleet Street, joylessly soaking it up, brought together remorselessly by their one common interest.

That empty, bibulous camaraderie was the essence of old Fleet Street. But Fleet Street itself no longer has newspa-pers in it, and the practice of keeping up with your opposi-tion at the Stab and the Tip has gone with them. Thank God. I have already offered an alternative autobiography as an Australian horseman: I could easily have written another.

87

Glenn McGrath was out of the second Test match, having crocked his ankle while sodding about with a rugby ball. To my father, who has no embarrassment about parti-sanship, this was unambiguously good news. Me, I would normally make out a case for bringing on the best, and if England are good enough to win, they'd win. That is, if you like, the philosophical stance I have reached about the question of partisanship. The job of the telling of the tale would be too hard if partisanship was all-consuming: most sportswriters will hold the same kind of belief.

But I confess that, on this occasion, the philosophy didn't entirely stand up to close inspection. The notion that Australia had lost one of the finest fast bowlers that had ever played the game, the bowler who had destroyed them at Lord's, was not at all unattractive. My patriotism for the nation of excellence was ever so slightly undermined by a serious delight in the fact that England had been given a second chance. I badly wanted to see if they were good enough to seize it. What then, of the Pete Sampras? Of the quality of Redgrave? Do I contradict myself? Very well, I contradict myself.

McGrath's tumble was followed by Ricky Ponting's decision to ask England to bat. I would still defend this as an astute piece of captaincy, for all that it was the decision that turned the series in England's favour. The reason I would defend it is because it ought to have worked. England were a beaten side at Lord's. The knife had been inserted. If ever there was a moment to twist it, it was now.

But it didn't happen. England responded to the contemptuous insult of the insertion, and did so with neurotic violence. They scored 407 runs in the day. Australia looked a beaten side by lunch. I watched all this with my father, between visits to the beach with my family, pasty lunches, clifftop walks with buzzard and raven and, yes, peregrine, and trips to the ice cream place called Nauti But Ice and glasses of Pimm's and champagne. The cricket gave a certain fizz to the week. So, mind you, did the peregrines: there are few things quite so wonderful as the peregrine's fizzing clifftop glide. These birds seem to possess a perfect self-certainty in their role as killing machines, deeply secure in their fierce and terrible beauty.

And then Flintoff. Flintoff, in his own fierce and terrible beauty. Andrew Flintoff did that rare all-rounder's thing of batting and bowling at the top of his form in the same match. Over the course of three and a half days he became a giant. It is a fine thing, to watch the construction of a hero before your eyes. Heroes are the stuff of sport: without a hero there is no tale; without the truly exceptional performer, the narrative loses its fizz. The world has a huge hunger for heroes: it is the hunger that created Ben Johnson, Ayrton Senna and Steve Redgrave.

Humans are a species of fabulists. We live for the tale, for the revelation of character, for the triumph of good, or for that matter, the triumph of evil. And here was Flintoff, before our eyes shedding his past as a cricketer of much talent, and assuming the role of match-winner, occasion-seizer, triumph-bringer. It is a process in which an athlete takes a mythic aspect on himself.

Flintoff's story has so much resonance: a hulking boy of matchless talent, who proved that it is eminently possible to get by on talent alone, particularly if getting by is all you want. And so this affable, companionable and thirsty fellow got by, and became one of the better cameo-cricketers of our time. A couple of years earlier, various things had all happened round about the same time. Bobby Simpson, his Australian coach at Lancashire, had lost patience with him and told him in all frankness that he was a cunt. His management team of Neil Fairbrother and Chubby (not, I believe, his baptismal name) Chandler had given him a more protracted bollocking, and told him he was a wastrel. And he had met a girl, fallen in love, had a child.

And so Flintoff had become a man and thus, by easy stages, a hero. Unruly fellows are often looking out for a woman who will keep them in order: Flintoff seized his chance, and as a result, became a masterly seizer of chances. In that match, he took seven wickets and made 141 runs. Heroically.

88

My father, a religious man, chose to go to church on Sunday morning. It was a sound decision. Me, I stayed in front of the television to watch England take the last couple of wickets. My father, to profoundly mixed emotions, returned to see Australia still batting. He got to see some cricket: but it was cricket with Australia getting closer and closer to the target, with Brett Lee, the fast bowler, batting with unexpected self-certainty. England were losing the match in slow-motion. It was one of the most agonising pieces of sport I had ever experienced, and it was partisanship that made it so painful. I recall a friend of mine saying that as the last ball of the match was bowled, he was putting the lead on his dog. 'I'd tried everything else to take a wicket and nothing had worked.'

How often have I wished, with all England teams, with all British contenders in individual sports, that you could call on a closer. You can in baseball, after all: send for someone whose explicit job is to pitch the last inning or two, to finish the match, to safeguard the winning position, to add that touch of uncomplicated ruthlessness that will bring the match and the tale to its conclusion. With Tim Henman, with the England football team, with the England rugby team, I have frequently been dismayed at the team's or the individual's inability to close the match out.

This is generally interpreted as a failing in the British or the English character. Would Tim Henman have won Wimbledon had he been – impossible thought – American? Had he been the number one player in a country whose number one players win most of the prizes in most of the world's sports, would he have thought that Wimbledon was his natural prize? Rather than being something forever just a fraction beyond his reach? Why did he lose that rain-soaked semi-final against Goran Ivanisevic in 2001? Was it the Englishness in Henman, or was it the Henmanness in the Englishman? Did Henman lose because of his nurture, or because of his nature?

Sir Steve Redgrave is English, and yet he is also the quintessential sporting winner. Does that make him an exceptional Englishman? Or merely an exceptional man? Is he a cuckoo in England's nest, or are winners of his type rare in any society?

Certainly, we are aware of a diffidence in the English: an embarrassment, a sense of apology. Most English feel it in themselves when they are abroad, and certainly we notice it in certain competitors. Certain aspects of the national teams seem to reflect our own English embarrassment at the idea of seeming to impose overmuch. At the same time, we can also identify an equally English sense of bluster, one that ineffectually masks a sense of defeat.

But England also produced Redgrave, Martin Johnson, Ian Botham, Sebastian Coe, Ellen MacArthur, Kelly Holmes: people who would be exceptional in any society. So perhaps this notion of England as the land of the losers is the effect of partisanship in which it is natural to see only the weakness of your own side, only the strengths of the opposition. Perhaps every nation sees itself as a nation of losers. The idea that every other nation is spared the agonies that a British and especially an English supporter must undergo is surely misplaced.

All the same, England came within two runs of losing a Test that they dominated throughout. Their one weakness was in the finishing: as if they couldn't quite believe that it was them – little them – who were actually beating enormous old Australia. In the end, English talent beat English diffidence; but it was a damned close-run thing.

The match ended in a perfectly heroic manner: the last ball from Harmison ripping through and taking Michael Kafprowicz's glove, and Flintoff's spontaneous reaction to this moment of ultimate achievement was not to whoop and air-punch and hug team-mates, but to turn to the stricken Lee at the other end and offer a word of comfort. It was a fine gesture from a human being: and finer still from a hero.

89

The pleasures of the second Test were quite doubled by the fact that I shared them with my father. It might even have been a three-generation thing, but it wasn't. My own older son, Joseph, aged 11, didn't watch a ball. He stayed out in the garden, getting on with whatever he was getting on with. As soon as he could walk, he was naturally given footballs and cricket balls and tennis balls to play with. Every time, he would throw the ball into the nearest bush and walk away to get on with something else. His cousin, Max was in Cornwall with us. He had never watched cricket before, but by a strange instinct, he was drawn in. He watched a little and then more and more; and by the end, he was watching with total and heartfelt involvement. Sport gets to him.

But some people just don't understand sport. Others believe that an indifference to sport is a proof of intellectual superiority, as already discussed in these pages. But some people simply don't get it. They are, as it were, tone-deaf as regards sport. They like stories as much as the next human being, but for some reason, the stories that sport supplies come in the wrong form and fail to resonate on the mind.

I haven't, to use the traditional parent's expression, thrust sport down Joe's throat. I have been at great pains to allow him to make his own mind up, with the result that he is utterly indifferent to sport. It is something that other people do.

This is not a disappointment to me. I won't be taking Joe to the Test match, but never mind. A couple of weeks before we went to Cornwall, he and I went to Cardigan Bay and to look for dolphins, and we saw them leaping and wheeling and revelling in a glorious day, and it was one of the great shared expeditions, though not quite as good as the trip we made the previous year to the Luangwa Valley in Zambia (we stayed with Jess, naturally). There are people who think wildlife is a life and death matter. They're fools. It's much more important than that.

90

Round about this time, I was careless enough to fall off a horse. My young one, of course. Had I been a better rider, I would still have fallen off: the business involved a three-quarter stand and a 180-degree spin, both accomplished simultaneously and in an instant of time. I 'came out the side-door', as horsepeople say, and landed, alas, on my arse: it happened too quickly for me to get my feet down first. And no, I didn't get straight back on, the fall was far too uncomfortable, though I worked the horse hard from the ground for a decent while before finishing the session. That was not for my pride, but so that she didn't reach the conclusion that the act of dumping her rider gave her all sorts of personal advantages. It was not a bad fall, as these things go, though there comes a time in your life when you no longer bounce, and I was a long way past that. I had compression in the lower spine and whiplash at the top. I was back riding within the week; that wasn't the problem. The only things I found difficult were sitting still for long periods of time, especially in cars and trains. Travelling around England watching Test matches was, then, a suboptimal experience, at least physically. But these things are never wasted: it is always useful to feel a touch of physical failure, not to mention pain. And then the fear if – when – you get on the horse again. It is always a good idea to take fear seriously: to write about fear from personal experience.

Sport is nothing without fear. If you cannot feel something of the athlete's fear, you cannot write well about sport: or, for that matter, enjoy watching sport. Matthew Pinsent was so fearful before his final in Athens that he threw up over the side of the boat. It's a common experience, found among the toughest. Competitors in many sports must face a physical fear: in all sports, they face a fear of failure. But it is above all a fear of being put to the test: a fear not of other people but of oneself. Not exactly a fear of failure, no, nor even a fear of success. Rather, a fear of the process of testing: a fear of being found wanting, of being found out. And I know about that: I remember how, before every cross-country event I ever rode in, I would find myself five minutes before the start suffering from rather bad peritonitis, and wanting to approach the starter and say, excuse me, I'm awfully sorry, but I won't be able to compete today, because I have rather bad peritonitis, and *it wouldn't be fair to the horse*. And the thing that really scared the crap out of me was the certain knowledge that I was going to do no such thing.

You write everything, at least to an extent, from your own experience: even when you write about greatness. You write, not from having been great, but from experiencing one or two glimpses, times when you start in fear and end up creating something beyond your own expectations: beyond, in fact, your own capabilities. The achievements themselves may be pitifully low when measured against the world: but the feeling of reaching beyond is a common human experience. We have all experienced it, in a million different ways. The best writing also involves a testing; it is improved by a little mild terror, and is the better, too, for the occasional reminder that the ground is still so very hard.

91

The leisurely pace, protracted timescale and almost infinite number of variables gives a Test series a formidable narrative drive. The one-day match is a short story, a Test match is a novel, a five-match series is a *roman fleuve*. Previous Ashes series have cast Steve Waugh as a kind of glorious cricketing Widmerpool – the ghastly power-drunk Widmerpool being the central character of Anthony Powell's great *roman fleuve*, *A Dance to the Music of Time*. I have admired few cricketers as much as Waugh: his reinvention of Test cricket, his deployment of a hugely talented collection of cricketers, his culture of excellence, above all, his extortion of humility from all opponents: this was masterly. Waugh was cricket's Sampras, cricket's Redgrave. There is no higher praise.

Now, under Ricky Ponting's leadership, Australia's

savage and terrible mask of mastery was no longer in place. The Australian side had a goat, for example. Goat is an American term for the calamity-prone member of a team, one whose contribution to the common cause is almost heart-rendingly comic. Jason Gillespie, a fearsome bowler at his best, went to pieces. Like a disaster during the washing-up, he simply came apart in England's hands. In the three matches he played, he took three wickets at 100 runs each. The once-fearsome Australian batting line-up had its flaws exposed by astute bowling plans and bowlers bouncing in with conviction. The batsmen found it hard to make the adjustment from flat-track bullies to fighters.

That term, 'flat-track bully', has become one of the most useful in sport. It was coined by John Bracewell, a former New Zealand spin bowler, for Graeme Hick, the Zimbabwe-born England batsman who murdered county bowling but was found wanting against savage and purposeful Test attacks. In point of fact, being a flat-track bully is an under-rated talent: over the years, I have wished that Tim Henman and the England football team had some of Hick's mastery over the second-rate.

In the third Test in Manchester, Australia struggled as England refused to be bullied. Bullying failed: and there seemed to be no plan B. What emerged most clearly was the extraordinary nature of Shane Warne. Beaten in more or less every session of the match, Australia managed to hang on for a draw, and the principal reason they managed it was the will of Warne.

Warne is possibly the greatest bowler that ever drew breath. He has the gift of a genuinely exceptional cricket brain, an attribute which might be defined as a profound understanding of the opposition as individuals and as a team. Still, Warne was not the bowler he once was. Not, that is, in terms of the balls he bowled, of the variety he used to possess in his leg-spinner's repertoire. But the intelligence was keener with experience: and the mind utterly unsated by past triumphs. He loved, above all, the gladiatorial confrontations of Test match cricket; and that real relish was at the heart of everything he did in that series. He thought people out. I don't just mean that he used guile. He also used a kind of mental force.

There was a character in *The Incredible Hulk* comics called The Leader. He had been exposed to the same demonic gamma rays as poor Bruce Banner, but instead of turning into a creature of monstrous strength, he became a creature of monstrous mind. He could slay people and destroy buildings by means of mental bolts. That was Warne in that series: forever firing mental bolts at English batsmen, seeking to destroy them by the might of pure mind.

At Old Trafford, England roared to a decent first innings total with a gorgeous innings from the captain, Michael Vaughan. England failed to run away with the match thanks entirely to Warne's four wickets. The Australian top-order batsmen then all failed, but Warne scored 90. He is not supposed to be a batsman: not even a serious all-rounder. But it seems that mental powers work even at the things you are not good at. England then batted and declared, and then tried to bowl Australia out.

They couldn't do it. The striking of the killer blow had been almost beyond them at Edgbaston, and it was beyond them altogether this time. The last pair, Glenn McGrath and Brett Lee, saw off the last 24 balls.

It was clear enough that if Warne had been captain — if Warne had, indeed, been recognised as The Leader — Australia would at this stage have been two-up in the series at least. So why wasn't he? Australia likes to pretend that it is a country of take-as-you-find, one that prefers rough-and-ready virtue to prim respectability. But Warne's various indiscretions meant that when Waugh retired, the respectable Ponting got the job, and the scandal-prone Warne did not. It was an egregious error. By the third Test, Ponting's leadership was in the process of falling apart. The Test series provided a kind of Petri dish for the testing of the curious culture of Ponting's captaincy: and we all watched as it shrivelled and died. Instead, the side was held together by the strength of Warne's mind. Had he been The Leader, I believe that Warne would have made sure that Australia retained the Ashes. As it was, Warne had the most extraordinary series, with the ball and with the bat, and it was not enough.

But it seemed possible, almost to the end, that Warne might do it despite everything. As the series continued, I found myself thrilling more and more to his relish for the contest, his ability to believe a dozen impossible things before breakfast and then to bring them into actuality. Here was a great sportsman, no question of that, and certainly the greatest player taking part in the series.

Greatness. For all my partisanship for Warne's opponents that summer, the part of me that remained a patriot of the land of greatness was an increasingly devoted supporter of Warne. I wouldn't have been entirely disappointed to see Warne turn the series around and win it on his own.

As it was, England were in the most desperate need of someone who could close out a cricket match. All the certainty was with the second-best side: all the uncertainty with the side that was winning most of the battles.

92

That surreal Monday morning. Travelling to Old Trafford for the final day of the Test, to find thousands upon thousands of supporters walking in the wrong direction: away from the ground. I couldn't fathom it. Only once I was in the press-box, looking out at the stands packed full to bursting with excitable folk in holiday humour, did I work it out. The walkers-away had failed to get in. They were too late. The ground was full by breakfast. It was a perfect demonstration of the way the Ashes summer had the entire country rapt, enthralled, unable to look away, as if held by the eye of the Ancient Mariner. So inevitably, there was a lot of media talk about this extraordinary phenomenon: the new surge of interest in cricket – cricket, the new football. You know.

But cricket was not making a comeback. The truth of the matter was that cricket had never gone away. You don't extirpate more than a century of national life with a few disappointments. Cricket had been part of national life even in the worst of times, when England navigated their way from batting collapse to batting collapse. They were years in which every player in the team seemed to be playing for himself, the batting collapse becoming the ultimate expression of trade union solidarity: if we all fail, then no one has failed. Right?

Cricket remained in the national consciousness as a kind of aching joke. But behind the gallows humour was a hope that some day, things might be different. England sank to the bottom place in the rankings after a defeat by New Zealand, but people did not give up on cricket. A huge fuss was made of the disappointment, and the captain, Nasser Hussain, was booed on the balcony after the final Test of that year, 1999. The England team may have given up winning, but the English people certainly hadn't stopped caring.

And so, when it came to 2005, and a visit from Australia, traditionally the most important Test series, all it took was a little hope and a great rush of latent enthusiasm was released. It was not surprising at all. Winning is, as we have established, more exciting than losing, but the *possibility* of winning is more exciting than either. I remember sitting on a committee asking 'whither showjumping', and being asked what the sport needed to re-establish itself in the nation's hearts. An Olympic gold medal, I said.

Remember the curling boom? At the Winter Olympic Games of 2002, millions of Brits stayed up after midnight to watch Rhona Martin and her immortals win a gold medal for Britain in the sport of curling. I was one of them. It was wonderful. Best game of curling I've ever watched.

Clearly, then, the possibility of the England team winning an Ashes series was rather more than wonderful. The nation was entranced by the story; every day brought absurd and impossible new twists. The nation were junkies, demanding every day a further fix of the tale. It was the unputdownable summer. So how do you think I felt? Like Scheherazade.

How many more twists could the tale produce? At Old Trafford, on the way to that sumptuous century, Michael Vaughan was dropped by Adam Gilchrist on 42, off the miraculously fit-again Glenn McGrath. The ball after that, he was clean-bowled. But it was a no-ball.

You wouldn't write it in a comic-book story. That is one of sport's oldest conceits: the notion that sport gives you, as a matter of routine, stuff so improbable that you would hesitate to write it in a tale intended for sophisticated ten-year olds. But sport has a way of telling these absurd and improbable tales and acting them out for real before us: to the incontinent delight of our ten-year-old selves.

93

Our attitude to youth is deeply ambiguous. We despise certain ideas and forms of behaviour (like sport) as childish: and yet we seek to retain our own youthfulness. We want firm skin, flat bellies and vigorous bodies; we turn up our noses at the naïve, the wet-behind-the ears and the half-baked. Our attitude to youth has always been difficult, complex and contradictory.

One of the significant aspects of the development of *Homo sapiens* has been the retention of youthful characteristics: neotony, to use the scientific term. Stephen Jay Gould, the great writer on evolution and science, explained: 'We have evolved by retaining to adulthood the originally juvenile features of our ancestors.' An adult and a baby chimpanzee are hugely dissimilar, especially when compared to the obvious similarities between an adult and a baby human. But the skulls of a baby chimpanzee and a baby human are markedly similar. The chimpanzee develops: the human retains the look of youth. Part of the human evolutionary advantage lay in this retention of juvenile features.

Early studies of humanity made it clear that white European types developed more fully than other races: that 'negroes' especially tended to retain youthful – childish – characteristics. This, of course, proved the superiority of white races over black. Then the phenomenon of neotony was understood as a crucial part of human advances. So scientists then discovered that 'negroes' tend to develop, while white races are more prone to retaining youthful characteristics. Which shows us that science is as much a product of human culture as art and, for that matter, sport.

But certainly, we humans – of all races – retain in adult life a lot of stuff that other animals lose. Grown elephants do not play with each other: grown humans do. We hang on to the frivolous and childish delight in play, in messing about. The sort of thing that in a wild animal is preparation for grown-up life, is in humans carried into adulthood. As Gould put it: 'We… never grow up, although we do, alas, grow old.' So we retain the taste for play, even if we frequently delegate the actual playing to others. And call it professional sport.

We also retain the child's taste for stories. A bed-time story is every child's earliest intellectual delight, and the taste for a good story stays with every adult. Especially if it has a happy ending.

94
As the summer continued, it became increasingly clear that England had an edge in all their dealings against Australia, save the area of finishing. The more this grew clear, the more the greatness of Shane Warne became apparent. In the course of the series he became the first bowler to take 600 Test match wickets; he was to take 96 Test wickets in the calendar year, another record. And the more the series seemed to be slipping away from Australia, the more Warne relished each confrontation and savoured each triumph. He was untiring, his will unrelenting, his appetite unsated.

A Dance to the Music of Time contains a scene in which the characters discuss Casanova. '"Why should he be considered a great man just because he had a lot of women? Most men would have ended by being bored to death."

"That's why he was a great man," said Moreland. "It wasn't the number of women he had, it was the fact that he didn't get bored."'

The immunity from boredom is an aspect of sporting greatness. Perhaps this quality is better understood as the ability to devote life and heart and mind and soul to a single thing. This is a much more unusual ability than you might think. Most people in sport who are considered great leave behind a series of championships, a collection of medals. Longevity is very frequently an aspect of greatness: Redgrave, Sampras, Warne.

This is not invariably the case: Jesse Owens became one of the greatest of all time in a few summer days in 1936. Bob Beamon became great in the course of a handful of seconds: the unconscionably long time he spent in the air between the take-off board and the sandpit in Mexico at the Olympic Games of 1968; the long-jump world record he set that day stood for a quarter of a century.

But under normal circumstances, we find greatness in the people who go on and on: who amass triumph after triumph, who meet rivals and adversity along the way and yet who are apparently never daunted, never downhearted. Always ready for one more great battle.

Greatness requires a kind of perpetual thirst. Over the course of the summer, Warne showed that he was one of the Great Unslaked. It is the weak ones who get bored.

95

Somehow, England managed to finish the fourth Test at Trent Bridge. At the heart of the victory was a gloriously meticulous and grown-up century from Andrew Flintoff. As a result, Australia had to follow on, the first time they had done so against England for 20 years, and

England were left needing 129 runs to win. Even then, the will of Shane Warne almost stopped them; along with the speed of Brett Lee. England lost seven wickets, four to Warne including the first three, as they staggered towards the total they needed. When you require an exquisite cover drive from Matthew Hoggard for a win, you know that you have at least given disaster a fair chance. But England thoroughly deserved their win: it would have been a travesty of justice had Australia won.

Did you ever hear such nonsense? Justice? Deserts? Yet the concept of justice is one of the most cherished in sport. Aston Villa are two goals up and just about deserve it. West Bromwich Albion won by a single goal in an extraordinary miscarriage of justice... these are stock phrases, and like all stock phrases, they reveal the important assumptions people make about the matter in question.

And yes, we really do think that a side that missed the goal 12 times is more deserving of a victory than a side that had one attempt and succeeded. In football, we feel that a side that plays an attacking game has a greater moral right to a victory than a team that relies on an impeccable defence. Does this mean that the side that gives us more entertainment is more deserving of victory? Not entirely. There is also an idea that a sporting victory should have a moral dimension. This has nothing to do with the way sport is actually played: but a very great deal to do with the way people – including professional athletes – understand sport.

Sport is a kind of morality play: and it is bemusing, therefore, that so often, the bad end happily and the good unhappily, that justice so often fails to be done. Partisanship also conveys a moral sense to the sport, in the sense that most matches put the good guys against the bad guys. But on the other hand, if England win a football match against the run of play, a spectator will say: 'We won, but we didn't deserve it.'

But there are no undeserved victories in sport. If you win because your opponent is unable to make his superiority of craft or strength or opportunity tell against you, then you, rather than the opponent, deserve victory. Bettina Hoy may not agree with this, but it is true for all that. If your defensive guile is more effective than his attacking brio, then again, you deserve victory. Victory, in sport as in warfare, does not depend on justice: it defines justice. And that is a truth that you will scarcely ever find acknowledged anywhere in sport.

96

I began as a patriot for the nation of excellence, I ended up a chauvinist for the land of rain. As the fifth and final Test approached, with England needing just a draw to win the Ashes, many people had been expressing the view that five days of rain would be just about perfect.

I was a for-God's-saker myself. I took a much more manly view, and very becoming it was too. For God's sake, I said, let's have a bloody cricket match. Let's go out and win the damn thing or lose the damn thing: let's not cower behind rainclouds. This view was sound, butch, sporty and, above all, consistent with the way I think and write about sport. Walt Whitman wrote, in 'Song of Myself': 'I also say it is good to fall, battles are lost in the same spirit in which they are won.'

But by the time that England were slithering inevitably towards defeat, a deeper truth had been revealed. I wanted rain. I wanted bad light, as a reasonable second-best. I didn't want the contest, I wanted the result. I was aware that this was a contradiction that amounted to a betrayal, but I wanted England to win the Ashes, and I was looking not for heroism, but for the easy way out. I wanted not the conclusion but the anticlimax. I didn't want the natural and inevitable result, brought about by the collision of the wills of the participants: I wanted a deus ex machina to decide the summer irrevocably in England's favour. I wanted it for the memory of my grandfather, I wanted it for my father's sake, but I couldn't hide behind those pious sentiments. Most of all, I wanted it for my sake. I wanted to win.

To tell the tale, yes, of course to tell the tale, a victory would be far, far greater than a tale of defeat. But most of all, I wanted England to win, because that would mean they had won. Walt Whitman again:

Do I contradict myself?
Very well then I contradict myself,
(I am large, I contain multitudes.)

We are all large: and perhaps there is something inherently life-denying about consistency, about forcing everything into a coherent body of thought. In saying so, of course, I subvert the very foundation of this book. But this book is also at least fairlylarge. It was written by a human, and it represents the thoughts of a human in all his mental chaos and contradiction.

And, more importantly, sport is also large: it is peaceful warfare, it is a duel without rancour, it is a serious triviality, it is a meaningful nonsense. It is inevitable that our approaches to it should also be contradictory.

Humans are contradictory creatures. This matter is familiar to us all: we want at the same time to be married, to be free; to be wildly promiscuous, to be forever faithful; to travel, to stay at home; to seek adventures, to remain in safety; to be idle, to be rewardingly busy; to revel in company, to be contentedly alone. And sport, being a human pursuit, is naturally filled with contradictions. We relish the brilliance of a great opponent; we delight in the fact that he has trodden on a cricket ball and can't play; we want to see genius in action; we want the team we support to render genius ineffectual.

I wanted to see great action in the final Test: I wanted to see a green field on which the autumn rain fell unrelentingly. English supporters, who had paid good money to be present, raised umbrellas to a dry sky, imploring the rain to come, while Australians in the crowd removed their shirts and put on their sunglasses. The absurdity of the situation was lost on no one. And by lunchtime on the last day with England five wickets down and Andrew Flintoff out, it was clear that rain and only rain could give England victory in the Ashes.

97

It is a commonplace of sport, as we have seen. You couldn't make it up, people say. It seems that one of sport's most addictive factors is that of belief-beggaring. My three novels are all more or less naturalistic, and I am very much aware, therefore, of the need to write matters that can be believed without too much strain. The central character of my first novel was loosely based on an African ornithologist of my acquaintance. In order to make him believable, I toned down his eccentricities. For example, I cut out the detail about his rolling his cigarettes from the *Guardian Weekly*. My second novel, set in Hong Kong, brought the comment from a friend: 'Did we really drink as much as that?' No, we did not. Much more. I edited the consumption in the interests of credibility.

But in sport, essentially a kind of fiction played out in real life, there need be no such concession to the reader's good taste and delicate sensibilities. Sport, as a matter of routine, brings us events that are past serious credence. Liverpool's European Cup Final in Istanbul was just such an event: the final day of the Ashes series was another.

The greatest player on either side made a howler: Shane Warne dropped Kevin Pietersen on fifteen. Australia's most effective fast bowler, Brett Lee, made a sustained and violent assault on Pietersen. And Pietersen responded with an innings of disturbing, unbalanced aggression. It was a performance based essentially on absurdity. England needed to bat all day to save the series. It was a day for safety, for caution, for defence. And Pietersen played an innings based on risk piled on risk. He hit seven sixes. He risked looking the most titanic bloody fool in sport. He scored 158 runs, and England won the Ashes.

It made for a day of surreal perfection. Grown men played a game of stick and ball, and grown people across the country found the whole business fraught almost beyond bearing. At the final victory, the outpouring of joy, mixed liberally with relief, swept over the nation. It was, everyone agreed, the greatest cricketing summer that had ever been played. Everyone wanted to talk about it and think about it and to read about it. And me, I told the tale.

98 Young people write to me asking what they have to do in order to get my job. Often, they write asking me what they should read at university: should they read journalism or media studies? I always reply: think about it. You could spend three years reading me, or three years reading Shakespeare. Who has more to say? My nephew, reading media studies against my advice, is completing three years of paralysed boredom. He groaned when I mentioned this, not for the first time. 'It's not even as good as reading you. It's reading academic treatises on the history of journalism.'

Academic institutions come up with all kinds of courses these days and they all look very sexy on the prospectus: sexy, and exactly the sort of thing that you don't do in school. They provide an entry, or so it seems, into all that is most amusing about being a grownup. Better still, how to be a grownup without actually growing up – no wonder so many people want to work in sports journalism. So universities come up with courses on sports journalism, or television, or fashion, and congratulate themselves on a job well done. They then sit down at a later a date and some one asks: 'What are we going to teach the people who get onto our course?' An ugly silence reigns. And then some one else remarks: 'There, I think you might have hit on the one snag in the entire scheme.'

And then young people ask me: what should I to do train my mind for sports journalism? Should I watch a lot of sport? Yes, but far more important than that, read. Read anything. Ready everything. Read Shakespeare, Proust, Joyce: read *The Times*, read sporting autobiographies, read Ian Fleming, read CLR James, read Brian Glanville. For a writer – any kind of writer – reading is your training pitch. You are seeking to tell a tale: read tales, then. Make the telling of tales the central part of the way your mind works. Read the best tale-tellers, read the tale-tellers who talk to you, and then go out and tell the tales yourself. And while you are doing so, don't stop reading. After all, a great sportsman never stops practising. Gary Player said that the more he practised, the luckier he got. The more you read, the more the right way to turn the tale will come to you: sometimes after long pondering, more often, in sports journalism, as a thought that takes you by surprise the moment before your deadline does the same thing. You don't need to study the history of the newspaper in popular culture: you need to study words, words, words, words.

99 At the heart of the story of the Ashes was the story of Andrew Flintoff. Flintoff: the Man Who Changed. The story of his conversion to training and application has already been touched on in these pages: but the Test series turned England's way because something changed in Flintoff in between the first and the second Test. In the first, Flintoff, took six wickets – pretty good going – but scored nought and three, and was part of England's House-of-Usher collapse. In the second Test, he took seven wickets and scored 68 and 73, and England won.

Somewhere between the first and the second test, Flintoff became the bull elephant who drinks at the coolest part of the water hole. Somehow, in between the two great matches, he became a cricketer who had the beating of every batsman and every bowler. Somehow, he acquired the knowledge that the most important place of all belonged to him as a matter of right. He had only to give a certain look – he didn't even have to flap his ears or shake his tusks – and he would be given what he wanted. Not willingly, not easily – just inevitably. He had acquired the quality known as Redgrave.

And so he set the tone for the series, making England's second win at Trent Bridge possible with his century, and paving the way for Kevin Pietersen's series-saving innings at the Oval by taking five wickets, as Australia lost seven wickets for 44 runs and lost their position of dominance. Central to England's success throughout the summer was the fact that Adam Gilchrist, Australia's greatest destructive batsman, failed to post a decent score all series. Flintoff's bull-elephant domination of Gilchrist — taking his wicket four times in nine innings and troubling him greatly in all nine — was a core part of England's strategy.

I can tell the tale of the way it worked: the increasingly fraught and febrile batsman, the increasingly puff-chested and flint-eyed bowler — but I can't tell you why. No one can. Not even a bull elephant, and not Flintoff either. I know, I asked him. I had a long session with him after the series, and found him a delightful fellow, very generous not only with his time but also in his efforts to answer questions in a meaningful fashion rather than hide behind stock phrases. But he didn't know how he became the top elephant. He just went to the water hole one day and found that everyone else gave way to him. So he drank: drank the coolest water, as was his right.

100

Not all luck is earned luck, not all luck is the kind of luck you earn by practising. No indeed. I realised that when I went to Belize in the early summer of that year, and kissed Darryl Hannah and saw a jaguar. I am glad I didn't get offered a choice, because I would certainly have taken the jaguar. I am glad I didn't miss the matey — but certainly hearty — at least on my part — cheek-kiss with the star of *Roxanne*, *Splash*, *Kill Bill* and of course, *The Attack of the Fifty-Foot Woman*.

I was travelling with the World Land Trust, an organisation

that is buying up chunks of endangered habitat across the world, and is buying bits of Belize in order to save its rainforest. I was writing my wildlife column of that week from there; Darryl, if I may be so matey – one really shouldn't presume on a wartime commission – was there to do a photo-shoot for *Hello!* magazine, in order to publicise the Trust, she being a big fan of rainforests and so forth.

So this was a fairly reckless mixture of people. The group comprised Darryl and her gofer, a female PR, a female celeb writer, a female fashion photographer, a male make-up artist, a nature writer for *Country Life*, me, and John Burton, head honcho of the World Land Trust. I got on OK with Darryl because I was able to ask the question so few men can ask sincerely of a woman: 'How are your horses?'

The Belize forest is a wonderful and vivid experience. I was there for five days, and on my third day, I saw a jaguar: big, butch and male, and with a neck like Mike Tyson. That gloriously patterned coat. An eternity-long pause as we crashed to a halt and he looked at us and we looked at him, and then he padded with slow certainty back into the maw of the forest.

Vladimir Rodriguez has worked as a field naturalist for Programme for Belize for six years: this was his fourteenth jaguar. Ramon Pachero has worked as a station manager in the forest for eight years: this was his eighth. Burton had made upwards of 20 trips to Belize, and had never seen one before. And he didn't see one this time, either, because he wasn't in the vehicle. As a result, he is not a man to whom I can say 'jaguar' very often. He has seen jaguarundi, which he says is much more interesting. He is entitled to his view: and also to my disbelief.

Now I have spent many hours and days and weeks and months in the Luangwa Valley in Zambia, and I have earned all the luck I have had there. I have put in the hours; I have done the hard yards; and as a direct result, I have seen untold wonders. I have seen leopard kill on three occasions; I have followed the fortunes of a pride of lion; I have seen aardvark and serval; I have seen bat-hawk and seen a thousand carmine bee-eaters at once; I have recorded two new birds for the Valley. I have also had many quiet days, and have enjoyed the quieter sense of wonder they bring. These days, I go into the bush with no urgent need to see anything, and the relaxed certainty that I will revel in anything that turns up. Any more wonders: well, I have earned them.

I hadn't earned the luck I had in Belize. England had luck in the Ashes series: and a lot of it was the sort that *is* earned: the kind Gary Player talked about, Luangwa Luck. England had a strong team of improving players exploiting the conditions better, playing for each other and within their physical limits. These things can be put down, at least in part, to good preparation and serious hard work. You can't go into any modern professional sporting contest without these things.

But right at the last, they had a slice of what you might call Jaguar Luck, and it came when Warne dropped Pietersen. The chance came to him at first slip, and it was not hard as these things go, coming swift but not crazy-swift, at face height. Reverse the hands, let the ball arrive, let the hands close around the ball and the arms ride with the impact. Routine. Warne – was he wanting victory too strongly? Was he thinking about the demonic variations with which he would bamboozle Pietersen when he bowled to him? – spilled it. It was Warne's fault, so in one sense, as already discussed, England did indeed deserve to win the series, since you are perfectly permitted to profit from your opponent's errors.

But in another sense – am I contradicting myself again? – this was unearned luck. This was luck beyond the routine, the luck that is not explained or justified by hours of seeking for it. Napoleon's eternal question of his generals – 'Has he luck?' – was nothing to do with Gary Player Luck. Presumably all good generals have that. Napoleon was talking about Jaguar Luck. England not only had it: they had it when they needed it. And that made all the difference.

101

A couple of weeks or so after the Ashes had ended, I bumped into Paul Hayward, chief sportswriter for the *Daily Mail*. 'I know it sounds precious,' he said. Paul does not have a reputation for preciousness. 'But I felt shattered after the Ashes. Drained.' So I told him about Gerry Nowicki, an actor and playwright who used to play for Tewin Irregulars, the weekend village-green cricket team I was involved with for some years. Gerry, as theatrical in his cricket as he was in everything else in his life, had bowled himself, if not the opposition, to a standstill. My sister asked him – 'breezily', she recalls – if he had been having fun. He replied: 'I – have – nothing – left – to – give!'

Paul laughed and said he felt much the same. As indeed, did I, though I most certainly have a reputation for being precious, despite my taste for walking with lions and training young horses (the lady doth protest too much). But obviously, if you throw your heart into a story, you are going to feel a reaction when it is all over. If you don't, it is because you have failed to throw your heart far enough.

102

I was not a great cricketer. Nor even a semi-competent one, though I had a lot of fun – unlike Gerry Nowicki – doing it. Never at school: there, I took every opportunity to avoid sport, especially rugby, the playing of which at junior level came close to putting me off sport for life. Why, I used to wonder, do people think that compulsory games are good for our souls? The junior house matches involved up to 30 boys who loathed every second of what they were doing. Cold, wet, muddy, miserable. The standard tactic was to give the ball to some oaf who had reached puberty at nine, and watch him trot the length of the pitch while the opposition tried to look as they were making a gallant attempt at a tackle. A favoured move was the pass into touch, performed when there was the smallest danger of being tackled yourself. Junior house sports was a deeply dispiriting business, and I took every chance to avoid it in whatever form it was presented.

I didn't play regular cricket till I was in my 30s. The

cricket press-boxes are full of people who have played cricket somewhat better and more extensively: Derek Pringle, Angus Fraser and Mike Selvey have all played Test cricket for England. Is it possible to cover cricket without having played it properly? Is it possible to cover cricket without training as a journalist? Obviously, the answer to both questions is yes.

But are the reports of ex-cricketers infinitely better than those of non-cricketers? Infinitely more perceptive? If you tried a blind tasting of all the match reports written for the same day's play, it would not be obvious which author had played Test cricket and which had not. Christopher Martin-Jenkins and Scyld Berry are among the best in the business, and they never played first-class cricket. CMJ played one match that was billed as first-class but was subsequently demoted, depriving him of a first-class wicket. Both rightly pride themselves on a good eye for technique and tactic. Peter Roebuck, already mentioned in these pages, played country cricket, but never made the Test team. It is not about how good a cricketer you were, it is about how good a writer you are.

You do not have to experience what you are writing about in order to write about it meaningfully. Marcel Proust wrote *Swann in Love* without being fully heterosexual; Anthony Burgess wrote *Earthly Powers* without being homosexual; James Joyce wrote the Molly Bloom soliloquy without being a woman; Fyodor Dostoyevsky wrote *Crime and Punishment* without being a murderer; Homer wrote *The Odyssey* without being a god.

Writing does not depend on direct experience, it

depends on the imaginative strength of the writer. I don't mean imagination as in the ability to make things up: I mean imagination as in the ability to understand what something is like for somebody else. The entirety of human society depends on the ability to imagine what it is like for another person: we tend to avoid situations in which we imagine that another person will feel pain, discomfort and distress: we tend to create circumstances in which another person feels content.

I have never been a great performer at sport. I kept goal in football, I kept wicket in cricket, later becoming a bowler of non-turning off-breaks (which I varied, of course, with the one that goes on with the arm). I was actually not bad at riding horses in competition, especially cross-country, in which you go as fast as you can over a series of reasonably terrifying obstacles. But I never had the ability to finish things off: the understanding of what it takes to win, and the certainty that I had it. I lacked all trace of the talent called Redgrave.

But I know what it is to struggle, and I can see — sometimes I can see very vividly — what is happening in the course of the struggle, the places where the doubts and the certainties are to be found.

103 When writing about disappointment, I have plenty of personal experience to bring to bear on the subject of sport. Diving for the ball and feeling it hard and red on the middle of the glove: the glove instantly turning to ferro-concrete, the ball falling ignominiously to the ground, my ears full of the never-uttered reproaches of my team-mates. Moving forward to collect an overhit through-ball and misjudging the bounce, for we used to play on a concrete pitch when I lived in Hong Kong and I kept goal for Gwai-Loong FC. And the ball, bouncing almost vertically in front of my shocked face, looping onwards unerringly into the goal: has anyone ever looked such a fool? Or the perfect showjumping round ridden in the highest class of the day: foot-perfect: landing over the last with a feeling of pure delight: and hearing that sweet musical Chinese-block clonk of wood hitting ground, for we had whiffed the top pole of the last fence and ever-so-gently rolled it out of its cups; and then a soft, involuntary sigh of disappointment from the spectators.

But I have also known perfection. Not perfection as Andrew Flintoff or Steve Gerrard know it (or as Mike Selvey, Derek Pringle, Angus Fraser and Peter Roebuck know) but I too have had the experience of excess: of exceeding not just my own expectations but my own abilities. And often, often I write of that experience when I observe it in others. Could I have written about it had I not experienced these moments of perfection? Perhaps not. But perhaps such moments are something we all know, in different forms.

Tewin Irregulars 78 for eight in reply to 240 for four declared: a dozen or so overs to go. And Marcus Williams and I batted them out for the draw: naturally, Marcus and I talk about it still. Or going for that beautiful diagonal cross, realising I would never make it, and seeing the perfect loop-ing header going towards the top corner: I can still see the expression of satisfaction on the face of the forward, expe-riencing a moment of perfection himself. And then I was diving up and backwards, as if we were performing a ballet long-rehearsed, and I had my hand underneath the ball and was propelling it with gentle certainty over the bar, and I was performing a backward roll on the concrete into the net. I know I can't play as well as that. So how come I did?

Shortly after the Ashes were over, I went out with my young horse, a friend riding my older mare. And we went to a place the young horse had never been before, and I asked her to take the lead, and, overwhelmed, she expressed her unhappiness by going into a canter-through-treacle routine. So I asked my friend to take the lead instead, and my horse responded with a fierce series of bucks, of which I took no notice whatsoever. Didn't hit her, didn't hold on for dear life: I just sat. Then, turning for home, I again took the lead, and this time we went on at a good clip. So I asked for more: and the little mare, ridicu-lously excited, responded by putting her head between her knees and throwing in three enormous bucks. I sat still, slipped the reins through to the buckle to give her a feeling of total freedom, and nudged her with my heels to ask her to go forward. And she took off like a rocket: a joyful rock-et, the first time she had ever galloped with a rider on board, and she stopped when I asked too, an agreeable bonus.

I had got three things right at the same time. Horsemanship, physical ability, nerve. As a result, I flew. I have never experienced greatness in sport, not by a million mules, but I know what triumph is and I know what disaster is: and so does everybody else who watches sport.

At one stage, Tewin Irregulars presented the annual Barnes-Davies Merit Award, given to the player who produced something beyond his own capacity. The recipient was chosen by me and Robert 'Roob' Davies, my brother-in-law and captain of the Irregulars. One year it went to Tim Goodwin, for clean-bowling an obnoxious show-off of a batsman who was within sight of his century; another year it went to Father Bernard Boylan, a Catholic priest, ungainly and uncoordinated, who pulled off the finest catch I have ever seen in a match I have been playing in: an extraordinary, diving, wrong-handed catch at gully. And one year it went to Gerry Nowicki, the already-mentioned actor, who was once – only once – asked to open the batting and was out in the second over for 30.

There is greatness in us all. We can't all be champions of the world: but we have all had moments in our lives when we get it absolutely right: mind, body and sprit combining to produce something beyond our normal capacity. Not only in sport, but in all kinds of areas of our normal lives: moments when we become champions of ourselves. We feel the resonance of those rare, never-forgotten moments of triumph – triumph that may be unnoticed by anybody else – when we watch sport; when we read about sport; and I certainly feel it when I write about sport. No, I am not Fred Flintoff, nor was I meant to be. But I have gone where Flintoff goes a thousand times: not in my dreams but in my waking life. And so have we all. That, too, is what sport means. Sport shows us not just what we might have been, but what we are.

104

It seems that every once in a while, we have to find someone to tear apart. Does us good. That is why the England football team has a manager or coach. If you take on the job, you get torn apart. It is the contract. We expect the prime minister to fail, we expect the Queen to fail, we expect the Archbishop of Canterbury to fail. But we expect the England football team to win every match, or by God we'll know the reason why. It stands to reason, then, if reason is the mot juste, that in the inevitable event of failure, someone must be torn apart. Because failure must be somebody's fault. It cannot possibly be because the other side had better players. It must be because someone has betrayed us and must therefore be punished.

And that is the function of the England coach: to be available for punishment, to be there for the tearing-apart, to suffer a ritual death. As the king must die when the crops fail, so the England manager must go when his team fails. No doubt the process satisfies the same atavistic urge: we seek, in football, in life, a repository for blame, the process of blaming to be followed by the glowing promise of the fresh start. It's not supposed to be fair. The king can't make the rains come to order; the England manager can't stop Brazil playing like gods. But in either case, the result is failure and therefore the manager-king must go.

A doctorate-level anthropological thesis on the cult of the England manager would be an illuminating document. Sir Alf Ramsey, World Cup winner, was fired after England failed to qualify in 1974. Don Revie saw trouble coming and, in a crazed panic, ran for safety and dollars in the Middle East. So he was called a traitor anyway. He said afterwards: 'As soon as it dawned on me that we were short of players who combined skill and commitment, I should have forgotten all about trying to play more controlled, attractive football, and settled for a real bastard of a team.' But it still wouldn't have worked. That's because if England win, the manager is still likely to be torn apart because England won the wrong way. That is another, if lesser kind of treachery. And, if England lose while playing the wrong way, God help the manager.

All England managers are traitors, apart from (a) when they are first appointed and (b) when they win the World Cup. In both these cases, they are world-beaters. Sir Bobby Robson took England to the semi-finals of the World Cup in 1990, and he was the subject of headlines like 'in the name of God go' and 'in the name of Allah go'. Graham Taylor is a greatly likeable man of considerable decency; so much so that he had the decency to tear himself apart.

Terry Venables is always regarded, not least by himself, as the smartest England coach of them all – so smart he ran for his life after getting England to the semi-finals of the European Championship with home advantage, ever afterwards posing as a man who would have taken England to the loftiest heights of the game but for foul conspiracy. There are people who actually believe this stuff, and that, surely, is Venables' greatest triumph. He kept one step ahead of the tearer-aparters, rightly understanding that it is better to be known as the man who might have won the World Cup, rather than the man who couldn't get England to the finals of a lesser tournament in their own backyard.

Glenn Hoddle used David Beckham as a shield after going out of the 1998 World Cup finals, which worked pretty well for a while. But as his results in qualifying matches got poorer and poorer, he had the foolishness to talk about his own eccentric made-up religion. Thus he became the first Englishman to be sacked for heresy since Thomas Cramner, though Hoddle was spared the actual burning. He had to go because the nation was ready to tear him apart, and he has considered himself ever after the victim of a foul injustice. But, had he been winning football matches, he would never have been sacked.

Kevin Keegan, another likeable and fair man, also had the decency to do his own tearing apart, resigning in tears with the gloriously honest self-assessment that he wasn't good enough to do the job. Had the nation not been so excited by the idea of the tearing-apart, we might have given him some credit for this.

So then came Sven-Goran Eriksson, a man who mixed serenity of demeanour with an ability to take his trousers off in Olympic time. At the time of his appointment, England football followers were craving consistency, rationality, common sense: Eriksson's long suits. So naturally, he has subsequently suffered minor tearings-apart for the failure of his consistent team to be exceptional: against Brazil in 2002, against France and Portugal in 2004. We wanted the team to be consistent: like Walt Whitman, football followers feel no urge for consistency in themselves.

The early autumn was marked out by a further and more comprehensive tearing-apart of Eriksson. He was menaced and snarled at rather than actually savaged, but it was an unenviable experience. Eriksson brought some rationality to English football, but true rationality, at least on the subject of football, is an impossibility.

England lost a friendly to Denmark 4-1, won a World Cup qualifier against Wales by a subfusc 1-0, and then, hideously, lost 1-0 to Northern Ireland. Eriksson's mind, tactical nous and record were examined. Poor Svennis K! He did not know what he had done wrong. He did not know what rules he had broken. He did not know to whom he might explain himself, or what explanations might be acceptable. He did not know if he was on trial and, if so, who was the judge and who the executioner. Now qualifiers against Austria and Poland lay ahead, if Eriksson were to take England to Germany, where the manager and his team might read Franz Kafka in the original.

105 The prevailing mythology, perpetrated by football and television, is that all attacks on the England manager, and for that matter all information that is not entirely to the credit of football and footballing people, is something to do with the press. Pariahs, parasites, evil people determined to spoil the game. Everyone in football,

everyone in television, and everyone who watches football knows that the press are mere troublemakers.

This leaves out one essential aspect of the business. Who buys the newspapers? We are not forced to buy newspapers, we are not forced to read Sven-Must-Go stories. The essential aspect of the newspaper business is to give the public what they want: if newspapers were so far out of tune with readers' wishes as to produce stories to which the readership were violently opposed, they would rapidly go out of business.

In all sports to some extent, but in football to a major extent, the press is the enemy. This view, this certainty is expressed time and again on television, and is parroted by those who watch football – even while they get their information from newspapers. The notion that the England manager must be torn apart is one that comes from football supporters, or they wouldn't buy the newspapers that lead the assault on the beleaguered manager. The most extreme opinions about England managers are to be found in the most popular newspapers in the country. A rum coincidence, I am sure you will agree. But, as capable as Walt Whitman of contradictory ideas, newspaper readers also feel that the press is vicious, vindictive and unfair. And then buy next day's paper.

Watch how television interviews a footballing person involved in the latest scandal. 'The press have been saying...' A lovely likeable football insider like me wouldn't stoop so low, of course, but here's the microphone: please deny as much as you please in your best clichés. 'Yes, of course I agree, it's not your fault, it's the fault of all those horrid people outside the cosy world we share.' Television is hugely sycophantic to everyone in football, because television wants to keep football on the box and on our channel.

The ultimate example of television sycophancy came after *The Times* told the world that Glenn Hoddle believed that disabled people were paying for sins they had committed in former incarnations. Hoddle appeared on the BBC's *Football Focus*, was warmly invited to make a full denial, and happily did so. 'I feel sorry for the reporter,' he said. 'I never said them things.' Alas, poor Glenda: my colleague Matt Dickinson had a full note in his perfect Tee-line shorthand, and that made Hoddle a liar as well as a heretic. And at the end of the interview, Steve Rider faced the camera with a satisfied smile and said: 'Well, let's hope that's the last we hear of *that*.' Yes, the power of television had got rid of another bit of mischievous nonsense in the press. It was the perfect example of lackey television. There was no hint of the only question that actually mattered: do you actually believe it, Mr Hoddle? But then you see, the object of the exercise was not truth, but the maintenance of the cosy conspiracy between television and football.

So Sven-Goran Eriksson carried on believing that the press were against him, and certainly, the zest of the oppositional questioning would not have disabused him of that notion.

And behind the press, there was a population of discontented football fans in the midst of an angry despair. It was all going badly wrong; England fans really do believe that England ought to win every game they play, but now each time they played, they were filled with a passionate uncertainty. It was like the scene in *The Voyage of the Dawn Treader* from the great Chronicles of Narnia, when the ship can't sail away from dreadful dark island: 'He's steering us wrong. We're going round and round in circles. We shall never get out.'

As always happens when the England team has a run of indifferent results, there was a huge feeling of hurt and betrayal. The press responded to this with undisguised enthusiasm. Me, I thought England had half a chance of winning the World Cup. Was everybody else out of step?

106 So England qualified after all for the World Cup Finals, and Wayne Rooney had a blinder in the final qualifier against Poland, and suddenly England were a great team again. Why, they could win the World Cup. The country was filled with delight, which was quite doubled when England had a streaky 3-2 win against Argentina in a friendly in Switzerland, a suitably neutral venue.

Quite a journey, then: from no-hopers to world-beaters in a couple of weeks. My position remained the same: that England had a chance of winning the World Cup if Rooney was fit and at the top of his game. On the downside, England had blown 1-0 leads against the finest possible opposition – Brazil in 2002, France in 2004. Barring Northern Ireland, England seemed to have mastered consistency against ordinary teams. It was the exceptional – on the rare occasions is needed – that they had consistently failed to find. Thus do teams take their tone from the coach.

But I felt, as the qualifiers ended, that the exceptional was within England's scope, so long as Rooney remained fit. I was, in short, being boringly consistent, and I very much hoped that, come Germany and June, both England and I would be reaching for the exceptional. It would, after all, be so drab and predictable to end up writing Where Sven Went Wrong, as the tearing-apart took place.

107

The profession of sportswriting will occasionally send you a very silly day. That is no doubt because sportswriting is a very silly profession. I had just such a day in mid-autumn: getting up at four at very short notice in order to fly to Basle to cover a tennis tournament. Tim Henman and Andrew Murray were playing for the future of British tennis. It was a very agreeable story. So I got to the stadium about lunch-time, and wrote 1,000 words on the importance of nature reserves for the RSPB's magazine *Birds*, for which I write a column, and for which I had set aside a day. Then I watched the tennis, and Murray won a stirring contest two sets to one. 'I've passed on the torch,' Henman said afterwards. 'Or is it the baton? Well, whatever it is, I'm more than happy for Andy to have it.'

I then wrote the back page and then the inside piece and did the press conference, by which time I was a mite weary. This was a lovely tournament, full of kind people eager to help you. They gave me two cold beers, which I drank before going back to my hotel, determined to swallow a bite of food before passing out. The phone rang just as I was leaving my room for a restaurant. 'Er, I know you've done a lot today.'

'But?'

'George Best is dying.'

Why does everything happen to me?

108

I decided to write two or three paragraphs, have a meal, and then come back and finish. So I switched on the laptop and in 20 minutes I had written perhaps the best 900 words of the year. Why not? I had been researching Best for nearly 40 years. Writing is sometimes a rum business: you find yourself writing stuff that is absolutely heartfelt, and yet you hadn't previously been aware that your heart felt such a thing.

Because as soon as I began to write, I found that I had no wish to ask the immortal question of where it all went wrong – that's a reference to the oldest and the best Best story, should by some extraordinary omission you have failed to hear it, in which Best is in a hotel room with Miss World (sometimes the detail is added of a huge coup in the casino as well, with carrier bags full of fivers festooning the room) and the floor-waiter arrives with champagne (add caviar if you wish) and says: 'Do you mind if I ask you one thing, Mr Best?'

'No, I don't.'

'Tell me – where did it all go wrong?'

Of course it all went wrong, things always all went wrong with Best. But the modern morality tale is common-place. The greater and far more beautiful mystery is where it all went right. And I found myself writing that Best was, indeed, the best, the best I had ever seen. And yet he was a man almost entirely without the quality of Redgrave. He didn't have great longevity, retiring as a Manchester United player at 27. He didn't amass a collection of trophies – one European Cup and two league championships, that was all.

The greatest footballers have the talent to build a team around themselves and somehow infect the players around them with their own vision, their own skill, their own belief: Pele, Franz Beckenbauer, Diego Maradona. Best had none of that. He was never given any sort of responsibility, and it wouldn't have suited him anyway. But when it came to playing football, beating a man, scoring a goal, he was the best, the bravest and the most beautiful and he made a lasting impression on me and on everyone else who saw him play. Perhaps it's Best's fault that I came into sports journalism, and learned to value so highly attributes that Best never possessed: the attributes of Redgrave and Sampras.

In admiring Best, I contradict myself once again. But there are more ways than one of enjoying sport, and beauty is as important as partisanship and the search for greatness. You can always upset a footballing person, player, coach, chairman, supporter, by saying that his team may be effective, but it is insufficiently beautiful – it doesn't play 'the right way'. Sport not only constructs myths and creates archetypes. It also creates, mostly as a by-product of the striving for victory, a majestic and impromptu beauty. Like the great stories and the great heroes, beauty also catches our imagination.

So no, Best did not create an oeuvre. He left no lasting substantial masterpiece, like *Ulysses* or five Olympic gold medals or a World Cup. Rather, he left a series of minor pieces, perfect, unforgettable, and, in their delicacy, perhaps more meaningful than the thumping Wagnerian triumphs of the great champions.

Best was the greatest of all the illusionists: greater even than Federer. Like Federer, he made his opponents look as if they were co-operating with him, the great illusion of complicity. But Best's opponents were not just trying to beat him: they were also trying to kick him, in the great clogging free-for-all of 60s football. Best played at a time when defensive football was a form of assault, and yet he seemed to turn battle into a dance of joy. I have said, again and again, that it is the hero and the tale that enthral me. But beauty is also enthralling, and it is to be found time and again in sport: a by-product, to be sure, an incidental thing.

With Best, you could watch a match and be struck forever by a moment of beauty, regardless of the fact that Best's team lost. This is a truth that subverts much of what I have written here, and much of sport itself. It must nevertheless be faced. Golfers, as we know, say the same thing: of course it's a horribly difficult and frustrating game but it's all worthwhile for that one moment of sweet connexion when the ball takes wing and flies straight and high and true. I have mentioned some all-worthwhile moments from my own less-than-all-conquering sporting life.

Not all athletes feel that: or perhaps I mean admit that. Peter Shilton told me he had no idea what his best save was: he remembered only the great matches in which his team had won. William Fox-Pitt, after a brilliant cross-country round at Badminton, was asked in the press conference (by a ten-year-old girl) which fence he had enjoyed jumping most, and he answered 'the last'.

But some great competitors do, indeed, value the small moment of perfection as well as the greater, more mercenary, notion of mere victory. Bob Taylor will tell you exactly which was his favourite wicket-keeping dismissal (catching Mike Smith of Middlesex off an inside edge down the legside); Ian Stark, riding in the three-day event at the Olympic Games in Barcelona, on a disappointing day for his team, nevertheless described jumping one particularly fearsome obstacle: 'There's nothing better in the world. Except maybe sex.' The crucial word in this sentence is 'maybe'. And I suspect that Best – who used to get sexually aroused before matches – would have agreed. It is a quixotic thing, a cavalier thing, the idea that the struggle, and even the defeat, is made worthwhile by one moment of perfection. But the Cavalier and the Roundhead live side by side not just in sport, but in the hearts and minds of those who watch it. We are contradictory creatures, and we understand the world (and sport) by means of antitheses. Contradiction is life. Best's career was a disappointment, Best's talent was unfulfilled: Best was the best, Best was perfect. Leaving us unsatisfied.

109

Carl Lewis said that there would never be drugs-free sport until we had a drugs-free society. There are many drugs in sport, but George Best died from sport's drug of choice. In Western culture, sport and booze are inseparable: the one an enabler of the other. Whether you play sport, or you watch sport, alcohol is almost always there, and in some areas, its consumption is considered more or less de rigueur. And very agreeable it is too, it must be said.

I remember sitting at a table with a couple of colleagues during the World Cup of 1994 (the one in the United States) and I was asked, in deference to the supposed excesses of my hippy past, to name the most dangerous drug I had ever consumed. I raised my glass: 'Gentlemen, we are consuming it.' This led, I am sorry to say, to the most terrible row, after which, inevitably, we pissed and made up.

People don't accept that alcohol is a drug or that it is dangerous, despite all the evidence you could wish for in support of this notion. And sport is constructed and organised in order to facilitate the consumption of this drug: beer at football, Pimm's at Wimbledon, champagne at the races. Sport's oldest motto: win or lose, on the booze. You drink for celebration you drink for consolation: a wonderfully versatile sort of drug, the drug for all seasons, the drug for all sorts and conditions of men and women. I have drunk beer in the Lamma Island Bar after playing football, I have been to the Plume of Feathers after Tewin Irregulars had contrived another defeat from a position of overwhelming supremacy and, after cross-country rounds of unforgettable ferocity, I have shared beers with my horse.

Booze and sport is a wonderful combination, and like everything to do with booze, it regularly drags its victims to disaster and despair: the victims being not only the drinkers but those around them – wives, children, colleagues, friends, pedestrians, motorists.

Best was a man who had his being in excess. He was excessively talented at his sport, and expressed this excess in a manner that no other played has rivalled. He was also a man of heroic, ludicrous excess with women and with drink. Football, sex, booze: the lads' great trilogy of passions, or vices. No one has mastered any single one of them to the extent that Best did: to pull off the treble was extraordinary. And it destroyed him, and it was the booze that was the chief destroyer. Booze will destroy anyone it can, the worst of us and the best.

And sport, since it works hand in hand with booze, is also a destroyer, or at least, the destroyer's accomplice. Alcohol is a glorious thing, something that we enjoy for the greater glory of life. In the Catholic Church, wine is more than a symbol of life: it is life.

Sport does not exist for alcohol, nor alcohol for sport: but the two are blood brothers. And alcohol, like riding horses fast, is glorious and dangerous and addictive and I wouldn't wish to live without either.

110
Towards the end of the year, I went to Zambia. Not for sport, not for wildlife, but to write about wind-up radios. This was for Freeplay Foundation, one of the Christmas charities adopted by *The Times*. I went to places deep in the bush: villages in which the school building was a tree, the only teaching aid a blackboard the colour of dirty milk, the pupils shoeless, the few exercise books as tattered and treasured as Shakespeare first folios, and the teacher untrained and unpaid but fed, clothed and cherished by the community. And from the radio, in a land where batteries are never seen and cash is a rarity, issued the broadcasts, which gave the schoolday its structure and the community its hope.

Hope is always in the next generation, which is the only old-age pension in the Third World. In a community of subsistence farmers, hope lies also in the belief that perhaps one or two or even some of the children will be educated enough to find a job and bring cash into the system, and the cycle of poverty will be broken.

I visited one village that was building its own school. They had moulded bricks from mud, 4,000 of them, and then built a kiln and baked them for four days, and then dried them for six weeks. The day I arrived, they had just begun to dig the foundations; the chairman of the school's board of governors was up to his waist in a trench in the noon sun. We in the rich countries imagine that Africa is a beggar moping on the side of the road with its hand held out: in this village, there were people building a school off their own bat, as a break from tending their fields.

I found myself addressing a village meeting, talking with parents and teachers and children and committee men and powerful women and everywhere finding the most extraordinary and enlivening feeling of hope. It was an unforgettable trip, and I wrote about it with enthusiasm and love when I got back.

The trip didn't make me feel that sport was trivial, or even that sportswriting was trivial. Certainly, I wished I could write about Africa every day, and that every day it would change the lives of thousands and bring to life the hope of Africans, but alas, that is beyond the power of my laptop, and perhaps of anyone else's. We suffer readily from compassion-fatigue, but rarely, it seems from sports-fatigue. But this was one occasion in which the stuff I wrote did more than entertain. At the thrilling and mind-boggling heart of the matter was the fact that what I wrote was actually able to do something. To bring something about. *The Times* raised £170,000 for Freeplay: it was good, more than good, to be a part of that.

111
The great David Attenborough, when miles above the earth in a balloon, or on the polar ice-cap, or deep in a cave in Borneo, would say, in those always imitated but ultimately inimitable tones: 'And – even here – there is life.'

Where there is true poverty there is no rubbish. Everything is valuable. And in village after village, I saw an example of one of the great masterpieces of African recycling, a thing made with 100 plastic bags and a fair amount of string. It was one of the treasures of the village. A football, what else? – for the playing of barefoot football. In any form of life beyond desperation, you find sport. Sport, it seems, is the first luxury of human life. At village after village, I wanted to turn to camera and say: 'And – even here – there is sport.'

112

A horse died: and divided the nation. Best Mate, three times winner of the Cheltenham Gold Cup, dropped dead from a heart attack on the racecourse in the early stages of preparing for a dart at a fourth. Many people were saddened by this: a great racehorse, a horse with more than a touch of Redgrave, dying in a distressingly public way. Others thought it was ridiculous to make a fuss about such an occurrence: it was only a horse. Still others preferred to be angry, blaming the racing industry for its cruelty and callousness.

There is no statute of limitation on love, and therefore no statute of limitation on grief. Rather, there is a hierarchy. It is sentimental to think that your dog understands every word you say and will go woofing up to doggy-heaven to play with the angel-bunnies when he dies, but it is not sentimental to love your dog and to be sad when he dies. I do not think my dog is human, but I will grieve when she is gone, for she is a companion who greets me with uncritical affection, and with whom I share many good times.

The Times carried a dead-horse cartoon the day after Best Mate's death, making some political point or other. A political cartoonist like Peter Brookes takes plenty of risks, uses dodgy materials whenever possible, and dares to go close to the edge. This one was a mite too close for many: certainly, it set the phones ringing in Wapping. It was only a horse, but people had strong feelings about it.

I took a few risks myself with the piece I wrote, though of the opposite kind. I tried to write about the right to grieve for any champion, even an equine one, and to celebrate the life of a horse that, as serial champions do, acquired a million owners, a million people who revelled in the horse's life and so were fully entitled to grieve at the horse's death. I risked being seen not as a heartless bastard but – perhaps worse, at least for a writer – as a sentimental old fool.

There are always plenty who are ready to call horse-people cruel. Some years ago, a bunch of heroes chained themselves to a fence at Badminton in protest at the event's cruelty to the horses. But a Badminton horse has a great life: the best food, plenty of company, every need catered for, stirring, complex forms of exercise and occasional thrilling adventures. If you want to protest about cruelty to animals, then chain yourself to the fried-chicken stand. Performance horses are not required to go through the debeaking machine in order to avoid cannibalistic practices, after all.

I spent two or three years working almost exclusively in horsey journalism, and I enjoyed it very much, especially when I was able to grab a chance ride. I got to ride champion endurance horses; I performed passage and piaffe on a grand prix dressage horse; I led Jeremy Noseda's string out across Newmarket Heath; I rode polo ponies; I rode cutting horses and Western reining horses; I rode Ian Balding's hack, the not inaptly named Quirk, out across Watership Down – 'He usually bucks when the string goes past'. (He did, though not catastrophically.)

The affinity between horse and human is one of the most extraordinary aspects of modern life. The horse is a genius of evolution: by going so wholeheartedly for the strategy of domestication, the horse has survived and prospered where most wild equids are endangered or extinct. (I am obviously not, should this need saying, talking about conscious choice here.)

But this affinity between horses and humans is – as is so often the case – expressed most vividly in sport: in this case, in our human striving to prove that our horse is better, faster, braver, that our relationship with our horse is tighter, stronger and more meaningful. Horse sports do not work by means of cruelty and subjection: they work by co-operation. That is true whether you are Sheikh Mohammed, Aidan O'Brien, Leslie Law, Bettina Hoy, or me.

This is not to sentimentalise all horse-people as universally kind and gentle: far from it. That would be the same as saying that all husbands and all wives are kind and gentle. But in both cases, the relationship works better with co-operation and understanding. I recall a visit to Ballydoyle to meet Aidan O'Brien, the great racehorse trainer, a man whose shyness is almost physically painful to watch. For some reason he insisted on being put through an interview, which he enjoyed every bit as much as I enjoyed root canal treatment. But then he took me for a tour of the property and a meeting with a few horses, including the great Istabraq, three times winner of the Champion Hurdle. To see him with that flawed, edgy, nervous, brilliant animal was to see a man whose genius is in understanding, in softness, in knowing his horse's capabilities. And side by side in a Land Rover, freed from the burden of eye contact, we talked the usual sort of horsey drivel, and I told him about Western horses, and how I had been taught to ride the classic cowboy crash-halt, in which the horse sits down like a dog – and had then done it while riding a horse that had no bridle. 'How would he be doing that?' So we talked the eternal horsey talk of training, which is nothing more than seeking an understanding of this strange species, a species which is at the same time half comprehensible and utterly remote.

I have five horses at home, and one of them at least is totally useless. She was my old competition mare, with whom I have shared moments of almost ludicrous excitement and joy, a horse that would jump over a house if you put one in the way: she never once stopped when I pointed her at a jump, anyway. She has borne me two foals, one of which I still have – that's the one I dismounted from so incontinently during the Ashes series – but she herself can no longer be ridden. She suffered an accident in the field, and has been eating and flirting outrageously with her field companion ever since. When she got the injury, I did a deal with her: so long as she still gets a kick out of life, she gets a kick out of life. I have kept to that for nine years, and I am still in her debt.

And if you think that makes me sentimental, you are entitled to your opinion. I don't treat her as a human, and I don't give her cake for tea every day. She will die, and I will deal with it well enough, though not without grief. It's all part of the business of loving: that is to say, part of the business of being alive. If nothing can make you sad, then you are not really alive.

113

But I still haven't mentioned my charging lion. I met him in Zambia in the process of looking for a palmnut vulture. We – damn it, the story is unexceptional enough, and you can find it, should you wish, in my novel *Rogue Lion Safaris*, told without embellishment, indeed, if anything, toned down, in chapter four. I love to go bird-watching on foot in the Luangwa Valley, preferably with my old friend Bob Stjernstedt, the *Guardian Weekly* man. Once, looking for Angola pitta together, we wandered into the middle of a herd of elephant. We have been charged by elephant, menaced by hippo, have waded in crocodile-infested rivers and driven through bandit country, all in pursuit of birds. We once nearly got ourselves killed by a train in Wales; saw some great birds once we had survived.

Was it all for the birds themselves? Or for the crazy joys of walking through the bush?

I am not foolhardy, not an adrenaline junkie. But the Angola pitta and the palmnut vulture are two of the great birds of my life... and I never even saw the pitta.

114

The year ended. The subs' party was held. Tim Hallissey and I met to discuss the following year: what else should I do, apart from the World Cup? Two intercontinental jaunts for the cricket, certainly. And, as the World Cup was discussed, I felt that familiar sense of mild terror: the fans, the travel, the deadlines and, above all, the fact that when England played, I would be read. Perhaps as never before. And then we discussed the year just past. The quiet year, the odd-numbered year. In which Liverpool won the European Cup in Istanbul, London was awarded the Olympic Games and England won the Ashes. Three of the biggest and best stories I have had the privilege of telling. Was this the kind of quietness I required for the next twelve months? Or something with a bit less predictability?

115

There is a story about the footballer who went to the theatre, and went to see – well, let's say it was Ben Travers's *Thark*. And somebody asked him: 'Was it a farce?' and he answered: 'No – it was quite good, actually.'

I wish I could believe the story, but no matter. The fact is that in all sports, but in football especially, we are only ever a finger's breadth from farce. True farce, I mean, of the kind defined in *The Cambridge Guide to Literature in English* as 'A type of broad comedy in which extreme crisis for the characters is amusing for the audience.' It is amusing because the conventions of naturalism have been abandoned, and the characters themselves and the events that happen to them are beyond serious credence.

We can go along with sport for an awfully long way, and weep real tears of emotion when England, say, win the Ashes, or when David Beckham's penalty hits the net against Argentina. But the willingness to take sport at its own valuation – the willingness to suspend our disbelief – is a very delicate thing, and its balance can be disturbed in an instant, sending us tumbling from epic into farce.

At least Sven-Goran Eriksson kept his trousers on for this outbreak of farce, but he lost quite a lot of other things. He was trapped by the *News of the World*'s infamous fake sheik, who promised to buy an English Premiership club and put Eriksson in charge. Eriksson, inevitably flattered, spoke of his willingness to leave his job as England coach before his contract ended, and as a bonus, said a few indiscreet things about some members of the England team. It was not the biggest deal of all time, then, but it had a lot of people very excited, calling Eriksson a traitor and demanding his immediate removal.

In truth, the whole business was nothing more than a practical joke. It revealed the fact that Eriksson is gullible, and ambitious and is keen on money. All these things we knew already, but their restatement, in the exotic context of the fake sheik, caused a certain stir: and all of it totally spurious. At the same time, the Luton Town manager, Mike Newell, declared roundly that the game was corrupt and said that he had been offered bribes. My colleague at *The Times*, Matt Dickinson, wrote that it was a pity that the resources of a great newspaper had been employed to bring us the non-revelations about Eriksson, rather than a serious investigation of the bung culture.

But the *News of the World*, rather than begin a moral crusade, preferred to feed the nation's apparently insatiable taste for farce. The following week, they gave us a second ration of Eriksson's remarks to the fake sheikh, and these contained a candid – and casual – acceptance of the fact that many people in football are corrupt. A couple of days later, it was announced that Eriksson had to go at the end of the World Cup.

Eriksson had embarrassed his employers too many times with his willingness to consider other employment. But the biggest embarrassment of all is the certainty that a culture of illicit payments runs right through football, and that there is a total unwillingness to do anything about it. The Football Association is not even willing to accept that corrupt practices exist, which is the only possible starting point for making things better. The Jockey Club showed this truth to the sporting world when it attempted to seize some kind of control of the racing industry.

Eriksson had to go, as all England managers have to go. Eriksson's crime was – well, there wasn't any crime, really.

Only a punishment. But Eriksson is Swedish, and that fact can certainly be levelled against him. It is for this reason that many people have wanted to get rid of Eriksson right from the start, regardless of his results. Eriksson, in the end, made it easy for them. Me, I wondered if the certainty that he was leaving at the end of the World Cup would add a joyous sense of abandon to his last campaign as England coach: whether a certain demob-happiness, the fact that he had already said 'thank you and good-bye', would be the missing ingredient that his tournament campaigns had so far lacked.

David McGilivray, in his series of plays about Farndale Avenue Women's Institute, wrote a parody of a French farce. The set comprises nothing but doors. It is called *Chase Me Down Farndale Avenue, S'il Vous Plait*. Come on, then, Sven. Chase me round Soho Square, s'il vous plait.

116 So the fake sheik won. He got rid of Sven all right.

It was agreed that Sven Goran Eriksson would stay in place for the World Cup finals that lay a few months ahead, but that he would go straight afterwards, rather than seeing out the remaining two years of his contract. A comparatively modest pay-off was agreed. All parties seemed relieved.

I have already written in these pages about the English need to tear apart an England head coach or manager every now and then: he must be punished for disappointments that are not necessarily his fault. But this dismissal of Eriksson set a precedent. He was dismissed without any disappointments to be punished for – certainly not in qualification. In fact, he had just succeeded in getting England through the most recent qualification tournament with a match to spare: an unheard-of luxury. Why, then, was everybody so keen to get rid of him?

Certainly, it is a fact that Eriksson had enemies as soon as he took office. He is not English. He was making a lot of money. Many English people resented those two things. They wanted a man with an emotional rather than a written contract. Eriksson played his hand poorly, in public relations terms, with his public flirtations with Manchester United and Chelsea and then the business of the fake sheik. But the fact is that England qualified and qualified well: so why the need to punish him between qualification and the tournament proper?

It is like being a member of the royal family. No one can come out well from the kind of tabloid scrutiny that Sven had brought on himself. In *Manhattan*, Woody Allen's character, whose ex-wife is writing an account of their marriage, says: 'Not that I have anything to hide, because, you know… but there are a few disgusting little moments that I regret.' So it is with us all. For years I thought that the only possible defence was to keep on winning football matches: but even that extreme step was not enough to keep Eriksson safe. An England coach has but one function: his own destruction.

Most columnists on the sports pages of English newspaper have more or less consistently taken a Sven-must-go line from the first moment that this was tenable. To write such stuff certainly makes you look tough, hard-minded and controversial. The truth, in fact, is the exact opposite. From an actuarial point of view, it is more likely that an England team will lose a major tournament than that they will win one. The odds, then, are most emphatically with the snipers and the sneerers and the begrudgers. To come up with harsh criticism of the England manager makes you look as if you are sticking your neck on the block, when you are actually making the safest of safe bets. You are backing a near-certainty. England has not won a major tournament for 40 years. And so the columnist works up the atavistic notion that England have the right to win every match and every tournament they enter. It is a view, deep-seated and ineradicable, that makes England-head-coach-knocking the perfect, for-all-seasons, percentage ploy.

And so, in January, Eriksson was dismissed at a rather silly press conference at the headquarters of the Football Association: and the fact remained that he might yet have a very good World Cup. It was even possible – low-double-figure odds – that England could win the damn thing, as I had been so foolishly suggesting since the European championships. The most intriguing thing about the whole business is that winning football matches was the last thing anybody was worried about. The newspaper, the newspaper's readers and the FA were all intoxicated by power: the fact that together, they had the power to get rid of an England football manager. Perhaps that, rather than religious outrage, was the reason for Hoddle's departure after all. Scent, pursuit and capture. From a drag to a chase, from a chase to a view, from a view to a death in the morning.

Something that lies very deep in national life was profoundly satisfied by the whole process of the hunting of the Sven. And can you believe it, no sooner had it happened than there were people falling over themselves to fill the vacancy. Sam Allardyce, Guus Hiddink, Martin O'Neill: well, never mind. Whoever it is, we'll get you. The hounds will soon pick up your scent. Kill the coach: it is the greatest sport of them all, is it not?

117

At one stage I was all set to go to the Winter Olympics in Turin, and then at a later stage I wasn't. I was in some ways disappointed: I have never covered a winter Games. In other ways I was relieved: I don't care for the cold. If they could hold the Winter Olympics in Belize, say, or Zambia…

So I watched the Games from Suffolk, and found the experience very agreeable. I found the action consistently dizzying, even the curling. This was because I went down with labyrinthitis, an affliction of the balancing mechanism of the inner ear. It leaves you for some weeks seasick on dry land. I was effectively grounded. As a result, I was able to enjoy the splendid biodiversity of the cold weather sports: all these games that matter so much to the participants, and which we Brits don't watch from one quadrennium to the next.

My pleasure in the Winter Games made me more irritated than usual with the ever-more-popular notion that only football matters. It has reached the point when to admit to a liking for any sport other than football is a confession that you are homosexual, and worse, way behind the times. Only football is cool.

Sport has become a monoculture: a thing that I know a lot about, as I live in an area full of arable farming. Though the countryside is changing for the better, there are still many open windy acres around me, places where the hedges have been grubbed out, the trees felled, and all that remains is a horizon-to-horizon prairie of winter-sown wheat. There is more biodiversity in your house than on those fields. Diversity is what gives life its resilience, and, if you like, its meaning. The process of life works by creating more and more different species. Specification is the basic mechanism of life, nothing less.

Monoculture is anti-life. That is because it is so vulnerable to disaster. It was monoculture that created the potato famine in Ireland in the nineteenthth century: all those acres of spuds, all the same variety: there was no slack in the system. Once disease struck the crop, it all went.

Life does best in teeming chaos, in contradiction, in multiplicity and multifariousness. And we humans, being mammals ourselves, respond to that. Certainly I do. My delighted anticipation of the Chelsea v Barcelona match that lay ahead was in no way compromised by my enjoyment of the men's and the women's downhill, or the barmy contortions of the snowboarders, or the esoteric slithering of the curling and, perhaps best, the flight of the birdy-boned birdmen of the ski-jumping hills.

Why cut yourself off from pleasure on a point of principle? Why limit yourself? The inability or unwillingness to enjoy art is called philistinism. The term is always used abusively. I could – though I don't – describe those who don't care for *Ulysses* as philistines, or those who find their musical tastes met by Classic FM.

But certainly, I describe those non-AS Byatt intellectuals who don't care for sport as philistines. It is closing your eyes to pleasure and meaning and instruction. Sport's own prevailing culture of football-or-nothing is another form of philistinism. Both forms are simply a way of making slightly less of your life. CLR James said it in his most famous line: 'What do they know of cricket who only cricket know?' The same is true of football, or for that matter, of sport: or of any other specialised approach to life. What do they know of *Ulysses*, who only *Ulysses* know?

118
For that matter, what do they know of sport, who only *Ulysses* know? Quite a bit, actually, because *Ulysses* is in fact a sports book. The central event is the Ascot Gold Cup, won by the dark horse Throwaway. Of almost equal importance is the boxing match between Myler Keogh (Dublin's pet lamb) and Sergeantmajor Percy Bennett, the Portobello bruiser. There is also mention of a significant bowls match, meditations on Gaelic sports, especially the putting of the sixteen-pound shot, discussion of the virtues of tennis, cycling races and even some thoughts about

cricket. (*Finnegans Wake* goes better here, and has two pages devoted to cricket.) There are sections on motor-racing, swimming, shooting and gymnastics. In *Ulysses*, much thought is given to the exercises of the primordial strong man, Eugene Sandow – sport, or at least vigorous physical exercise, as a vision of the idealised self, the ultimately *improved* self – the custom of exercise being, of course, more honoured in the breach than the observance.

There is more than sport in *Ulysses*, just as there is more than sport in sport. *Ulysses* is encyclopaedic: a book about absolutely everything. Sport is an unending tale, an ever-flowing river of stories, and sport too, is encyclopaedic: about absolutely everything. It is foolish to limit sport as it is to limit yourself.

119

All things are about sport. Or perhaps sport is about all things. That is the way with all metaphors. And so, reading Christopher Ricks and his manic evisceration of the lyrics of Bob Dylan, I find myself coming back to sport again. As usual. 'Like the great athlete, the great artist is both highly trained and deeply instinctual,' Ricks writes. Which is why most athletes and most artists are deeply reluctant to talk about the process of doing what they do. A footballer says that he 'takes each match as it comes'; Ian Botham would only describe his outbursts of brilliance with the phrase 'it sort of clicks'; Dylan said he was 'just a song and dance man'. If you look at your own talent too searchingly, it might cease to be what it is. If you bring these highly trained but deeply instinctual matters to the level of conscious thought, the magic stuff might never happen again.

Dylan, quoted by Ricks, says: 'As you get older, you get smarter and that can hinder you because you try to gain control over the creative impulse. Creativity is not like a freight train going down the tracks. It's something that has to be caressed and treated with a great deal of respect. If your mind is intellectually in the way, it will stop you. You've got to programme your brain not to think too much.'

Pete Sampras knew that. And much of our enjoyment of sport and everything else – say, the songs of Bob Dylan – is at an unthinking, instinctual level. We can thrill to the entwinement of Louise and her lover without a line-by-line analysis of such questions as who is Louise, whether her lover is Dylan or someone else quite different, and whether Johanna is real or imagined. In the same way, we thrill to a great piece of sport without needing to know its meaning.

But there is a meaning all the same: to sport, to 'Visions of Johanna'. Or rather, many meanings, for meaning, in all great matters, is obscure, shifting, Protean, never more clearly missed than when most confidently seized. In a sense, sport means everything, because it is a giant, ever-changing, all-purpose metaphor. All human learning depends on a perception of similarity and dissimilarity, and that is why the greatest of all talents is to be a master of metaphor: this, again, is Ricks, who is quoting Aristotle. Everything is found in sport: everything is also found in the work of the encyclopaedic writers – Shakespeare, Dante, Homer, Joyce. And perhaps one might make a case for including the shape-shifter and name-changer from Hibbing, Minnesota: pop music's only genius.

120

I enjoyed the skiing, the Nordic skiing, the ski-jumping, the snowboarding, the skating, the tobogganing. I watched, and wondered about sport. The Winter Games are all about sliding. How many different ways of sliding can you think of? They have already come up with far more than you could have imagined. I have written earlier about the search for flight: well, the Winter Games give the illusion of the breaking of the laws of gravity by means of their conquest of the laws of friction. Or, for any proper physicists who may be reading, the apparent conquest. I can skate, just about, and it's fun: take one step, and it goes on forever. Take another: that one takes you still further. Speed up, and you are faster that you could run. You've got something for nothing, and it's a fine feeling. It's the feeling of flight: skate around a frozen lake, and you are a gull, riding the updraughts and eddies of the cliff-face.

It all takes you back to the child and the icy puddle. It just has to be slid. 'You run ten yards, stop running, and you travel ten yards further all the same. It's magic. It's irresistible, and you have to do it again. Sliding: great fun if you're a kid. But a grown-up is normally a little reticent about running up to an icy puddle and going 'wheee!'

This thought led me to the going-whee theory of sport. Do all sports have as their origin something that's fun to do when you are a child? Throwing a stone, hitting a stone with a stick, kicking anything that doesn't make your foot hurt. They are things that you do, that a child does, for their own sake. So then the child says: I slid ten yards. And the other says, well, I can slide eleven. All right then. Show me.

What is the Lowest Common Denominator – or do I mean Highest Common Factor? – of sport? Is it competition? Or does it all begin with the delight in the actual doing: the throwing, the hitting, the sliding? Is competition really an excuse to get back to the doing? Or is it something that adds to the doing? Certainly there are many sporty activities that people do without competing: walking, running, swimming, skiing, riding horses. There is a competitive structure available for those who wish for it, but for many, the doing is all.

I rode because I loved, and still love to ride, but I also loved to compete. Competition was a bonus, a secondary thing. There is a snobbery among horse-people: if you don't compete, you are something of a lesser being. A 'happy hacker': someone who is not fully serious about horses, who doesn't really understand what horses are for. All the same, happy hackers represent the majority: people who love the doing, and don't wish to be the best at doing.

You might think that football can only ever be competitive: but kicking a ball is one of life's small pleasures, and children everywhere play elaborate uncompetitive football games, kickabout, against the wall, three goals and in. The sport of lions is competitive all right, but there is never an outright winner. The game is seamless, never-ending, and every one wins, like the caucus race in *Alice*. A formal competitive structure is an add-on to the natural pleasure we take in the doing, and to the secondary pleasure we take in the outdoing. But it is the formal structure that creates the tales and their heroes. Sports starts by going whee: it ends up as myth.

121

Graham Gooch was never regarded as a verbal genius in his time as England cricket captain, but he faced life with a certain honesty, and could express it uncompromisingly. I bumped into him on a flight to Edinburgh earlier that same year for the England-Scotland rugby match – he was almost unrecognisable without his moustache – and we talked briefly about rugby and cricket and so forth, and then moved on. And later that day, I remembered Gooch saying to me: 'Losing is part of your life as a sportsman.'

Coping with defeat has to become part of your routine. If it is not, then you will find yourself unable to deal with it when it comes: as Arsenal did when their long unbeaten run ended with the battle of the buffet. An ability to absorb defeat and then to come back, if not stronger then at least not too greatly diminished, is part of the stock-in-trade of all professional athletes. Everybody loses: it is the way you deal with defeat that separates the good from the great.

Chelsea lost to Barcelona in the Champions League and

Jose Mourinho was quite unable to cope with it. Mourinho had become the new Clough: the same arrogance, the same self-conscious air of brilliance, the same air of being about three steps ahead of everyone else, the same way of both protecting and dominating his own players, the same love of being centre-stage, the players mere extensions of his will. Clough called himself 'Old Bighead'; Mourinho, with rather less irony, called himself 'a special one'.

The changing of the order of English football, fuelled by the money of the owner, Roman Abramovich, was vastly intriguing. Harold Wilson wanted Labour to become 'the natural party of government'. As Chelsea established themselves as the natural league champions of England, I watched with fascination. Mourinho converted millions of roubles into a match-winning machine. It was deeply impressive.

But naturally, he wanted more. These days, it is by European Cups that you measure greatness in English football. And in recent years, one manager after another has battered himself into a decline in pursuit of this trophy. Even those who have won it are only briefly satisfied: for within a few months, the mania and the quest must begin again. The grail brings immortality: and then takes it away again. The European Cup was once a glorious bonus; now it has become a necessity. And more often than not, it is the most colossal disappointment: the ultimate proving ground in which the English champions so often fail to be proven. All of which had made Liverpool's victory so astonishing the previous year.

And once again, Mourinho's season was crushed under

the wheels of the great juggernaut of the European Cup. The previous season, Liverpool had beaten Chelsea in that competition, thanks to a goal Mourinho disputes to this day. In that season he set up the most bitter feud with Barcelona. And so, inevitably, Chelsea were drawn with Barcelona the following year. The crucial incident was a sending-off in the first leg at Stamford Bridge. I was there, unable to see the incident, of course, because it took place in the blind-spot from the press box. But the television was uncompromising. Lionel Messi was ludicrously fouled by Asier del Horno, and del Horno had to go. Mourinho gave a histrionic press conference in which he accused Messi of acting, of cheating. Some observers read this as the usual clever gamesmanship from Mourinho; to me it looked like derangement, a total inability to believe certain unacceptable truths.

This incident was followed by a spat with Bryan Robson, manager of West Bromwich Albion. Mourinho brought his players out late for the second half, a naked piece of gamesmanship, and Robson expressed his irritation. So we had a Mourinho I'm-smarter-than-you smirk and then the now-traditional refusal to shake hands: and you know, I was beginning to find it all rather tiresome and so, I suspect was everybody else.

Too many spats, too many feuds, too many accusations of conspiracy, too many opponents cheating; too few apologies, too few admissions of Chelsea's own failings; too much theatricality, not enough substance. I was reminded, and wrote at the time, about the scene in *Sunday Bloody Sunday* when a woman arrives at a social gathering late and drunk, picks a fight, throws a scene and starts taking her clothes off. And a fellow-guest sighs: 'Not those tired old tits again.'

What was once thrilling, attractive, audacious and dangerous had become the most frightful bore. That's the danger with playing the lead character in sport: people get to see far too much of you. Put your frock back on and put them away, Jose: we've all seen them before. If you try and do your stuff entirely by force of character, it is best not to be too predictable. Brian Clough knew that, but then he was better at it.

122

There are countries, cultures, civilisations with which you instantly feel a rapport, others that are forever alien. It is not a matter of how close the civilisation is to your own. The English have always found France alien territory – a view expressed either by quiet hostility or by overloud admiration – despite or because of the millennia of shared history. The English have far less in common with Italy, but, for all the great differences of emphasis and temperament and history, the English are in general much more comfortable there. I have already mentioned in these pages the deep sense of belonging I had in Japan. Not everyone shares that, of course. It is a matter of who you are. I knew an Australian couple who lived there for a couple of years: she loved the sense of order and appositeness; he would stand on a train platform *willing* the train to be late. In the

United States, I find Los Angeles deeply alien, but find a great answering spark in New York, even when unable to find a publisher willing to talk about me.

The British – or do I mean the English? You must decide that one for yourself – have always felt a huge affinity with India. I suspect that this is only partly because of the shared history, the imposition of British culture on India, the infiltration of Indian culture into the British mind. I believe that these things happened because there is some kind of complementary mind. Like a good married couple, each civilisation finds some completion in the other.

And this is most finely expressed in the game of cricket. The book *The Tao of Cricket*, by Ashis Nandy, famously begins: 'Cricket is an Indian game accidentally discovered by the English'. Certainly there is something about cricket that is gloriously suited to the Indian mind; but then unquestionably, cricket is also immensely suited to the English mind. Each approaches the game in a different way: if England and America are divided by a common language, then England and the entire subcontinent are divided by a common game.

And so I travelled out to India for two Test matches. India has always been a deep and important place for me. From the first moment I arrived, to have an adventure in my early 20s, I felt both thrilled by the exoticism and deeply at home. I responded not just to the Englishness of India, but to the Indianness of England. And astonishingly, sport expresses both the cultural division and the cultural union.

It is strange, then, that most England cricket tours of

India are dominated by a sense of hardship: a feeling that the entire country, the weather, the food, the beggars, the taxi-drivers and the sacred cows that roam the streets are all against them. I remember, years ago, checking in at Heathrow just in front of a touring club cricket side: they were all making loud jokes about their bowels. It is perhaps an example of the English genius: to turn one of the world's most ancient and profound cultures into a lavatory joke. Me, I have never suffered any digestive malaise in India, in five visits. Something to do with being a vegetarian: a cultural advance I made towards the country on my first visit. English visitors fill themselves with jabs and malaria prophylactics and never drink the tap-water and won't touch a salad or an ice-cube, but they carry on eating meat, the hardest food to cook hygienically. Meat has a symbolic and cultural meaning, as well as a nutritional one. But I am supposed to be writing about sport...

The point, then, is that making friends with your environment is one of the great skills of the performer. Sports psychologists are always encouraging their clients to get the stadium on their side. Many tours of India have been conducted by groups of young men all making a deliberate enemy of the environment in which they find themselves. Don't go out: stay in the hotel and eat steak. I remember arriving uncommonly early at an event, and watching a sixteen-year-old gymnast coming into the hall two hours before the scheduled start. After some suppling exercises and some careful, graceful tumbles, she settled herself down for a good half-hour sit. She was getting the hall on her side. She was, then, a great deal more grownup than many international cricket sides that visit India.

In the days when cricketers were allowed to pick and choose their tours, India was always the one the English teams took off. But hardship is a double-edged thing – like most things. It can destroy; it can inspire. It all depends, as I say, on the kind of person you are.

123

Frank Keating writes the sports column in *The Spectator*. He was the first to write the column; I was the second. I took over because the *Guardian* asked Frank to stop; later, *The Times* asked me to stop, both deciding that the magazine was direct competition. In retirement, Frank is now writing *The Spectator* sports column again, and in a post-Christmas piece, he wrote that he had been reading a pair of heavyweight social histories: one of Britain in the late nineteenth century, another of Britain in the 1950s. Frank wrote that he had hugely enjoyed them both. But here's the truly astonishing thing: neither book mentioned sport. Neither WG Grace nor Denis Compton was important enough to make the pages. Neither man was important, of course, in terms of what he did, but both were massively important in terms of what they meant. Grace was a symbol of brashness, manliness, and all-conquering British rightness: a country that produced such a man was surely right to rule the world. Compton was a symbol of style, elegance, and British brilliance: a symbol of hope after the endless years of war. You can't contemplate British social history without these figures, yet contemplate it the historians did. Didn't want to compromise their reputation for seriousness, I suppose.

As time goes on and other histories come to be written, will they too be written without reference to sport? Does the notion that sport trivialises all it touches affect the chroniclers of the ages so deeply? If so, how will they be able to tell the story of the emergence of South Africa from the era of apartheid? For it was the international sporting boycott that informed South Africans, as nothing else did, that this was a pariah nation. It is not possible to document the last years of apartheid without reference to D'Oliveira, rebel tours, the suspension from the Olympic Games, the protests in Britain and New Zealand – and, above all, the 1995 rugby World Cup. If I had been Nelson Mandela, I would have banned rugby forever, as the sport of the Boers, the sport of the oppressors, the sport of the inventors and upholders of apartheid. Instead, Mandela welcomed the sport, held the World Cup in South Africa and at the final, in a political stunt of genius, he turned up wearing a Springbok shirt, making the symbol of apartheid a symbol of reunion: more, of forgiveness. On the back of the shirt, the name of the Afrikaner captain, Francois van Pieasnaar.

And when it comes to writing a social, or for that matter, political and economic history of India, the historians would do well not to ignore a significant date: the date on which India changed forever. After independence on August 15, 1947, the next most significant date is June 25 1983: the day India won the cricket World Cup. In terms of the development of nationalism, Midnight's

Children became Tea-time's Adolescents.

Since that time, India has changed. More prosperous, much more nationalistic, far less subservient, very quick to jump on any perceived slight by England touring teams. This is a modern, self-confident nation, obsessed with consumerism, most certainly in the big cities, most obviously in Bombay – or Mumbai, as we must now call it in the new nationalistic nation. What would Roebuck say? Alas, he wasn't there to ask. An Indian once told me that India was the richest country in the world, because it was almost exclusively populated by people who didn't want anything more than they already had. That is no longer the case. Like all changes, this is good news and bad news. But as a result, India's cricketers are millionaires, and India is the financial powerhouse of the world game. The World Cup was held on the subcontinent in 1987, and then again in 1996: no longer a poor relation, you see. Ashis Nandy was right, but not in the way he thought: cricket really is an Indian game now. It's their ball. And whether cricket is a symptom or a prime mover of change, it is impossible to consider modern Indian history seriously without attempting to understand cricket.

124

During the Mohali Test in March 2006, I managed to catch the last 20 or so overs of the extraordinary one-day match between South Africa and Australia. Australia made 434 runs and lost. It was reckoned to be the finest game of cricket ever played. I watched it on Indian television. There were adverts at the end of every over, and sly little captions and pop-ups and moving strips kept sneaking onto the screen when the cricket was going on. After it was over I had dinner with CMJ (the *Times* cricket correspondent, Christopher Martin-Jenkins) and I told him: 'You do realise, don't you, that we've been privileged to catch a glimpse of the future. That's what cricket will become: nothing but sixes and adverts.'

The Test in Mohali was fascinating: each side manoeuvring for the mastery, one good session for one side followed by a good session for the opposition. It was a wicket on which bowlers, if they got it right, could bowl, and batters, if they got it right, could bat. The ground was at times no more than a quarter-full, filling up at weekends, and then again at the end, when India got on top at last and there was blood in the water. Indians, post-1983 World Cup, prefer the one-day game, in which they can wave flags and Mexicans and blow horns. For the Indians, one-day cricket is *tamasha*, festival: and a patriotic festival at that. Test match cricket is less gratifying: a bit Raj.

Tamasha cricket, relished all over the world, is not about a balance between bat and ball: it is about bowlers teeing it up for batsmen on flat wickets. One-day cricket, with its new gimmicks of power-plays and supersubs (an experiment now dropped) is aimed to encourage big hitting, discourage bowlers. Like Twenty-20, it is cricket for people who don't like cricket. Cricket is doing all it can to bring in the fickle, the sensation-seekers: assuming that the heartland audience will always be there.

The truth of the matter is that a betrayed heartland is

perfectly capable of moving on, while people who enjoy the favours of the fickle should not be surprised when the fickle find something else more amusing. He who enjoys the fruits of caprice must accustom himself to bear caprice's lash, as Mr Deacon remarks in *A Dance to the Music of Time*.

That is true whether you are running a sport or a newspaper or a television station or any kind of business. It is also true of politics: general election campaigns are now targeted exclusively at the capricious voters in marginal constituencies. You assume the heartland voters will always be with you. The Conservative party made that assumption in 1997.

Another thing also occurred to me as I watched the incessant advertisements between the sixes. In the 1960s, the West saw India as the repository of all that was right and true and meaningful. Every student had on the bookshelf an unread copy of the Penguin Classics *Bhagavad Gita*. People tried to take from India all that was most profound in its culture. And largely failed. In more recent times, India has seen the West as the repository of all that is new and thrilling and amusing – mostly money – and tried to take from the West all that is most silly in its culture. And here, India has succeeded not wisely but too well. You need only watch the cricket to understand such a matter.

125 The third Test in Mumbai ended, and I spoke to Tim Hallissey back in London. Two pieces required, sure,

great. 'Er, do you think you have another Flintoff piece in you?' Well, I had already written five in the past fortnight, and my reply was unequivocal. I'll have another Flintoff piece for every edition of the newspaper for the next five years if Flintoff carries on amazing me from one day to the next: every day creating a new story, every day showing new aspects of himself, every day adding new deeds.

It was a glorious triumph out of adversity. The Ashes team had been blown apart, both captain and vice-captain unable to make the tour. Flintoff came in as the stand-in stand-in captain, the best bowler missing, the best batsman missing, the crucial spinner missing, illness, tiredness and injury running through the squad. Flintoff's wife Rachael had given birth to their second child, but Flintoff had decided to stay on in India to take on the captaincy. He took on the job and did it with all his heart. But that's the way Flintoff does everything.

When we met for that long session after the Ashes, I had brought up the captaincy question. Flintoff had said that he could only ever take on captaincy 'as one of the lads'. I winced. A captain can never be one of the lads. Whatever else, I thought, don't give Flintoff the captaincy. He would do it badly, quite obviously; and besides, it would spoil him, at least for a while, as the England captaincy spoiled Ian Botham.

England won the third Test in Mumbai and levelled the series, their first victory in India for more than 20 years, and it was, above all else, a triumph of captaincy. Or, if you prefer, a triumph of ladmanship. Flintoff worked by means of corporate ethic: he actually succeeded in leading by being one of the lads. So I was wrong, then. My theory of captaincy was right and remains right. But the point is that theories don't always work for exceptional people, and Flintoff is certainly in that category.

With my commitment to the idea of sport as myth, as living mythology, I naturally worked up the idea of the *Freddiad*, or better, the *Freddieyana*, since I was reading the *Ramayana* at the time. Both the *Freddieyana* and the *Ramayana* are stories of exile: in each case, an exile undertaken for noble and pure reasons. Rama turned down kingship on a point of honour: Flintoff accepted leadership for the same reason. Neither Rama nor Flintoff were ever downhearted: always seeing a reason to fight on, despite the horrendous odds, the effectiveness of their opponents and the boundless adversity of circumstance.

The parallel is not entirely facetious. Perhaps I mean not at all facetious. I wrote, facetiously, that Flintoff was not the earthly form of a god, but that he was at least the nearest English cricket was going to get. Sport is always creating stories like this, always creating situations that have a need for a hero. And sometimes, a mere human can fill the niche. Such heroes fulfil their part in the story and we make more of them than they actually are. That is how humans respond to stories: to living mythologies. Flintoff remains a man, and therefore fallible: but with his triumph in Mumbai we celebrated not only his humanity, but his capacity to rise beyond his humanity – at least in the imagination of those who relished the story. In India, the land of a million gods and godlings, what difference does one more make?

I have written in these pages about sport and the illusion

of morality, the bogosity of the notion that victory is the reward for some kind of moral virtue. Perhaps I should contradict myself again, then. For Flintoff's triumph in Mumbai really did seem the reward for – not for saintly virtues, in the manner of Rama, of course not, but at least for an inherent decency. Flintoff stayed in India because he believed, after much heart-searching, that it was the right thing to do. He made a success of it because he took on the job with a full heart. And it worked because his method was of cheerful optimism, backed up by a hugely inclusive nature. It seemed that the England players wanted to give their all for Flintoff because they liked him: because his decency was of a compelling and inescapable kind.

To say that a captain 'leads by example' is usually to say that he has no idea of tactics and hasn't a clue about man-management, but he's not a bad player. Flintoff led by example in the Test series in India: but did so in a genuine and profound sense of this phrase. It was not that he showed people how to bat and bowl and field, but he certainly showed people how to play cricket: by making an ungrudging gift of himself every day of the match, and by being the disperser of good vibes and stick-together companionship throughout the tour, in good circumstances and in bad. This approach got its reward in Mumbai. It was hard not to imagine that it was meant: that it was some kind of divine reward for meaningful virtues. We like stories like that. We like heroes like that. It's what sport is for.

126 *Juventus* means youth. So does sport. At the beginning of the Mass, the priest tells the server *Introibo al altare Dei* (incidentally, the first words of dialogue in *Ulysses*), which translates as 'I shall go unto the altar of God'. The server replies, *Ad Deum Qui laetificat juventem meam*, which, as well I remember from my own devout boyhood, is 'Even unto the God of my joy and gladness', a fine phrase. A more literal translation, however, is 'To the God Who gives joy to my youth'. My youth, my *juventus*.

And so Juventus, the football team from Turin, came to play Arsenal in the quarter-finals of the European Cup, and it was indeed a festival of youth. But it was Juventus that came with a slick, professional outfit of wily and expensively bought old pros: and it was Arsenal that supplied all the juvenesence (not, as TS Eliot preferred, juvesence; maybe his spell-checker wasn't working that day). A bunch of home-reared, hand-reared boys beat the great Juve – *juventus* beating Juventus, and Arsenal were inspired by a mesmerising performance from Francesc Fabregas, aged eighteen. He was distractingly good: I could hardly concentrate on what I was doing – writing about Arsenal – for the pleasure Arsenal in general and Fabregas in particular were giving me.

Do I sound like an Arsenal supporter here? I am not. I am a supporter, I suppose, not of Juventus but of *juventus*: and if I could only manage faith and belief a bit better, I would be a worshipper of the God who lights up youths other than my own.

Sport is always about youth. There are not many walks of life in which you are at your peak in your mid-20s, well past it at 30 and retired five years after that, at the age when most of us are *nel mezzo del cammin di nostra vita*. In many sports, particularly female sports, you peak much younger than your mid-20s: Steffi Graf did her only Grand Slam at nineteen, most gymnasts are finished before they reach 20, many swimmers peak in their teens, Martina Hingis retired at 22, and made a comeback in her dotage, aged 25.

It's not just the running about in sports that demands youth. Even the sports that you wear ordinary clothes for – well, fairly ordinary – and can smoke while playing, insist on youth. Golfers abruptly fade in their 30s, and so do snooker players. Clearly, it's not the legs that go in snooker. Perhaps it's the mind, the competitive nerve, or perhaps it's the perfection of handeye coordination required in long-potting. But these days, snooker players don't go on and on, any more than footballers or gymnasts.

It is a strange thing for the rest of us to consider. In my mid-20s, I was scarcely at the foothills of professional life: by 30, when an athlete is committed to the downslope, I was just beginning to have an idea of what it was all about. By 35, when most athletes retire, I was considered a person of some promise; I was actually beginning to get somewhere. I got the chief's job when I had turned 50. If I had been an athlete, I would by then have been living on memories, show-us-yer-medals bravado and hoping to stay employed by the media I once prided myself on despising. And getting the big job at 50 makes me look absolutely infantile compared to, say, the pope. By the time most popes get the job, they are 40 years older than an athlete at his highest level of ability.

Sport's Moloch-like desire for youth – youth that is stridently demanded and willingly offered, youth that is sacrificed on its altars, youth that is consumed with never-sated appetite – gives it a strangely accelerated rhythm. A sporting lifetime lasts little more than a decade. The lifespan of a great team is little longer. In real life, empires and dynasties last for centuries. In sport, an empire that dominates the world is come and gone in the blinking of an eye. Think of the great teams, the teams that struck fear into every heart, the teams that seemed certain to dominate their sport forever, and you feel like the traveller from an antique land who contemplated the crumbled statue of Ozymandias. Consider them now: West Indies cricket team, Wigan rugby league, Liverpool Football Club, the Welsh rugby union side of the 70s, San Francisco 49ers, Ferrari, the Manchester United side of the 90s. Look on my works, ye mighty and despair.

And yet it is perfectly possible, if this book survives at all, that these names will rise again, and again, and that a new reader coming across these words, might say: but look here, Liverpool dominate football now, West Indies rule cricket, no one can beat Wigan. For as empires slide and crumble, so they arise again. Or if not, new ones arise to take their place.

It is a matter of youth. Youth fades fast, and is replaced fast. What is true of the world is truer than ever of sport: here is no continuing city, here is no abiding stay. Sport is real life on fast forward: lives, empires and dynasties flash across our knowing and are gone, to be replaced by more, at a dizzying rate. Real life can't provide us with myths in quite the same way, because real life takes so long to be lived. But sport takes place at a breakneck pace: the great performers are with us, and then before we know it, they are gone. There is nostalgia even in the first flickerings of youthful promise. In every thrilling beginning, we can already see the sad and celebrated end. They come, they go; they play, they move on; they face a huge test, they pass and are forgotten with the rest... or, sometimes, the very best are remembered not as themselves, but as the people they once were – the greying, ever heavier, ever more boozy shell a living embarrassment to the mythologies of his own past.

127 Turin to Glasgow: not an obvious journey,

but one made in pursuit of youth. I went to Turin, that oddly unItalian city, to see Arsenal play a highly competent 0-0 against Juventus, with Francesc Fabregas again impressive. Musing on youth and the chimera of promise, I flew to Glasgow via Gatwick so that I might watch Andy Murray play Davis Cup tennis.

My enduring memory of the place is of a shopping centre. In order to get to the Braehead Arena, you get dropped off at Marks and Spencer, walk through food and gents' clothes, then along an avenue lined with Waterstones and Clinton Cards and Vodafone, and you end up in a sports arena. Rather rum. And Murray didn't play the singles, because he was crocked. He and Greg Rusedski played the doubles on Saturday and lost, and Murray said fuck to the umpire and got into trouble. Great Britain went on to lose the tie – it was against Serbia and Montenegro, and it would have been hard enough with just Serbia, ho ho – and I didn't have much of a tale to tell, but I did what I could. Sometimes sport just doesn't work out.

Sometimes youth doesn't work out either, but promise is always a joy, and the idea that Murray could train on – that the Arsenal boys, Wenger's Weanlings, could train on, that Wayne Rooney could train on: this is intoxicating. The best part of any football season is early August, when every pitch is like a green duvet, every new signing is a genius, every old hand is better and keener than ever before, and every team is a champion. The best horse in racing is an unraced two-year-old, for it might do anything. I remember talking to the great American trainer, Charlie Whittingham, then in his 80s, and asking why he didn't retire. 'Simon, I got a young horse.' Meaning that he had hundreds. 'And no one with a young horse ever committed suicide.' Because any young horse might just turn out to be the greatest race-horse that ever drew breath. It *probably* won't be, but you can't say that it *definitely* won't be. No one can. That's the joy of it. That's why you have to stay alive: to see what happens next. You can't take the chance of it not being Nijinsky, after all.

So Fabregas might be the greatest midfielder that ever drew breath, Murray might win Wimbledon, Rooney might drive England to victory in the World Cup: and might do so in not very many weeks. The fizz of anticipation: in sport, you never know the answer to the question, what happens next? The same is true of a career, and the thrill of ignorance is that much more intense with a young person of almost, it seems, boundless promise. Cyril Connolly famously said: 'Whom the gods wish to destroy, they first call promising.' But not invariably. Every so often, promise is fulfilled. Promise is kept. It happened with Pele, with Diego Maradona, with Pete Sampras.

So what might Murray do? Top 20? Better? Does he have a Grand Slam in him? The process of finding out will be enthralling: and almost certainly disappointing. But we can't say for certain that Murray will not win Wimbledon, that Rooney will not lead England to victory. When we sight promise in any sphere, we are inclined to hope that little bit too much. That is because where there is hope, there is life. Sport brings us hope, in many different forms: and then, at fantastic speed, shows us what happens next. Shows us the inevitable disappointment... and sometimes something else. Life is, if you like, a process of coming to terms with disappointment, a strategic retreat – a procedure which at times constitutes a rout – from perfectionism. But every now and then, perfection strikes, and when it strikes in sport, it touches us very deeply.

But really, only the unfinished is perfect. There is more beauty in the Leonardo cartoon in the National Gallery than there is in his greatest completed masterpieces, because every completion is a kind of spoiling. A few lines of a lost great poem, a fragment of a sculpture: these things have a perfection that not even the greatest finished piece of work can ever rival. The reason is that we can fill in the gaps with ourselves. We can elevate the promise into an imagined perfection that can never, in the harshness of the real world, actually exist. And so, with Rooney, with Fabregas, with Murray, we see an infinite potential, and convert it in our minds to perfection. It is a perfection that cannot be spoiled by anything save each passing second of time.

128

I was watching the match on television, and a good one it was, too, Manchester United, inspired by Rooney, raging against the dying of the season, unhappily conceding to Chelsea the title of the natural champions of England. And almost at the end, a Rooney charge on goal, a tackle, and Rooney was down. Christ, I said at once, his one's a metatarsal. Proving, at least, that we are all experts now. In 2002, there was David Beckham's metatarsal, and then Gary Neville's (the forgotten metatarsal, and arguably at least, the one that cost England more dearly in the World Cup of that year) and in 2004, there was Rooney's.

Now it was Rooney's again. I had, against the tide, and for two years, been suggesting that England could do well in the World Cup of 2006: no weakness in any position and in Rooney, a player who gives the side the glorious quality of devil. Sven-Goran Eriksson, always caricatured as a man without an adventurous bone in his body, was gambling on Rooney's precocious ability before Rooney's then club manager, David Moyes. Rooney was what gave England an edge as they went into the competition. Now Rooney was crocked.

And so the country was at once plunged into hideous mourning: a deep gloom that lived alongside a crazed optimism. Everyone was convinced that Rooney would take no part in the tournament, and that all England's chances had gone; everyone was equally enthused with a wild belief that Rooney would be back in the England team in time to set the tournament aflame. The two beliefs co-existed without any apparent contradiction. As I began to get my mind around the coming World Cup, I grew more and more aware that there were two views of England's chances in the World Cup. They were contradictory, were held simultaneously, and by the same people the length and breadth of the country. The two beliefs were held by people who cared very deeply about football and sport and the England team, and also by people who cared almost nothing for football in the general run of things.

People believed that England had no chance whatsoever, and yet at the same time, they felt that an England failure would be the most shattering surprise. At the same time, people had extremely low hopes and extraordinarily high expectations. At the same time, people were prepared to honour the men who achieved the impossible, and to revile forever the men who brought about the shocking event of failure. Triumph was both inevitable and impossible: the players were at once world-beaters and no-hopers.

For most people, sport is an area of life in which you are let off rational thought. Very few people, no matter how much given to analysis, are prepared to turn these powers to sport. Sport is instead an emotional free-for-all, in which chaos and contradiction can be given full rein. Count that rule double for football, double again when football is seen from a determinedly partisan point of view, and double once again when you throw in a bit of serious nationalism.

129

The miracle did not take place. Not Arsenal's miracle, anyway. I watched the tense 1-0 win over Villareal at Highbury, and the tenser 0-0 draw away. I stayed in a very nice class of cell in a windswept out-of-season seaside hotel outside Valencia, and wondered where the adventure would take us all.

Paris was the literal answer, of course: a trip to the Stade de France for the European Cup Final against Barcelona. It was called The Purist's Final. I thought this was a bad title. If you want your football to be beautiful as well as effective, you are not a purist. You want football adulterated by beauty: victory muddled by aestheticism. Surely it was the old Arsenal of George Graham and Tony Adams, which specialised in the brutal functionality of the 1-0 win, that was pure.

Both Barcelona and Arsenal at their best, played with a sense of style, which was effective, certainly, but was additionally delightful, and pleasing to the eye and the mind. Impure football, then – or is beautiful football actually the pure form of football, football unsullied by the pursuit of victory? My grandmother would agree with that idea: few footballers, whether creators of beauty or not, would go along with her.

Football can bring deep delight without recourse to beauty, of course; certainly, without recourse to beauty of execution. We have grown used to miracles when English clubs reach the European Cup Final: there was Manchester United's extraordinary comeback in 1999, there was Liverpool's equally extraordinary achievement in Istanbul. Neither of these were beautiful, in the sense that the football the teams produced pleased the eye, but the narrative they created was full of beauty. And for getting on for an hour on a warm and rainswept Parisian evening, I thought that the usual miracle would indeed take place as scheduled. Arsenal were down to ten men after the goalkeeper, Jens Lehmann, was sent off for bringing down the opposing forward, Samuel Eto'o. Arsenal grabbed an unsightly yet undeniably beautiful set-piece goal against the run of play; and held on... and held on... and then, when you could almost smell the incense, the miracle vanished, Barcelona scored twice and that was it. It was, I suppose, almost beautiful. Certainly, there was a sad poetry in the defeat. I took a strange route home via Amsterdam, trying to find the sad poetry in a book on German history (my mind increasingly on the World Cup) and ended up in Norwich, an hour from home. A fair result, on the whole.

130 There is a story I love to tell about Rob

Hughes, a colleague from *The Sunday Times* who is, it must be said, occasionally prone to taking himself with a fairly uncompromising seriousness. It happened at the three-day event at the Barcelona Olympic Games of 1992. I was walking the cross-country course with Jenny MacArthur, the *Times* equestrian correspondent, and we bumped into Rob at one of the more imposing fences. 'Good morning, Rob.'

'Right here.'

'What's that?'

'Right here.'

'Elaborate,' I said tolerantly.

'This event is going to be won and lost right here.'

'I'm sure you're right, Rob. It's certainly going to be an influential fence.' A pause to savour the moment: the greatest competition in the greatest of all sports about to start: a relentlessly beautiful Spanish morning. 'This is all right, isn't it?' I said. 'I've got a feeling I'm really going to enjoy it today.'

A black, bitter look from Rob. 'Yes. You can enjoy it. I've got to understand it.'

I was, naturally, overjoyed by this. I have, it is true, very deeply enjoyed the sport over the years, to the extent, at least of taking part in it (dodgy dressage, gungho cross-country, imprecise showjumping). I love eventing. It is the supreme sport. It tests all the horsey skills: that is to say courage, skill, nerve, will-to-win, sensitivity, co-operation, toughness and gentleness. And having taken part in the sport at the lowest levels (in terms of both hierarchy and the height I got above the ground) I know what it feels like. I have felt the terror at the start, the surge of joy as the first (and the last) fence passes beneath one, I have felt the fierce concentration (part competitive, part survival-based) as one moves from jump to jump; I have even felt the rhythm that comes when things are going right: when the solution to the next puzzle is but the natural corollary to the problems of the previous one.

And so every year I go to Badminton, to celebrate the great event, and the delightful, brilliant and modest people who compete there. It is a special weekend for me; and I love to make much of it. Eventing is, perhaps, the most dangerous of all sports. In rugby and football, you are always going to get biffs and bangs: in eventing you risk death. In the dreadful year of 1999, five riders were killed. Since then, much work has been done to make the sport safer – but there is still no getting away from the fact that risk is at the very heart of the sport. Shared risk, because the sport is, at the end of it, the testing of trust.

Eventing is, then, the ultimate team sport. I am not talking here about the team events you get at the Olympic Games, in which four riders compete for the team, and the worst score is discarded, and if you fall in the water you have let the whole country down. These things certainly make for very good sport indeed: but the essential team in eventing is not the team of four humans, it is the team of two. Human; horse. No, I am not being anthropomorphic. Try and get a horse over a jump if he doesn't trust you: it can't be done. Try and jump an obstacle with a horse you don't trust: you have failed before you start.

For years people have celebrated sport as something that breaks down barriers. In a team, boundaries dissolve: the boundaries between races, religions, nationalities, colours, in some rare cases (eventing being one example) even the boundary between the sexes. But in eventing, the last frontier is broken down. In eventing, the team-work and the co-operation cross the boundaries of species. If you don't co-operate with your horse, and vice versa, you won't win.

It reminds me of the philosophical work of Peter Singer, who proposes that the history of human civilisation has been about expanding areas of concern. As society has developed, so a sense of responsibility – a sense of kinship – has expanded: moving beyond family, beyond tribe, beyond region, beyond nation, beyond religion, beyond race, beyond gender. And now we are at the next frontier: and coming to the realisation that it is the one that lies between humans and other species of animal. That's how I understand the sport, anyway. And that's how I enjoy it as well, come to that.

Andrew Hoy won Badminton from the front: a startlingly cool and clean dressage, then a cross-country round full of rhythm, in which it seemed that the fences had been lowered a couple of feet into the ground for Hoy's arrival, and then raised again for everybody else. He had two fences in hand for the showjumping, but won like a champion, needing neither. Afterwards, he put it all down to the team of himself and his wife, Bettina Hoy (she who had gone through the start twice at the Athens Olympics). It was her preparation of the horse Moonfleet, that was the key, he said, and it was her brilliant dressage skills that gave the team of horse and rider the edge; and with it, the confidence. Hoy had been one of the top riders in eventing: all at once, he was the competitor in supreme control of his sport, like Schumacher, Federer, Tiger.

And I was reminded of a previous encounter with Mr and Mrs Hoy. They had marched into the press-tent at Badminton, Andrew in full riding gear including helmet, and carrying a whip. Someone asked cheerily: 'Is that for Andrew to use on you, or for you to use on him?' Bettina, small, German, minxsome, raised a blonde eyebrow and said: 'Actually, we both like it.' Team work, you see. It was team work that had put Andrew on top; and it seems they both like that.

131

I travelled back from Paris (via Amsterdam and Norwich) meditating on defeat. As a sportswriter, it is my job to celebrate victory, but defeat is by far the more common experience in sport. At the end of every match, every event, every season, there is but one winner. Everyone else is a loser. Sport is about losing. Mostly, it is the tales of victory that ensnare us; but every happy ending is based on someone else's misery. The barque of victory floats on the tears of the losers.

Thierry Henry dealt with Arsenal's defeat with bitter gibes about referees and diving. The course of the entire football season had been full of ugly reactions to defeat. Sir Alex Ferguson, Arsene Wenger, Jose Mourinho: once defeat had these men in its icy grip, all possibility of grace was extinguished. Defeat is too grave a matter for decency. Yet all must end up defeated. All save one; and even for the victor, victory is but a temporary respite in a world of defeat. For even the greatest champion, Beowulf's last dragon lies in wait.

Boris Becker said the right thing: a remark that has echoed across the years, a piece of teenage wisdom bursting out from the clichés of the press conference. After winning fifteen successive matches at Wimbledon, a sequence that included championship victories at the age of seventeen and then eighteen, he lost in the second round to a man named Peter Doohan. And Becker said – more or less blurted – 'I lost a tennis match. Nobody died.'

That's the point, of course. It was a metaphorical death, certainly – a fallen champion, nothing less. But Becker the man lived still, with a life of championships and tax problems and broom cupboards still stretching ahead of him. That is what sport means. Everybody struggles, everybody loses, nobody dies.

132

Lance Armstrong is one of the few people who has dared to talk about defeat in terms of life and death. 'Dying and losing, it's the same thing,' he said. No one else in sport has the qualifications to say that; but Armstrong has come as close to death as anybody alive. He survived cancer in his balls, his chest and his brain: and then won the Tour de France seven times in a row. He described the race as 'the obligation of the cured'. He was a man obsessed by the idea of winning, and to a frightening degree. He was victory's slave. For him, it was not just that defeat was death. It was also that victory was the only viable form of life: the only possible way of living. Frequently, it is those who take the trivialities of sport with the greatest seriousness that achieve the greatest things. As spectators we respond to that: so much so that if a competitor fails to perform as if sport were a life and death matter, we feel cheated. We need people to suffer. Sport is the ultimate theatre of cruelty, for without suffering there is no sport. And still nobody dies.

133

Some years ago – the year was 1999 – I was walking the course at Badminton with the great Mark Todd, the finest competitive rider I have ever seen. I was not there to give him advice on how to ride the course: it was a stunt for a piece. But he and I have always got on pretty well, so after we had reached the finish, Todd invited me for a beer in the competitors' tent. I was in there, chatting away, when I felt a tap on my shoulder. I turned round, and there was a face of incandescent loveliness about a foot from my own. For an instant I felt an intemperate urge to kiss it: then common sense prevailed. I have always regretted this.

I didn't think Peta Beckett and I were quite on snogging terms after a single meeting. She was a three-day eventer, witchingly pretty, very funny, utterly delightful. If I sound smitten, it's only because I was. I had visited her to write a piece. She'd showed me round her stables; I'd met her horses; she rode beautifully, showing off her flying changes (non-horsey readers need only know that this manoeuvre is very difficult and, when done right, wonderfully elegant) and we'd talked horsey talk for a long and lovely morning.

I wrote a very jolly and affectionate piece (so maybe a snoggette would have been all right, who knows?) and then I had the pleasure of bumping into her again at Badminton. And we talked horsey talk again and she thought she had a great chance and her horse was going well, and I finished my beer, wished her luck, and left. And – well, that's it, really. Not much of a story, I know. But I moved on into the day feeling that the world was a slightly better place.

A few weeks later she was dead. She died in competition. She saw a big stride at a particularly imposing jump and the horse failed to make it: flipped, and landed on top of her. That's a killing fall. A jockey in jump-racing is flung out of the saddle, because he is riding with very short stirrup leathers, and very little of his body is in contact with the horse. He is catapaulted to an uncomfortable safety. But an event-rider rides long, because an event-rider needs control and, particularly, control of lateral movement. And that can only be achieved by a long leg and close contact with the horse. So if a horse flips, the rider sticks: and is there when the killing weight descends.

I still mourn this lovely person I never knew: because she was so full of delight in living. All those who take part in risk sports will tell you that there is no death wish in what they do: the exact opposite. Peta Beckett's was not a wasted life. Her end is a matter of the most desperate sadness, but she did wonderful and beautiful things and made life seem an altogether splendid idea. I just wish she hadn't died in pursuit of these fine things.

134

I went to Paris for three nights to mug up on rivalries. The French Open tennis tournament was starting, unprecedentedly, on a Sunday, so I went out to inspect. First time I had done this one: a very well-set-up tournament, a hotel that was a pleasant enough walk from the courts, and a cell that was fine so long as you didn't attempt movement of any kind in the shower. Paris is full of them.

On the first day, I had Roger Federer; on the second, Rafael Nadal. First-round matches: both men won as they should. The point to relish was that Federer, seen by many as the best player ever, suddenly had a rival. At the time I went to Paris, Nadal had a 5-1 advantage over Federer, and was still in his teens. Nadal seemed unaffected by Federer's most potent weapon: his serenity. Perhaps in his crass teenage way, he didn't even notice it. And meanwhile, something about Nadal was very definitely getting to Federer. In their previous meeting in Rome, Nadal had won over five sets, saving two match points on the way.

I had a theory that the real problem was Nadal's exotic self-production. Nadal dresses up like Sylvester Stallone on the Rambo poster: all pneumatic biceps, silly trousers, headband and battle-tousled hair. He does this blind-force-of-nature act: an overdose of testosterone in calf-length shorts. The shirt's not made that can contain his muscles, that's why he has to wear the sleeveless vest. And all that too-strident macho stuff can unsettle a chap. Federer doesn't seem to care for the look-at-the-size-of-my-dick level of debate. He can out-tennis anybody: but he starts psychologically one-down once Nadal gets onto court with his wanna-feel-my-pecs strut. And Nadal can play, too: with a thunderous, booming aggression backed by supreme accuracy and a great feel for the ebb and flow of a rally.

What we needed next, I thought, was for Federer to get one back on Nadal: and then for Nadal to get one back at Federer. What we really wanted was not a brief battle for supremacy, but a serious long-term rivalry. If a feud is something that diminishes both parties, a rivalry is something that actually enriches both. This is something of a tennis speciality: Borg-McEnroe, Evert-Navratilova. In these relationships, the players were far more than friends. Each gave to the other something they could find in no other way, that is to say, their own brilliance. Each was the greater for the other – like two halves of the same genius. John McEnroe was never the same player again after Bjorn Borg retired. Chrissie Evert and Martina Navratilova went on slugging it out for match after match, never tiring of rivalry, never bitching, always relishing the next opportunity for confrontation.

The final result between the two was 43 matches to 37 in Navratilova's favour. In the course of this, Evert took women's tennis to new levels of directness and purpose while Navratilova took women's tennis to an athleticism never before considered possible. I remember a story in which one of Evert's beaten opponents said loudly in the locker-room: 'Thank God my happiness doesn't depend on the result of a tennis match.' Evert responded: 'Thank God mine does.'

All sports thrive on such rivalries – Alain Prost and Ayrton Senna – but they are rare, rare things, and much to be cherished. The normal pattern is for one great champion to be succeeded by another. It is when you get two great talents at the same time that sport gives us the best thing it is capable of giving. At such moments, sport brings one of the highest passive pleasures available to human beings – insofar as watching sport is passive. England and Brazil in 1970; Steve Ovett and Sebastian Coe in Moscow, 1980; England and Australia in 2005; and, perhaps the perfect vignette of this whole business, the fourth-set tie-break between Borg and McEnroe at Wimbledon in 1980. The final score was 18-16 to McEnroe: Borg won the fifth set 8-6. A year later, they met in the final at Wimbledon again and in another match of celestial dimensions, McEnroe won in four sets, and then did it again with the same result at the US Open the same year. So Borg retired, at the age of 25, just like that. And McEnroe was never quite as good again. He had lost not just an opponent: he had lost the better part of himself.

135 The rivalry between Ayrton Senna and Alain

Prost certainly had elements of the feud: most notably when Senna drove Prost off the track in Japan in 1990. It was after this, or perhaps some other transgression, that somebody suggested that this sort of behaviour was all wrong. The response tells you – almost – everything. 'But I am Senna.' Not aggressive: just a trifle bewildered that someone had failed to grasp that particular point.

But I am Senna. I have never met anyone quite like Senna. I met him just the once, at the Canadian Grand Prix in 1992. He agreed to give me an interview at a certain time and I was there, journo-like, good and early, outside the motorhome. It was a blazing hot day, and I stood there in the sun. Through the windows, I could see Senna, deep in conversation, hands occasionally raised to clasp a steering-wheel of air. He was talking technicalities and seeking perfection: he was driving and he was winning.

At last, he came out. After a brief handshake, the first question. It was received in an unnerving silence. I was about to try another: I had actually made the intake of breath when I was belatedly smart enough to shut up. I realised, in one of those sudden intuitive moments that can come in the strange social encounter of the interview, when you are focused entirely on the other person, that Senna was translating the question into Portuguese, pondering its traps and its philosophical implications, coming up with an answer, and then translating it into English. Senna was not a man given to compromises in anything he did. 'I still don't know how far I can go. I can only try what I believe I can do, but by trying, I often find I can do more. And I have to readjust.'

Eyes focused beyond me, staring down the slippery avenues of eternity. 'Many times, I find myself in a comfortable position and I don't feel happy about it. I feel it is right to slow down, but something inside of me, something very strong, pushes me on, makes me try to beat... myself. It is... an enormous desire to go further and further, to travel beyond my own limits.'

It was not like talking to a sportsman, a performer, an athlete, something I have naturally done again and again for year after year. No. This was more like talking to a mystic. A saint. 'Every time I have an idea about where my limits are, I go to check it. And most of the time I am wrong. So I have to adjust myself to going even further. It is very exciting, and it is a non-stop process.'

No bluster. No positive thinking. No modesty. No pride. Just a man perfectly convinced of his own singularity: of the fact that it was his destiny to be greater than us all. 'Power comes from my education, which, you would say, was privileged. I was privileged to grow up in a happy and healthy environment. I had my family always behind me, helping me when I have some doubt, some question. And on top of that, I have been able to experience God's power on earth.'

I returned to normal duties like a man waking from a dream: slightly unsure what was real and what was not, knowing that I had spent time with one of the greatest performers ever to take part in sport. I am convinced that had he been born five centuries earlier, he would indeed have been a saint.

But in modern life, sport also gives the opportunity for

extraordinary human beings to achieve extraordinary things, and all in an arena of pure and perfect frivolity.

If Senna had become a saint, he would presumably have been a martyr. And I can still recall the moment I heard about his death. Keith Blackmore, then deputy sports editor at *The Times*, rang me up. I answered at once: I was at my desk, despite it being a Sunday afternoon, despite the fact that I could have been watching Senna in pursuit of the ultimate perfection. I was working on a novel (one that had a martyr in it).

'Are you in a position to write something?'

'Sure, what's happening?'

'I think Ayrton Senna's dead.'

'Oh Christ.'

I hung up on him. Couldn't believe it. Couldn't accept it. I had been, you see, taken in by Senna's own mythologising of himself. I believed that he was beyond the cares of the rest of us. That such things couldn't happen to him. I mean, not him. He couldn't be dead. He was Senna.

A few minutes later, I called back, and agreed to write, and did so, recalling that meeting and those strange lines I have quoted above. I have never forgotten my meeting with the man who had felt God's power on earth: the eyes that were focused on infinity. They used to sell the *News of the World* under the slogan 'All human life is there.'

The slogan also works for sport. You can find everything you want in sport: absolutely everything. You can find fools, you can find heroes, you can find villains: and you can even find saints and martyrs. Martyred: but for what cause? Sport is everything: and it is therefore, among many other things, a cause that people are prepared to die for. Nor, again, does this make for a wasted life. I have been enriched by the life and by the death of Ayrton Senna, and of Peta Beckett. I wish they both lived still: but I can't reject what they have both given me in death. In me, and in many others, they live on. That is what life and death both mean. Someone once described Proust's big book as 'a theological work for a secular world.' Sport provides a secular world positively crammed with aspects of religion.

136

From Paris to Manchester, to watch England's pre-World Cup friendly against Hungary. Then, five days later, to Manchester again to watch another friendly against Jamaica. And it seemed that Sven-Goran Eriksson had been pondering on the essential frivolity of sport, because he was behaving with a wild, out-of-character recklessness. The man renowned for his caution selected Theo Walcott, aged seventeen, to play for England, despite the fact that he had never seen Walcott play, or that Walcott had yet to play for his club, Arsenal. Eriksson also tried some mad experiments in formation: odd for a man who arrived as England coach irretrievably wedded to 4-4-2. Give it a go, lads: it's only the World Cup.

I must say, I rather enjoyed this revelation of Eriksson's sudden intemperate wackiness. The problem with all England's efforts at every World Cup since 1970 has been the fact that it all becomes so, so desperately important. It's all about who wants it most: but, as I've said before, under Ed Smith's Law, it's often about who wants it least. The prize goes to the player or the team that can shrug off the twin shackles of hope and fear, and simply play the bloody ball. Perhaps England's post-metatarsal hope lay in the madness of King Sven. I wrote a piece saying as much with some relish.

Time, then, to get back to Suffolk and pack. Time, then, to go to Germany and watch the World Cup. Time to write the big one. Perhaps this should be the last reference to the two great wars: but certainly, it was time to go over the top.

137

There are times when the experience of the writer is very different to the experience of the people he is writing for. A World Cup is the most extreme example in sport. For the reader, the start of the World Cup is like standing at the top of the Cresta Run. For the writer, it is more like standing at the bottom of the North Face of the Eiger. For the reader, it will be wild, hectic fun, even if he ends up a little bruised at the bottom. For the writer the coming four-and-a-bit weeks will require concentration, tenacity and endurance. Plus a little bit of nerve.

In terms of intensity, it is the most draining item on the four-year agenda. A cricket tour takes much longer, but it has down days, quiet days, easy days: and your transport is all arranged. A World Cup is full on, all the time. The Olympic Games take place in a single city: a World Cup in many. You must move from city to city to city, fixing up your train travel as you do so. You lie in bed thinking not about the great lines you will write but about the trains you hope to travel on. On most days, you also have the mild terror of live match-reporting.

I'm not asking for pity. You're on a great story: perhaps, in terms of the readers who come to you, the best story of all. But you know one thing with great certainty: you will feel a little older by the time the competition is done.

138
So naturally, the first thing I did was to find the stadium media centre in Munich, and collect my accreditation. It was appallingly signposted, and I went to several wrong places first, muttering about German efficiency. Once there, the job was swift and easy, but I came out of the wrong door, since it was not clearly signed. I could see the exit gate 100 yards off, but a girl barred the way: 'You must not go out this way!' With heavy patience, I pointed out that that *was* the way out, so which way was I supposed to go out, if I wanted to go out. And then the small miracle of a smile, an inclination of the head: 'Go, jah?' I didn't think badly of her: she voz only disobeying orders.

We have all been let off trying to understand Germany. Instead, we keep our two nations separate by means of a Berlin Wall of jokes. Alas, I have put a brick or two there myself, with, for example, the Michael-Schumacher-is-

Herr-Flick piece, and, indeed, another when I compared Schumacher's podium triumphalism to the boy who sings 'Tomorrow Belongs to Me' in *Cabaret*.

In the same way, we are let off reading German literature. I would be embarrassed had I not read Flaubert, Dante, Homer, Dostoyevsky, Cervantes, Ibsen: but it had never occurred to me to read Goethe. Not my concern. Something to do with Germany. We punish them for losing the war by not reading their literature, by not engaging with their culture. I had never spent much time in Germany: when I was a wild boy-traveller, Germany was the place you raced through, praising the autobahns because they allowed you to dispense with Germany so quickly as you headed for Italy or Greece.

At the pre-World-Cup friendlies, some supporters had been wearing plastic World War I Tommy-Atkins helmets: honestly, herr policeman, it's a postmodern ironic helmet. Sport is always awkward when history gets in the way: as football matches between England and Germany, England and Argentina, England and any Celtic nation make clear. So for me, then, it was time to engage with Germany, to establish a relationship with the place, to stop making jokes, to read *Faust*, drink beer, eat spargel.

And listen to music. Now travelling with an iPod rather than the seventeen-quid Walkman, I had hour after hour of music to hand: and all of it German. What other music should any one listen to? All the great music has been written by German-speakers, and most of the second-greatest as well. And yet I never think of it as having much to do with Germany. Perhaps it doesn't. Perhaps anything or anyone that is as great as Bach has lost all claim to nationality. The music came from Germany, but Bach no more belongs to Germany than football does to England.

139

Coming back from an evening meal in Munich the day before the opening match, I encountered a group of Brazilians belting out a samba rhythm while two of their number engaged in the Brazilian dance-combat form called capoeira: twisting, turning, tumbling, cartwheeling, slashing never-landed blows with foot and hand, and not once losing the beat. I rang my old friend Simon Evans, who has been studying capoeira for years. 'It's not always done like that,' he said. 'Sometimes the blows are landed. It's a sport with no rules. Only rituals.'

140

When I lived on Lamma Island, outside Hong Kong, there was a lovely leaf-canopied glade with inviting benches and tables beneath its trees. Here my friends and I would gather on a Sunday evening and drink beer from cans purchased at the shop nearby, which was run by the engaging Cecelia. The place was rightly famous for its crepuscular mosquitoes, so one spent a lot of one's time slapping oneself enthusiastically. 'Let's go to Cecelia's,' we used to say, 'and do some Bavarian folk dancing.'

So there on the football pitch in Munich were several hundred men in lederhosen all slapping themselves with even greater enthusiasm. It was, I regret to say, the opening ceremony of the World Cup, and it concluded with Claudia Schiffer apparently marrying Pele and winning the World Cup. On then, to the football.

The World Cup had been held here before, in 1974: many people had been angry that Germany got the competition again. Not fair: somebody else's turn, most notably South Africa's. But the World Cup of 1974 had not, in fact, been held in Germany. It had been held in a no-longer-existing place called West Germany. It was, perhaps, an occasion to celebrate the emergence of a nation from years of strange and troubled history. Say 70 years, if you like – three score and ten – a human lifetime.

I met a lovely Brazilian woman, a journalist for one of the local papers, when I was covering a Grand Prix in Sao Paolo. It was years ago; I was there to write Ayrton Senna stories, being still smitten with the man after our meeting in Canada. And yes, I told her. Brazil's great, a wonderful place, and I hoped very much to visit the Amazon before all the trees were chopped down. Her face went hard with scorn: 'You chopped down your forests,' she said. And left me forever.

I wanted to tell her: no. No no no. I have never chopped down a forest in my life. The forests of England were chopped down by people several hundred years ago: people who had no understanding of the fact that forests were valuable and irreplaceable. Now all of humanity has advanced, understood that wanton destruction is not to the advantage of humankind. In short, do not blame an individual for the history of his country. Isn't it true that, for all of us, history is a nightmare from which we are trying to awake?

I thought of her as the opening match began: Germany against Costa Rica, a stadium full of cheering, a stadium full of German flags. You could, if you like, think about the Nuremberg rallies, but you couldn't have gone up to any single person in the stadium and said: you invaded Poland, you consented to the extermination camps, you voted for Hitler. It was other people. The people in the stadium, the people of Germany had more need than most to wake up from history's nightmare, and they were attempting to do so by means of sport. Not by denying the past, but by celebrating the present.

And so these people, these non-invaders of Poland seemed to have decided that it is now perfectly acceptable for a German to be patriotic: to sing and shout and wave a flag and to wear black-red-and-gold. Honestly, we can take it. It won't go to our heads. Patriotism is not quite the same as nationalism, despite Peter Roebuck. Cheering for your national team is not the same as thinking that your nation has the right to win the World Cup, that somebody must be punished if the team fails, that your nation must set the agenda for the world, and that anybody who disagrees with that notion is not just wrong but demented. Patriotism is often confused with nationalism, but it is not the same thing at all. Call patriotism a cheerful relationship with the place you live in. It is not unpatriotic to object to some of the rulers, the laws, the customs, and the culture of our country;

it is not unpatriotic to see one's country for what it is; it is not unpatriotic to keep all the ironies intact. A patriot does-n't demand the World Cup: he just hopes for a damn good ride down the Cresta Run. This German crowd felt more like patriots than nationalists to me.

Germany had sought to win the world's love by means of sport on two previous occasions. The most significant was the Munich Olympic Games in 1972, in which Germany was at pains to present itself as cheerful, friendly, laid-back, free. Many of the athletes were long-haired free spirits. But it was the point at which the great tidal wave of the 60s broke and rolled back: and it happened with the Black September atrocity, and me weeping quietly in a park with a no-longer-wanted cigar burning in my hand. Munich was not a new beginning but a new end.

The 1974 World Cup was another charm offensive: but the German team was seen by outsiders as typically soul-less, mechanical and effective. They won not friends but the World Cup. In the meantime, the world fell in love with the Total Football side of the Dutch and Johann Cruyff: artistry, self-expression, genius, as pleasing to the eye as it was dev-astating to the opposition. Germany – West Germany – beat them in the final. Method beat madness: prose beat poetry: logic beat intuition: science beat art: the respected beat the beloved.

So perhaps in 2006 it was time for a unified Germany to celebrate itself, in a way that hadn't really happened in those two muffed attempts at refinding global approval. Sport is, of course, always the best way to attract the attention of the world. But then sport has always been a continuation of politics by other means: and I suspect that Hitler was the first person to discover this. There is a famous picture of the England football team playing in Berlin in 1938, all lined up with arms extended in a Nazi salute. They had been ordered to do this by a craven British government, and the players were all sick with fury at having to do so. Stanley Matthews recalled a single, small Union Jack carried by two Englishmen who had somehow got into this celebration of Nazidom: and Matthews and his team gave their salute to this small symbol of opposition before they all put on a heroic performance and beat Germany 6-3. The Berlin Olympic Games of 1936 had a similar agenda of national and racial supremacy: upset, as we have seen, by the nonpareil Jesse Owens.

So there I was, at a World Cup that took place 70 years after the Berlin Olympics: and it was plain that this sporting festival was not designed to showcase Germany *über alles*, but Germany as a prosperous, unified democracy full of decent, free people all happy to enjoy the ride as long as their team survived and to put on a great show for the post-Cold-War World. And so Germany, victorious against Costa Rica, now had to play Poland. Sport loves to pulls strokes like that: just as it threw England and Argentina together at the previous World Cup. Sport frequently forces us to confront not only our opponents but ourselves.

141 There is a story still told about two journalists

of the doyen variety covering the World Cup in Germany in 1974. They were moving from one city to another by car in pursuit of the next match on the agenda, which involved the Total Football side of the Dutch. As they swooped – the driver was a swooper – along the autobahn out of Munich, the more reflective of the two said: 'Do you realise we've just driven past Dachau?'

There was an eternity-long pause. Then the driver said: 'Do you think Cruyff will score?'

142

England's first game was against Paraguay. They were ahead after four minutes, from an own goal, but it all went downhill after that. It was awful stuff. Rooney was on the bench, and ran about a bit in his bib – his training bib, this is not a joke about his age – but he didn't play. Afterwards, Sven-Goran Eriksson and the England players said the whole horrible unsatisfactory performance came about because it was too hot. It was 86 degrees. Looksherry!

When I lived on Lamma, we used to play football when it was 100 degrees and 100 per cent relative humidity – and we did so on a concrete pitch that reflected the heat upwards in a gloriously dismaying fashion. And we never played badly because of the heat. We played badly because we were bad footballers. But English athletes frequently believe that heat is unfair, that warm weather excuses any performance, however lamentable. Thus sport demonstrates the ineluctable provinciality of the English mind.

Paula Radcliffe blamed the heat (and many other things) in Athens two years earlier: other competitors wondered at the start why she needed a long and elaborate warm-up when the day was already coming up to the boil. Me, I recalled the Olympic Games of 1960. My first sporting hero – probably even pre-dating MJK Smith – was Don Thompson: *il topolino*, as the delighted Italian press called him. He won the 50-kilometre walk at the Rome Olympic Games at the first sporting event that truly seized my imagination. Amazing that this should happen, because at that time, the only part of the walks and the marathons that you saw on television was the finish: the entry into the stadium. I remember that wonderful triumphant lap: the Mighty Mouse walking in, all heels and elbows in the spindly comic hip-wobbling walk of the race-walker: and no one else even in sight. This, in Rome, in high summer, when it gets seriously warm. But Thompson had trained for the heat. He had done so in his bathroom. He carried heaters to his bathroom, he boiled kettles, he brought the temperature up to 100 degrees and there he performed a long series of exercises every day. He made the heat his friend: and so he won Britain's only athletics gold medal of the Games.

But for all the regrettable nature of the English football team against Paraguay and the deeply unsatisfactory nature of the English victory, it felt good to be writing about England at a World Cup again. This was not for the quality of the football, but for the way that the story would resonate with the nation. I knew that what happened at the World Cup, for good or ill, would become part of national life: part of English folklore. I felt as if I was about to write about Captain Oates's last walk, about Diana's funeral, about the small boats at Dunkirk. This World Cup story would become a national archetype: part of the way we understand the world and ourselves.

I knew, because this has been the case at every World Cup in which England have taken part. Start with 1966 and all that: go on to 1970, and the stolen bracelet and the mysterious poisoning of Gordon Banks; then to 1982 and the side that went out without losing a match; to 1986 and the Hand of God; to 1990 and Gazza's tears and the penalties against the Germans; to 1998 and Beckham's sending-off against Argentina and more penalties; to 2002 and Beckham's redemption, his penalty against Argentina. I would be telling a story as important to the English mind as the one about the man who paints the Forth Bridge. Could anything, for a writer, be better?

143

A strange thing happens at the World Cup once England have got their first match out of the way. You suddenly notice that this is a global tournament, and those with a taste for football get into the swing of watching football from all over the world: not for the sake of partisanship but for the sake of sport. The World Cup is simultaneously a festival of extreme partisanship and of extreme purity. People watch football for the sake of victory alone: and they also watch football for the sake of football itself. I felt this as Australia beat Japan from one down, scoring three times in the last eight minutes of play.

At the same time, all over the world, people were watching football in search of personal triumph and in search of objective beauty. I could see people across Germany, clad in the vesture of partisanship, watching in raptures at some other country's football: say, Argentina's sublime start to the competition. It is one of the perfect sporting contradictions.

The World Cup audience does not look only for victory. It begins to look for early signs of the player of the tournament, for the team that will carry all before it, for the stars that will dominate football for years to come, for new ways of playing, for old beauties in new forms. At the same time, the World Cup divides the world into cheerers for their own nation, and unites the world in a sporting conspiracy of excellence and beauty. Enmity and comradeship walk hand in hand.

144

'My priority is to ensure that players feel more amateur than professional. Thirty to 40 years ago, the effort was the other way. Now there is so much professionalism, we have to revert to urging players to like the game, to love it, do it with joy.' Words of Felipe Scolari, who coached Brazil to their World Cup victory in 2002, and who coached Portugal at the World Cup of 2006.

Sport matters more than ever, in the sense that there

is more money, bigger audiences, greater prizes, higher expectations, greater athleticism, higher stakes. Everything is tuned that much higher; every string is stretched to the point when another quarter-turn will snap it. So often, it is the person who, unoppressed by the great mattering of it all, simply plays the damn ball with a full heart and an empty mind. The World Cup has the same effect on the England football team as alcohol does on the act of love: it provokes the desire but it takes away the performance.

And so, then, to an extraordinary day in Nuremberg. England played an hour of fraught, angst-ridden football against Trinidad and Tobago; and all the time the crowd sang the name of the man who wasn't there. Wayne Rooney: who else? Rooney, not playing, had dominated every thought in England's build-up to the World Cup: now Rooney, not playing, was dominating every thought even as England toiled in desperate search for victory over Trinidad. There had been sightings of Rooney, running and stretching and shooting before the match, but he was just one of the substitutes. We had all heard before the match that Rooney was fit to play. The stadium was tingling with anticipation.

All the England outfielders were playing poorly. And then, in an instant, all the England outfielders were playing pretty well. One second, they were afraid; the next second, they were bold. One moment, they didn't know what they were about; the next moment, they were playing with power and purpose. I have watched a lot of football here and there, and I have never seen a substitution work that miracle.

Him. Yes, on the hour, Rooney came on, with all his bullocking runs into the box and his neat little lay-offs and his succinct passes and his vision and his passion: and it was England Unbound. The entire team responded to his mere presence by moving from incompetence to competence at a stroke, and a not-too-disgraceful 2-0 win. A happy simile occurred to me as I wrote: one of those small things that gives a writer a special pleasure. The image came from decades-distant memories of munchies-driven four-in-the-morning visits to the Venturer's café in Bristol, where I would drink pints of tea, eat bacon sandwiches and play pinball. And there are times when the silver ball hits a certain target, and every light on the table is illuminated, bells ring orgasmically and every score is multiplied by ten. Thus it was with Rooney's coming.

The story still had legs: ungainly, tottering, looking at every moment as if a fall must take place, but unquestionably still upright and moving approximately forward. The team was through to the round of sixteen: the final qualifying match against Sweden could not affect that. My wife reported strange goings-on in our local town in Suffolk: people unselfconsciously sprouting peculiar and undignified hats, white or red be-lioned shirts, and every other car bearing a St George's flag. The country was alight with hope, and hope had a name. The name of Rooney. The toboggan was gathering pace on the Cresta Run: me, I took a moment to bivouac on my ledge on the face. I did not look down: I'm too old a hand for that. I did not look up: that would be far worse.

145 Even for the most committed of writers, the World Cup is not a test of writing skills. It is a test of logistics. And I wish to report an extreme achievement here. At the stadium in Munich, the electrical equipment at the desks refused to accept the standard English adaptor that you use to make a continental plug-socket work. The sockets, surrounded by rubber collars, ever-so-gently spat them out again, like a child being fed an uncongenial meal. At the next stadium, the plugs were surrounded by a collar of hard plastic. With these, you could just about insert a plug and make contact, but after a while, unless you kept the plug jammed against knee or foot, it would slowly topple out. So I went to Mannheim, and spent an hour walking until I found the right place, a shop thrillingly called Bauhaus (as in 'Daddy wouldn't buy me a') and, practical as Walter Gropius, I bought a German plug and extension lead with three conventional, un-rubber-collared un-plastic-collared sockets. The plug fitted into the stadium sockets; the English adaptor fitted into the extension lead sockets. I was able to use my laptop without running out of battery at live matches. I was able to help my colleagues, too: don't worry, lads, plug into *my* socket. That's the sort of thing they should really give awards for. Simon Barnes: Extension Lead Buyer of the Year. It made all the difference to my World Cup: and I say this without a vestige of a joke. As EM Forster so rightly remarked: only connect. It is the sportswriter's ultimate truth. All else is flumdiddle.

146

I finished the five-and-a-half-hour train journey from Munich to Cologne and stepped into the first in a line of taxis. 'Hotel President,' I said, '*bitte.*' There isn't one, my charioteer told me. I checked my itinerary: sure there was. It says so here. But no, he insisted: no Hotel President, no August-Clemens Strasse either. I rummaged, produced some secondary documentation. Christ, it's in fucking Bonn. It was an authentic World Cup moment. My train had stopped in Bonn half an hour earlier. I had just made a complex train booking from Cologne. Perhaps I should have waited for the next train back to Bonn. And then again, perhaps not. 'Take me to Bonn,' I said, '*bitte.*'

I found myself eventually in Poppelsdorf, the sort of place that is technically known as 'a leafy suburb'. This was to teach me something important. In the meantime, I moved in, went to Bonn station, remade my train booking, dined out leafily on spargel and beer. On, then, to England's match the following day in Cologne. Germany were playing their own final group game as I walked bahnhofwards: the pavement cafés were full, standing room out into the road, the big screens belting out the match: a huge cheer, just as I left. A goal up, then.

Poppelsdorf deserted. Not a soul in sight. Quiet streets, with trees and their not inappropriate leaves. I was alone. And then the houses themselves cheered. Not a raucous, stadium-filling sound: more a cacophonous murmur as hidden viewers in every house along the street were united in the same moment of release. Yes! *Ja! Gol!* A shout in the street. And for some reason this was rather moving.

—The ways of the Creator are not our ways, Mr Deasy said. All history moves towards one great goal, the manifestation of God.

Stephen jerked his thumb towards the window, saying:

—That is God.

Hooray! Ay! Whrrwhee!

—What? Mr Deasy asked.

—A shout in the street, Stephen answered, shrugging his shoulders.

This from *Ulysses*, as Stephen and Mr Deasy discuss big subjects while the boys they teach are playing hockey. God: one great goal: a shout in the street.

It is not just the people who put paint on their faces and mug at the cameras who follow the World Cup. The event was also being followed in a seemly and decorous and understated fashion in leafy suburbs and dusty squares and remote villages all over the world. Football tries to sell itself by means of the message of fanaticism: but in truth, the World Cup has its life and its being among the legions of people – many of them once-in-a-quadrennium football followers – for whom the event is a treat: and perhaps the greatest treat of all is in the sharing. In England, the sofas of the nation concealed a population occasionally stealing horrified glances from behind their upholstered backs as the England team continued their faltering progress. Not waving flags, not dancing in fountains: just all sharing in one great story, and, occasionally, as all things moved towards their one great goal, a shout in the street – Hooray! Ay! Whrrwhee! I walked on to my train and Cologne in good heart.

147

Is it a claim to fame, to have invented a cliché? Or is it, on the other hand, a badge of shame? I don't really know, and besides, it is hard to know whether I was responsible for the invention, or whether I was merely on the leading edge of the wave as it swept into sporting journalism. The cliché is 'talisman', or 'talismanic', even 'talismanically'; the last two words accepted by Longman but not by the Shorter Oxford. All three words are now sporting clichés, showing signs of hard use along with such staples as leaping like a salmon and a sliderule pass. All these examples were initially pretty vivid, it must be said. Clichés generally become cliches because they once meant something important, or at least useful.

'Talisman' and 'talismanic player' are phrases used for any footballer who has some kind of emotional meaning for his team. Alan Shearer was Newcastle's talisman, Thierry Henry is Arsenal's talismanic striker, Eric Cantona's talismanically brilliant performances changed Manchester United into a great side.

I would argue that only one of these is a talisman, in the sense that I originally meant it. In fact, I am more or less certain that it was for Cantona that I first used the term. Shearer and Henry are or were essential to their clubs for what they do: scoring goals, mainly. Cantona changed Manchester United because of what he was. And that is quite a different matter. A talisman isn't only important for what he does himself. He is also important for what other people do when he is around. When Cantona first came to Manchester United with his collar under his ears, his shoulder blades touching and his insect-smearing walk, his club, and his team were transformed. They took his insufferable arrogance and made it their keynote: who are these lesser clubs? How dare they be on the same field as us? We are superior beings, no?

Around Cantona, every Manchester United player played better: with more purpose, more belief, more certainty. Cantona did not merely score goals: he set the tone. The other Manchester United players took the lead from him and were transformed. It was one of those curious effects of team dynamics: the right player at the right time. His signing must go down forever as Sir Alex Ferguson's moment of genius.

By my own strict definition, then, as well as by the cliché-user's imprecision, England has a talisman and, for the first time at the World Cup, Wayne Rooney actually started a match. What is more, the first-choice pair of strikers played together for the first time since November. But the second of these, Michael Owen, went down with ruptured knee ligaments in the first minutes, a strange, knock-kneed unilateral fall: the last time I had seen anything like it was with a day-old foal. It was a dreadful injury, and the prognosis was that he would be out for a year. This left England with three fit strikers in the squad, one of whom was seventeen, Theo Walcott, and one of whom was Peter Crouch. A crisis, in short.

All the same, England had an imperative first half, with Rooney looking, well, talismanic. Rooney should, perhaps have been credited with an assist for Joe Cole's wonderful goal: would Cole have been capable of such brilliance without Rooney on the pitch? England, certainly seemed briefly a team inspired. But Rooney wearied and faded in the second half, and so did England, taking, as teams must, their tone from their talisman. Sweden drew level not once but twice, thanks to some startlingly poor defending. But England were through to the round of 16, and in first place in their group, which meant that they missed meeting Germany, and were in the opposite side of the draw to Argentina. That, at least, went some way towards contradicting Nietzsche's theory of Eternal Recurrence.

148

So I got a half-term. Two days, three nights at home, between one England match and the next. Went to the zoo with Joe, and saluted the Olympic-ring-tailed lemurs. He loves wildlife. It's a shared thing, a great shared thing. We planned a trip to Scotland to chase the dolphins. And maybe – maybe – an orca, Now that would be something. With sport and with wildlife, you don't know what happens next. You never do. I rode my young horse without another horse to chaperone her: a huge leap into adulthood for her, and a day of great significance for me. I drank a

bottle of champagne with my wife. And I played football –
the only kind that matters – with Eddie, my five-year-old.
He has Down's syndrome. This isn't the place to write
about him: this is a sports book. But I will tell you that
Eddie has always loved a ball, and we played with one of his
new birthday-present footballs. We giggled and giggled:
and it was as if nothing as small as the World Cup had ever
meant anything to me, or for that matter, existed.

149

I got up in Munich in order to go to Stuttgart,
three hours away. I had to watch England play Ecuador in
the round of sixteen. And it was the most astonishing example of practical Cartesian dualism I have ever experienced
in my life. My mind got up to go, and my body said: no,
absolutely not, completely out of the question. I had gone
down with what CMJ, a martyr to sub-continental digestive
disasters, refers to as 'the Confounded Squitters'. Despite
this unpleasantness, I was convinced that I could cope, get
to Stuttgart, write a piece, get the train back. So I got up to
go; next thing I knew, it was four hours later and I was ringing the office to explain my predicament. After that, I slept
for another three hours, got up, did the match from television, wrote a piece about David Beckham's sumptuous goal
from a 30-yard free-kick and filed it. It seemed to go all
right. I pondered on the reasons for being in the stadium at
all, being in the country at all. Though I would have liked to
have seen that goal in three dimensions: the rainbow in the

vertical plane, the sharp left-hand curve in the h orizontal plain. That famous free-kick from Ronaldinho, which did for England in the World Cup of 2002, I saw that in the stadium, and I was in a direct line between Ronaldinho's shoulders and the goal. I could see that it was a goal – and that he 'meant it', as footballing people say – from the moment he began his run-up.

But I wrote my Ecuador piece from the – comparative – comfort of my cell. I completed a fast of 36 hours; in those 36 hours I slept 24. Perhaps the CS's were simply an expression of exhaustion brought on by overwork: the body ganging up on the mind. I was fine the next day. Had breakfast, lunch, dinner. Wrote a piece. Booked a train for Baden Baden. It was time to take the waters of cynicism.

150

A pleasant spa town, Baden Baden. It was the base for the England football team, and their troupe of wives and girlfriends. No holiday town ever feels quite the same as reality. Every seaside town out of season, every spa town, feels that little bit like the Village in the *The Prisoner*. In Baden Baden, I constantly expected to be asked to see Number Two, or to be told, in sinister tones: 'I'm sorry, sir. We only sell *local* maps'.

The eternal meeting and re-meeting of old acquaintances added to the strangeness of it all. The town was full of journalists of all kinds: talking earnestly in cafés, keeping the waiters up past their bedtimes in restaurants, meeting each other in the streets or in hotel lobbies. Paparazzi hung around Brenner's Park Hotel waiting for the girls to come in and out. A chance-met colleague told me of one of their nights out. The manager of the place in which it had taken place said happily: 'The first six bottles of champagne were on the house. The rest they paid for.' This was a foreign town in which I seemed to know most of the people. A rum do.

So out to the England training camp itself, half an hour from town. The essential thing about such visits is hanging about. Surely in no other profession do so many highly paid people spend so much time waiting on the convenience of others. We always arrive early; they always arrive late: thus our relative importance in life is re-established on a daily basis. Coffee was provided, snacks, mineral water, not enough desks. We gathered in groups and sneered about the England team.

Eventually Owen Hargreaves came in, and spoke pleasantly and articulately and politely. A strange thing: at the pre-World-Cup friendlies, he was booed every time he came onto the pitch. I wondered why this was. Partly, I thought, it is because he is not one of ours. His father is from Bolton, his mother Welsh: but Hargreaves père went out to Canada to work in the steel industry. Hargreaves *fils* played football, was good at it, and a coach in Calgary had a contact at Bayern Munich. So at sixteen, Hargreaves went to Germany to give it a go. He still plays for the club as I write, and is bilingual in German.

There is also the point that he tended to come on as a substitute every time Sven-Goran Eriksson decided to settle for a 1-0 win, or for a 1-1 draw. Thus he had become a physical manifestation of the coach's damnable caution. Perhaps it was the caution that was being booed: but it was Hargreaves that kept hearing it. Hargreaves stood for England's consistent failure to be brilliant.

But I think in the end, the booing has more to do with Hargreaves's strange cosmopolitan existence. It is not that it is unEnglish: it is worse than that. It has something almost middle class about it. And these days, though England supporters will embrace most players in the England side regardless of colour, it is perhaps class that is the true barrier. In the 1970s, football supporters greeted black players from opposing sides by making monkey noises and throwing bananas onto the pitch: I wondered if England supporters should greet Hargreaves by throwing books onto the pitch and making mock-upper-class eoh-eoh noises. Well, I don't care if he's read Nietzsche in the original or if he can sing Schiller's 'Ode to Joy' all the way through, if he can do a good job for the team, he's in the side.

The following morning, we were permitted to watch fifteen minutes of training. After the usual pause, the players arrived, started to do their stuff, and then we were hustled away. I could see security men up in the woods. The previous day, I had strolled there (blackcap, song thrush, goldcrest, blackbird), but I thought better of it that day. Couldn't face the misunderstanding. Though apparently some intrepid souls were regularly doing a jungle belly-crawl to sneak a look. Rumour was that England had practised penalties and hardly scored a single one.

Me, I went back to the tent, had two cheese rolls and a

Kit-Kat Chunky kindly provided by the FA, and worked on my anthropology. I continued my study of the Number Ones. That is to say, the group comprising the senior football writers on each of the the national dailies. They form an impenetrable group: self-enclosed, all-repelling. I get on quite well with some of them when they are on their own, but they hardly ever are on their own. En masse, they are extraordinary: a mixture of status-consciousness, fear, competitiveness and camaraderie. It is essential that they share things with each other, but equally essential to keep certain matters from each other. The air around them crackles with neuroses like static electricity.

And above them, a great pall of cynicism. England are useless. Awful. Beyond serious credence. Sven-Goran Eriksson is a fool. David Beckham can't play football. All they wanted was to get out of Baden Baden and see some 'real' football; Brazil, preferably, Argentina for second choice. (They could of course, do that if they wished, but that would involve foregoing their status as Number One, for a Number One's number one job is covering England.) I must say that theirs is not a job that I envy or am capable of doing. The pressure of not missing the next big story is intense. As I savoured the mad claustrophobia of Baden Baden and the big tent and the life of the Number One, I felt very strongly that cynicism is bad for the soul. The more so if you mistake it for realism.

151

The German newspapers were full of Bruno the bear: the first wild bear seen in Germany for 170 years, rambling into the country from a re-release scheme in Austria, and going on a rampage of destruction. The idea of a bear running loose around civilisation is a very powerful one – most fairy shows depend on that very image – and when Wayne Rooney turned up the following day to 'do' the press, I knew I was writing a bear story.

Rooney looks startlingly grown up on the pitch: mature in purpose, not the sort to arouse anybody's protective impulses. Close up, out of his comfort-zone, he looked vulnerable: alarmingly young: certainly not old enough to carry the nation's hopes on his admittedly broad shoulders. Being on the defensive didn't suit him either, knocking back questions with a reflex 'no' reely'. Was it hard to cope with being the focus of the nation's dreams, the talisman of the England side, the emotional leader of the side, the cutting edge of the England attack? No' reely, no' reely, no' reely, no' reeely. And perhaps he's sincere: perhaps he shrugs off the realities as easily as he does the questions. Perhaps that's the secret.

So I wrote about Rooney-as-Bruno, failed to persuade *The Times* to put Bruno on the cover of the World Cup supplement (he made it inside, though) and had a revelation. England, I thought, are in the quarter-finals of the World Cup. They hadn't played terribly well, it had to be said. Sides that had played better than England included Spain, Holland, Mexico, Australia, Ivory Coast, Ghana. All gone home. Only eight teams can now win, and one of them is England. I left Baden Baden and the chilling waters of cynicism, and re-grouped myself. Bugger the cynics: as I have said before, I will not have my agenda set by the mockers and the sneerers. So I wrote a piece containing 25 reasons why England could win the World Cup: and the greatest of these reasons was Rooney. England and the World Cup: it was all Rooney, Rooney, Rooney. By the time this was puffed on the front of the supplement, it was 25 reasons why England *can* in the World Cup. And by the time it was puffed on the front of the newspaper, it was 25 reasons why England *will* win the World Cup. I would seem to have staked my reputation on an England victory. But come: let's raise the stakes. Make it a quid.

152

Football is more or less unique as a sport in that you can win games while playing badly. I don't mean playing below your own standards, I mean actually playing worse that your opponents. Your opponents can play brilliantly, dominate possession, create thousands of chances, make you look as if you don't have a hope of winning a football ever against anybody, and yet they can fail to score. You can be on the receiving end of this marmalising, then your centre-half can profit from half-a-second's inattention from the world-beaters you are up against, score from a corner and hey presto, you've won.

In most other games, the side playing better almost

always wins. But in the unique democracy of football, the last can quite often be first and the race is quite often to the slow. The longer the run of matches, the more the better side's advantages will be shown. A league championship favours bigger sides, smaller sides have a better chance in a knock-out format. And a run of seven games – that's a World Cup – is not necessarily long enough to make the the the best side's advantages tell. At the World Cup of 2002, Germany played seven indifferent matches, and the only one they actually lost was the final. In 1990, England played six matches: the only one in which they played well was the one they lost (to West Germany, on penalties, on the night of Gazza's tears).

The reason for this is, again, the uniquely high value of football's currency. Football really is a funny old game. A goal changes everything. That is not true of every run or wicket in cricket. In rugby union, tries and penalties are gradually accumulated by the superior side. A score against the run of play happens, but it doesn't change everything all in an instant. Runs, wickets, points, games, sets: they are all small change compared to the golden sovereign of the goal in football.

In football, a goal is the most colossal thing. I went to Berlin to see Germany play Argentina: most people (with classic Number Ones' logic) had predicted an Argentina victory, on the spurious grounds that Argentina were capable of playing better football. Argentina looked good for much of the match but then decided to protect a 1-0 lead, taking off the play-maker, Juan Riquelme, and the forward, Hernàn Crespo. Can you be too much in thrall to the value of the goal? Argentina had one of the most brilliant young players in the world on the bench in Lionel Messi, but he never stepped onto the pitch. I can only assume that the Argentina coach, Jose Pekerman, choked: that his mind got befuddled by the lack of oxygen at that level of World Cup altitude. Germany, reinspired, drew level and eventually won, not through brilliance, but through desire and courage. Argentina learned that one goal is a huge thing, but it is never quite as good as two.

153

Never sell out your heartland. Never sell out your heartland. Never sell out your heartland. I state this rule here thrice, because it matters so much, and is so often ignored. Sport spends so much of its time trying to get more popular, to attract 'new audiences'. As a result they invented one-day cricket and then Twenty-20 cricket: cricket for people who don't really like cricket. New gimmicks and hoopla attend every event. Sport keeps losing faith with its powers of attraction. Perhaps rightly so: because if you gear your efforts towards attracting the fickle, you learn soon enough that they are the hardest audience to keep.

No sport has sold its heartland to so great an extent as football. Football matches are supposed to be decided by footballing means. But now we have television audiences of countless millions, many of whom don't really like football and can't take all that much of it. Why, they might reach for the zapper at any moment. And so, to come to terms with the demands of the television companies and their concern for the floating voters of the remote control, football matches on the great occasions are now decided by means of the penalty shoot-out, should the scores be level after 90 minutes and again after half an hour of extra time.

This is not football, but it is damn good drama. It is not sport, but it ramps up the ratings like nothing else on a peaceful earth. The penalty shoot-out is the ultimate example of sport for people who don't like sport: each kick carrying an almost absurd weight of importance. All sport is the theatre of cruelty: the penalty shoot-out is the theatre of gratuitous cruelty.

The argument goes: bring in the fickle, the uncommitted, the floating voters of sport, and give them what they want. Never mind what the heartland followers of the sport want: you've always got them. But have you? As I have said, belief is that if you take your heartland audience for granted, in the end they will go away. Sadly, and with many a backward glance, but go they will.

What has been bewildering has been the meek way that football has capitulated to the demands of television, has sold its integrity as a sport in order to provide television viewers with a thrilling lottery. Why are voices not raised in protest? Perhaps because football values its television-led prosperity higher than it does its integrity. Never mind about football: we are putting on a show here. And the supporters have accepted this, have accepted that the most important moments of their footballing lives are decided not by the footballing skills but by luck and nerve in sport's own version of Texas Hold'em.

All the same, the German are wonderfully good at it. Against Argentina they struck four penalties: all four unsaveable. Jens Lehmann saved two of Argentina's efforts, one a weak shot from Roberto Ayala, the other a well-struck ball from Esteban Cambiasso that he read brilliantly and reached superbly. If you must be subjected to the hideous indignities of sport's greatest sell-out, you might as well be good at them.

154

Look for your strengths: you will find them in the same place as your weaknesses. This is an elementary truth about life: it might be described as the essential truth of sport. Sport dramatises certain truths about life: and that particular truth is, as it were, showcased and made much of by the processes of sport.

For example, David Beckham's sense of self-esteem was at the heart of all the good things he has done on a football pitch. He believed in himself as a star: he adored playing the part – like an actor – of the England captain. He consciously cultivated his own fame as a sporting asset: the better he felt about himself, the better he was able to impose himself on his opponents. The classic example of this is his extraordinary game against Greece in the last qualifying match before the 2002 World Cup, in which he played in an increasing frenzy and eventually scored the vital goal himself in the last moments of the game. But this strength was seen for the weakness it also was in 1998, when Beckham had his sense of self-esteem pricked by the Argentina captain, Diego Simeone, who patronisingly ruffled Beckham's artfully tousled hair. Beckham's uncontrollable response was to kick out at Simeone: as a result, Beckham was sent off and England went out of the World Cup.

Wayne Rooney's great strength is his combative passion for football. He loves the maelstrom of sport: for the *sturm und drang* – storm and stress – of football. He is at his best in contact, in the collision of desperate bodies, in situations in which his own strength and his own strength of will come to the fore. He can time an opponent's body as he can time a football, riding the impact, busting through the restraint, using the momentum to create his own particular form of mayhem.

It stems from his love for the intimacies of combat: for the closeness, the contact, the struggle and the victory. Rooney is no precious ball player who finds opposition mildly dismaying: opposition is the wellspring of his footballing self. He likes people to drive at, to shrug off, to leave fallen, to leave confounded. That is his purpose in football. He bounces off opponents as a pinball bounces off the bumpers, springing back with redoubled force and energy.

This is not just a physical feat: it is also a mental one. Rooney doesn't play cold. He doesn't play in a serene, trance-like state. He is is not the one cool head in the heat of battle. No: he *is* the heat of battle. To play at his best, he has to be up, hot, in a mood of extravagant relish, bursting with hyper-confident don't-mess-with-me aggression. It's no great trick for him to get there, either. It's staying there that is the problem.

And so, when England played Portugal in the quarter-finals of the World Cup, Rooney stamped on Ricardo Carvalho's balls and was sent off. As a result, England, short-handed, failed to break down the Portuguese defence and, with the scores level after extra time, England lost on penalties.

Rooney insisted that he was hard-done-by. And to an extent, he had a point. Certainly, you could argue that Rooney was more fouled against than fouling, that he was not actually *aiming* at Carvalho's crotch, that Cristiano Ronaldo's intervention was unforgivable, that the referee was overly sympathetic to the divers and fakers and whingers of Portugal, that Ronaldo earned his shove in the chest by running at Rooney, that referees love to send off a big-name player, that had it been anyone else it would have been a yellow, or more fairly, a yellow for Carvalho and Ronaldo as well. Most of these arguments are valid: and they are also irrelevant.

The fact is that Rooney lost control. He lost his temper on the pitch, and so inevitably he got sent off. Rooney dares to play on the far edge of control: that is his strength. But inevitably, at some stage, he is going to topple over: and that is his weakness. If he can learn to play at his passionate best without toppling over into the pit of folly, he will be a great player. If he can't, he won't. In 1982, Diego Maradona was sent off against Italy at the World Cup, lashing out after being constantly kicked by Claudio Gentile. Four years later, master of himself, he and Argentina won the World Cup.

Rooney's fall was a very straightforward tale: that of a man grappling with his own nature, that of a man seeking his best and for that very reason, coming up against his worst. It has been told in many forms, again and again: find it in the pride of Achilles, the love of Othello, the generosity of Bloom. Sport dramatises these ancient tales, makes them vivid, makes them new. Partisanship adds an extra layer of vividness: Rooney is himself, and he is also us, turning hope into despair by the very act of hoping too hard. Another bloodless tragedy is enacted: Rooney, bowed but unblooded, went home protesting, having learned nothing, his innocence. And we, having learned much, can only wonder what sport holds for us next.

155

I wrote the first draft of the chapter about penalties and heartlands in the stadium media centre at Gelsenkirchen, in the hours before England played Portugal. And so I watched England lose on penalties yet again. It was the sixth penalty competition England have been involved in, the fifth defeat. They lost on penalties in the World Cup semi-finals to West Germany in 1990, in the European Championship of 1996 to Germany, in the 1998 World Cup to Argentina, in the 2004 European Championship to Portugal, and in the

2006 World Cup to Portugal again. The sole success was against Spain at Wembley in 1996.

In 2006, England had four penalties, of which three were saved. Saved easily. England had practised them this time: practised relentlessly at their pitch in the forest. And still each penalty-taker walked up as if foredoomed to fail, as if failure were totally acceptable.

Perhaps they are right. Certainly, England has long held the view that failed penalty-takers are more to be pitied than blamed. There was a series of Pizza Hut advertisements in which failed penalty-takers were treated with rueful affection. Why is this? But let us cast aside the ancient nonsense which holds that England is 'a nation of losers'. In the pages of this book, we have discussed such English successes as Sir Matthew Pinsent, Dame Kelly Holmes, the Ashes heroes, Martin Johnson and his immortals. We adore success: but unlike some nations, we also have a taste for gallant failure.

I don't see that as a bad thing. A failure to appreciate the beauties of defeat, a failure to see the point of heroism in a doomed cause, is a blindness to some of the big things in life. I don't think I would want to live in a place in which failed penalty-takers were held up to shame and spitting: to become national hate-objects. All the same, it is possible, I think, that the national sympathy for failed penalty-takers leads inexorably to failure from the penalty-spot. We all of us know that the penalty competition is unfair: thus for players as for spectators, failure is legitimised.

England still rejoices in the tale of Captain Scott, his doomed expedition to the Antarctic, and the suicidal self-sacrificing Captain Oates. It is a story that is beautiful, perfect, tragic, heroic, futile: and it touches our hearts. A nation that accepts poor Oates as a national hero will always find some measure, not just of pity, but also of sad admiration, for failing penalty-takers. And – perhaps as a direct result – a Germanic ruthlessness in penalty competitions seems to be beyond the scope of footballers playing for England.

So: yet another of sport's eternal contradictions. We want success; we respect gallant failure. But somehow the respect for gallant failure compromises the success we crave.

Neither winning nor losing is a simple matter. And sport, once again, tells us something about ourselves, as a nation, as individuals.

156

Sport is everything: sport is nothing. Sport is important: sport is trivial. Sport is packed with meaning: sport means nothing. Sport is an escape from real life: sport makes real life uncompromisingly vivid. Sport is packed with contradictions: sport is the most straightforward thing on the planet. Sport is simple: sport is complex. Sport is beautiful: sport is irredeemably ugly. Sport is only about winning: sport is mainly about losing. Sport is about courage: sport's main subject is fear. Sport is for fools: sport is for intellectuals. Sport is about the creation of a living mythology: sport is a soap opera of the tedious doings of tedious people. In sport you find the commonplace: in sport you cannot avoid the truly exceptional. Sport is about strength; about weakness. Sport is endlessly entertaining: sport is full of longueurs. Sport is predictable: the point of sport is that no one ever knows what happens next. Sport tells us nothing new: sport supplies us with one revelation after another. Sport is about partisanship: sport is about the search for an abstract and unaffiliated excellence. Sport is about breadth of vision: sport has its being in the narrow and the one-eyed. Sport is about perfection: sport is about the endless fallibility of humankind. Sport is about the heroic: sport is about the craven. Sport is about the audience: sport is about the performers. Sport is about learning the new: sport is about the reconfirming of prejudice. Sport is about sex: sport is homophobic and homocentric. People care deeply about sport: people know that sport means nothing. For a champion, sport is a matter of life and death: in sport, victory often goes to the person to whom it matters least. Sport is a modern invention: sport takes us back to the most ancient parts of ourselves. Sport is basically uncivilised: sport is the first luxury of the civilised human. Sport owes everything to the age of television: sport is 65 million years old. Sport is something you do: sport is something you watch. Sport is about action: sport is about personality. Sport is about ability: sport is about character. Sport is about discipline: sport is about excess. Sport is about self-control: sport is about letting go. Sport is a form of madness: sport is the ultimate sanity. Sport is foolish: sport is a great bringer of wisdom. Sport is a waste of time: sport is something that can enrich all who come

into contact with it. Sport is for the illiterate: sport is a joy
for the writer, and also, God willing, on occasions, for the
reader.

157

Above all, sport is to be found in the testing:
in the last strides of the 400 metres when the body's
oxygen debt seems unrepayable; in the innings you play
when your side is 49 for five; in the way you strike the
free-kick in time added on; in the way you hit the penalty
that must decide the game; in the way you deal with the
out-swinging corner when you've clung onto a 1-0 lead
for 80 minutes; at the point in the marathon when mind
and body rebel; or again in the marathon at the uphill finish
and your rival alongside; or in the way you rip the entry
from the ten-metre board in your final dive; or in the
southern ocean with time ticking away and only an alba-
tross for company; or in the way ball meets boot when
you go for the drop- kick in the game's last seconds; or in
the apparent width of the balance beam as you throw the
gold medal back-somersault; or in the impossible weight
you select for your final lift; or in the amount of air you
give the ball when Adam Gilchrist is in full song; or in the
way you hit the long-jump board in the sixth and final
round; or in the way you respond to a crude tackle or a
coarse insult in the biggest game of your life; or in the way
you hit your second serve at match-point in the pin-drop
hush; or in the way you ride into the final vertical with

nothing in hand after three days of competition; or the way you wait when you know that your horse has all the speed in the finish; or the way you row when you're still second with ten yards left and you've already given your all; or, above all, in the moment between handgrip and handgrip as you perform the kovacs. The truth is always and only in the action.

158

It ends too soon. We should have gone further: we should have done better. There was so much more to say. But instead, I was in a taxi on my way to Dortmund airport. Soon I would be in Suffolk, at least for 36 hours, before I went on to Wimbledon. It is time to end things, then: end things that should have been better. I had initially thought that the excellence of England's players would take them to the semi-finals of the World Cup at least. I then thought that some kind of bumbling inept luck-scarred series of performances would do the same thing: but it was not to be. England looked destiny in the face and blinked. Wayne Rooney faced a profound examination of his own nature and failed. Sven-Goran Eriksson showed that he was the man to take England to a certain level of achievement: thus far and nor further. And as I come to the end of this journey in search of the meaning of sport, I too must admit: thus far and no further. I should have gone further: I should have done better. All journeys in sport end in failure: for even the champion who retires at the top is admitting that he has been defeated by Time. All books end in failure too, at least for the author: there is no work so perfect that the writer had no more to give. Every book that was ever written lacks some things that the writer knew, but was somehow unable to set down. Like every runner, footballer, gymnast, golfer, boxer, leaper, hurler, lifter of weights, battler with waters, cyclist, diver, hitter of balls, grappler, swerver, fighter, slitherer, slider, defier of gravity and tamer of Pegasus; like every champion, runner-up, first-round loser, failed qualifier and for-all-time sporting great; and like every writer, painter, composer, sculptor, scribbler, dauber and hack; and, like the great Fernando Pessoa himself, I carry my awareness of defeat like a banner of victory.

Acknowledgements

Thanks to all at Short Books: this is perhaps a unique example of an author being in love with an entire publishing firm.

Thanks to Georgina Capel and all at Capel and Land for seeing me right, always.

At *The Times*, I owe many more debts of thanks: first to Robert Thomson, not least for standing firm during the Swedish Open.

Thanks to Keith Blackmore for making me chief sportswriter; thanks to Tim Hallissey for asking me to stay on. Further thanks to all those on the sports desk I have worked with, especially David Chappell, Jeremy Griffon and Craig Tregurtha.

Thanks also to the *Times* specialist writers I often work alongside: Matt Dickinson, David Hands, David Powell, Neil Harman, Jenny MacArthur, Craig Lord, Christopher Martin-Jenkins, Richard Hobson, John Hopkins and John Goodbody.

Finally, thanks to the most important person in newspaper publishing: the good sub. Especially Keith Pike, who gets more than his share of my stuff to look after.

BY THE SAME AUTHOR:

How to be a Bad Birdwatcher
To the greater glory of life
Simon Barnes
1-904095-95-X   £9.99

Look out of the window.
See a bird.
Enjoy it.
Congratulations. You are now a bad birdwatcher.

Anyone who has ever gazed up at the sky or stared out of the
window knows something about birds. In this funny, inspiring,
eye-opening book, Simon Barnes paints a riveting picture of
how bird-watching has framed his life and can help us all to a
better understanding of our place on this planet.

How to be a bad birdwatcher shows why birdwatching is not
the preserve of twitchers, but one of the simplest, cheapest
and most rewarding pastimes around.

"A delightful ode to the wild world outside
the kitchen window"
Daily Telegraph

A Bad Birdwatcher's Companion
A personal introduction to Britain's
50 most obvious birds
Simon Barnes
£9.99   ISBN 1-904977-39-1

Few books are more intimidating than a conventional field guide. There are simply too many birds in them. This book introduces the reader to Britain's most obvious birds. But it does more than that: it also explains them. It explains the way that different birds do different things, eat different food, sing different songs and live different lives, and it explains why they are different.

If you are a would-be birdwatcher but don't know where to start, A Bad Birdwatcher's Companion is for you. It will help you understand birdwatching: but far more important, it will help you begin to understand birds.

"Thoughtful, instructive, and full of simple wisdom"
Daily Mail

In case of difficulty in purchasing any Short Books
title through normal channels, please contact
BOOKPOST Tel: 01624 836000
Fax: 01624 837033
email: bookshop@enterprise.net
www.bookpost.co.uk
Please quote ref. 'Short Books'